**The Train
That Ran Away**

STEWART JOY

The Train
That Ran Away

A BUSINESS HISTORY
OF BRITISH RAILWAYS
1948-1968

LONDON
IAN ALLAN

First published 1973

ISBN 0 7110 0413 7 (casebound)
ISBN 0 7110 0428 5 (paperback)

*For Louise, Heidi and Rosemary
who twice crossed the world in
support of a lost cause*

Published by Ian Allan Ltd, Shepperton, Surrey
and printed in Great Britain by Biddles Ltd,
Guildford, Surrey

Contents

Preface

This book is neither pure history nor pure economics. It is business history, written from an incomplete set of records, and a passable knowledge of the economics and the technical process of the industry concerned. Its formal purpose is to explain the need for the railway provisions of the Transport Act of 1968. In doing this, it must give a necessarily disturbing account of the way in which a publicly funded organisation can waste national resources if it is given neither unambiguous direction nor self-correcting controls. The story of British Rail's first twenty years of public ownership is a repetitive tale of failure to exert adequate control at successive levels, from the Minister of Transport downwards. Concentrating on the factors which led to the recapitalisation, which was effectively an admission that a large proportion of BR's investment since nationalisation had been a dead loss, the narrative pays little attention to the technical development over the period.

The study was written in three distinct stages. Chapters Two to Seven were originally drafted in 1964, from notes made during my researches at the London School of Economics. Chapter One and Chapters Eight to Twelve arose out of my three periods as consultant to the Ministry of Transport on the railway matters leading to the Transport Act of 1968. I had originally planned this second stage as the basis of a book on the post—1968 Act performance of BR, but on joining BR I decided to limit the study to a narrative of the years leading to the Act and the capital reconstruction. Thus the third stage of the work has been the expansion of the earlier materials, to take account of new writing on the subject, and of my own improved understanding of the problem following a few years of grappling at close quarters with the contemporary problems of British Rail.

It will quickly be obvious that the book has not been written under the auspices, or with the records, of the British Railways Board. My aim is to enlighten and not necessarily to please. Thus it relies on published sources and my own analysis and personal experience; for much of Part Two the latter is my only source.

My thanks are due particularly to Michael Beesley and Christopher Foster who, by suggesting to Mrs. Barbara Castle, the then Minister of Transport, that I might be able to solve some of her railway problems, secured the revival of my own interest in 'the railway problem'. But this could not have happened without the generous granting of necessary leave by Donald Cochrane, Dean of the Faculty of Economics & Politics at Monash University. My subsequent wish to stay with the railway problem a little longer, by leaving Monash to take a post with British Rail, was a poor recompense for his initial willingness to have a colleague act as consultant to a client 14,000 miles away. With a book like this, written over an extended period of active involvement with the subject matter, it is difficult to remember all those with whom discussions injected new ideas or clarified my own analysis. But foremost among them are Gilbert Ponsonby, who supervised my researches at the LSE, and Michael Beesley, who first directed my interest to the problem of railway costs and gave me helpful criticism and advice in the final drafting of this book.

Discussions with many railwaymen about contemporary (post–1968) problems have sharpened my understanding of earlier events, and I forbear from naming them in case any (or all) of them are dissatisfied with the result. Errors of fact or analysis are all my own work.

Dulwich, July 1972   Stewart Joy

Introduction

'The purpose of writing business history is that it
makes it much easier to see where you might be going
in the future if you have precise knowledge of where
you have been in the past.'
W.A. Sinclair

At the end of 1968, the British Government cancelled £1,262 million of the capital debt of the British Railways Board. Such a massive capital write-down was the equivalent of saying, for an ordinary limited liability company in the private sector of the economy, that its £1 preference shares now had a value of only twenty-nine pence, and that in future interest would be paid on the lower amount. Ironically, by this cancellation of BR's debt to the Minister, the Government actually appeared to be saving money. In 1968, Government payments to BR totalled £147 million, in the form of a 'deficit grant' to make good its losses, but in 1969 they were only £76 million, in the form of grants for social passenger services and 'surplus capacity' grants. The Government clearly hoped that the assistance given to BR by the 1968 Act would provide a permanent solution to the railway problem, because in the same Act it deliberately removed its previous ability to pay 'deficit grants'. In future, it was prepared to pay generously for services it required to be run for social reasons, but it was no longer prepared to make good any losses on BR's 'commercial' services.*

In its short life, BR had had a dismal financial history, having incurred a loss on its railway operations in every year since 1956. In the early days of loss-making it was believed that profits would soon return, so the Government loaned the money to cover the deficits. But when it became obvious that these loans could never be repaid, the Government decided that simply to write a cheque at the end of each year to cover the deficit would be a much more hygienic method of keeping BR in operation. No private firm could ever have expected financial help on such a scale. But then, few other corporations in the country had ever *needed* help on such a scale; such 'needs' would in almost all other cases have been met at an early stage with a Government decision to close down the firm and, possibly, to start again with those parts which could be made profitable, or were considered to be vital to the national interest. But while this strategem might work with Rolls Royce or Upper Clyde Shipbuilders,† which

---

* The best definition of BR's 'commercial' service is: 'All those services which are not in receipt of government grants.' At present this includes all freight services and most Inter-City passenger services.

† An important difference with these two firms is that the capital reorganisations involved the liquidation of the original companies and a substantial renunciation of debts and other obligations to outside parties. With BR, however, its debts to outsiders were guaranteed by the Treasury, so that only its debts to the Government itself could be avoided.

were organised in separable productive units that a receiver in bankruptcy or new management could elect to keep or abandon, BR is a nation-wide, integrated productive process. Any change in the services it provides must be decided and implemented *through its existing management structure.* In fact, the interdependences in BR operations are such that any precipitate change forced by an outsider could very easily, in the hands of an uncooperative management, cause more real harm than apparent good. Railways are one industry, which must be given guidelines and constraints within which to solve their own problems. The real 'railway problem' between 1948 and 1968 was caused by successive Governments' unwillingness to specify either type of boundary to management discretion. The BR management cannot therefore be wholly blamed for the waste created by its unwise exploitation of the freedom given by Governments' failure to act responsibly.

It should be remembered that BR's past losses are not notable as railway losses go. In 1970, the Penn-Central railroad in the US lost £80 million plus an uncalculated pile-up of deferred maintenance which should really have been added to the accounting loss. The latest announced 'losses' of the German and French railways at that time were £689 million and £504 million respectively. What is it about the railways, that they can 'lose' such massive sums yet Governments willingly make good their losses, with the hope, so often unfulfilled, that they will do better next year?

The answer is a combination of a failure (or refusal) to understand the railways' commercial problem, pure romanticism, and the vital social need for *some* railway services. Much of the railways' losses are not really losses at all, but amounts which should have been paid by the Government for social services. The primary purpose of this study is to trace the other causes of British Rail's poor financial performance. We will see that serious mistakes have been made, both by the BR management and by successive Governments. It took twenty years of public ownership of BR before a Government was prepared to act realistically toward it. It was far easier for Governments to act *unrealistically* about BR, to set it an impossible task and then to write a cheque at the end of each year to cover the deficit, than to attempt, as Mrs Barbara Castle did as Minister for Transport, to clarify BR's role and to accept direct financial responsibility for non-commercial obligations imposed upon it. As our narrative proceeds, we will touch on many of the problems of actually managing a railway system in modern Britain. There will inevitably be less on the equally important task of managing the Government's relations with British Rail, which many who have attempted the task would argue is often more difficult than actually running the railway. There is one hundred and thirty years' accumulated experience of managing railway systems, but the British Government has had less than twenty-five years' experience at acting as the single shareholder and biggest customer of BR.

The purpose of the present study is to explain the need for the changes brought about by the Transport Act of 1968, and to draw some conclusions for the future. Being directed solely to that end, it is not a history of BR's first twenty years. It concentrates on the factors which led to the recapitalisation and pays little attention to the technical developments over the period. The plan of the study is, first, to set the scene by restating the cost to the nation of the railway services it had at the end of 1968, and then to go back to look for reasons for this heavy expenditure for so little tangible result. Then, in Part Two, we will look at the major issues leading to the specifically 'railway' provisions of the 1968 Act. This legislation was the outcome of the first fundamental review of inland transport regulation since the Road Traffic Act of 1933. For British Rail, the new arrangements were both equitable in concept and generous in implementation. They put BR in a position envied by all of its European counterparts. The creation of this new deal, after twenty years of strategic misdirection at both Government and Railways Board levels, should have signallled BR's maturity and independence from its Ministerial parent. But this has not happened in quite the way Mrs Castle said she intended. In the closing chapters we will look for explanations for the obvious divergence between intention and achievement.

The Train
That Ran Away

Part One

1 | The True Losses of BR, 1948-1968

'. . . if we can get the framework of the Railways Board set
up so that they are paid for those services that they are
required to provide for other than commercial reasons, they will
be in a much better position to produce the sort of accounts that
people expect a commercial business to produce.'
*Sir Stanley Raymond — to the Parliamentary Select
Committee on the Nationalised Industries, 27 April 1967*

Before we trace the history of 'the railway problem', it will help if we place the
apparent size of the problem in a truer perspective. Inevitably, there will be
some shocks, because the methods adopted in presenting BR's accounts hid the
cost of providing social services, and they also hid the truer picture of how badly
BR had performed in its commercial operations.

The annual accounts show that British Rail lost over £600 million (before
meeting interest charges) between 1948 and 1968, plus an uncalculated amount
of interest on £705 million of capital 'suspended' by the Transport Act, 1962.
This substantially understated the full financial losses, because from 1963 to
1968 the annual loss on operations and interest unpaid was met by the
Exchequer as a deficit grant. These deficit grants, which totalled £822 million in
the six years, injected a dangerous unreality into the financial discipline of the
BR management, and, for that matter, of the Ministry of Transport. Apart from
the annual embarrassment of having to announce yet another loss, BR could
start each year as if, financially speaking, the organisation had precisely broken
even in the previous year. And the Ministry could glibly refuse proposals to close
passenger services, arguing (to themselves) that 'it will only add a small amount
to the Board's deficit'.

From its inception, the financial structure of British Rail carried a number of
serious handicaps. First, the relationship between the capitalisation of the
business and its earning power, if any did exist, was accidental. The British
Transport Commission took over from the four main-line railways a rag-bag of
assets, worn out by the war, and in the main unprofitable in the last years of
normal operation before the war. The Commission's capital structure, on which
interest was required to be paid to the Treasury, was based on the share prices of
the former main line railway companies.

With hindsight, it is obvious that a set of assets which after heavy investment
could produce operating results like those of the late Fifties and Sixties was, in
aggregate, worth no more than scrap value at January 1st, 1948. But these assets
were taken into the accounts at their values in the accounts of the former main
line railway companies, ie, £941 million, financed, in the main, by three per cent
Transport Stock. In addition, the Commission's operations were expected to

provide for the amortisation of the capital debt over 99 years. In its very first annual report, the Commission complained of the absence of 'equity stock to absorb the reductions in earning power', which resulted 'in a certain rigidity of capital structure and a degree of vulnerability'.[1] This was still the complaint of the Commission in 1960, to the Parliamentary Select Committee on the Nationalised Industries,[2] which reported that even with equity capital the Commission would rarely have been able to pay a dividend. Whilst this is true, the crux of the Commission's (ie. the railway's) difficulties lay in the amount of capital to be serviced, and less in the method of servicing it. Had British Rail been organised as a separate enterprise with equity capital, its lack of profits would have prevented the raising of further equity capital and it would have been forced to use debentures to raise money. This would have been a much more costly source of funds than Exchequer loans at around 6 per cent and, later, interest-free deficit grants. No alternative form of finance would have led to a significantly different end-result for the railways. If their commencing capital had been treated as equity capital, on which dividends were to be paid only after setting aside adequate reserves, no dividends would have been paid and the Commission and its successor the Board would have had to finance all new investment out of the meagre early profits and fixed interest loans. In this case, and without the facility of deficit grants from the Exchequer, British Rail would have just run out of cash and liquid assets sometime about 1955. Put bluntly, it would have been insolvent, just like Rolls Royce or Upper Clyde Shipbuilders, with a large quantity of assets having, in aggregate, zero earning power.

The crux of BR's initial problem was that the assets it took over were, in terms of their aggregate earning power, worthless. Particular sub-groups of assets, such as profitable routes, may have had some value, but taken overall the losses exceeded the profits. We can establish this crucial point by analysing the 'net cash flows' over the period. To do this we take the 'railway' activities of the British Transport Commission, defined as including all those activities left with the Board after the 1962 Act. This includes shipping services, which in the early days were almost totally dependent upon the rail connections, and the hotels business, about half of which was train and station catering.[3] The steady stream of 'losses' on Collection and Delivery activities before they were incorporated into the railway operations section of the annual accounts in 1957 suggests that little or no attempt was made to secure a split of the charges which would have permitted the consideration of C & D as a separate activity.

The net cash flows in Column 4 of the Table below differ from the reported profits or losses on the activities concerned in that they ignore provisions for depreciations and amortisation, but include net investment. The function of annual provisions for depreciation or amortisation is to set aside from that year's net revenue an amount representing the consumption of *capital* assets during the year. Ideally, this should be calculated in terms of current costs. Otherwise, because of rising prices, a firm will be overstating its profits. By using historical cost for its depreciation calculations British Rail, in common with nearly every firm in Britain, has been overstating its profits or understating its losses throughout its life. The annual provisions for depreciation in British Railways' accounts have never been anything like the amount which needed to be spent in replacing worn out and obsolescent plant to maintain existing capacity. The difference, broadly speaking, represents the amounts by which annual profits were overstated and, in recent years, losses were understated.

For this reason, the net cash flow basis gives a truer picture of British Rail's financial results. Even if the original capital had been dividend-bearing equity shares, any *negative* net cash flows would have represented borrowings, and interest would have needed to be paid on these in subsequent years. Column 4 of the following Table shows the net cash flows on British Rail over the period, with imputed borrowings, (ie, negative net cash flows) in square brackets [] , and column 5 shows the net cash flows accumulated and compounded annually at 6 per cent, which roughly corresponds with the rate of interest on borrowings from the Government in those days.

British Rail Cash Flows, 1948–1968

Year	Net Operating Surplus[1] (1)	Depeciation and Amortisation[2] (2)	Investment[3] (3)	Net Cash Flow (4)	Cumulative Net Cash Flow (5)
	£m	£m	£m	£m	£m
1948	25.7	13.7	35.7	3.7	3.7
1949	11.9	14.5	38.6	[12.2]	[8.3]
1950	25.8	15.2	38.7	2.3	[6.5]
1951	34.2	16.0	42.7	7.5	0.6
1952	38.8	16.8	36.5	19.1	19.7
1953	33.5	17.6	50.4	0.7	21.6
1954	15.8	19.0	62.2	[27.4]	[4.5]
1955	1.7	20.4	72.2	[50.1]	[54.9]
1956	[14.9]	22.0	85.9	[78.8]	[137.0]
1957	[25.1]	24.3	116.3	[117.1]	[262.3]
1958	[45.9]	26.2	129.5	[149.2]	[427.2]
1959	[37.7]	28.7	146.1	[155.1]	[607.9]
1960	[63.2]	31.4	137.7	[169.5]	[813.9]
1961	[82.3]	34.7	121.4	[169.0]	[1031.7]
1962	[99.0]	37.1	96.2	[158.1]	[1251.7]
1963	[75.7]	58.5	95.2	[112.4]	[1439.2]
1964	[60.9]	60.7	107.8	[108.0]	[1633.6]
1965	[67.3]	62.3	120.6	[125.6]	[1857.2]
1966	[67.4]	64.7	106.5	[109.2]	[2077.6]
1967	[84.8]	66.4	95.4	[113.8]	[2316.3]
1968	[78.2]	67.5	87.1	[97.8]	[2553.1]

[] = Negative.   Source: *Annual Reports and Accounts.*
1 Excluding Harbours 1948-62.
2 Excluding Harbours 1948-62. Comparability BTC/BRB assumes implicit amortisation provision for way and structures in BTC Accounts.
3 Excluding Harbours 1948-62. Including interest charged to capital. Excluding operational land.

Thus by the end of 1968 BR appears to have absorbed £2,500 million (plus the original scrap value) to reach a position where, given its then current profit prospects, it was still, in aggregate, worth only the scrap value of its assets. But the true picture is a little less gloomy. The Transport Act of 1968 formalised a long-standing *de facto* expression of Government policy, that the nation values the services of stopping and suburban passengers trains more than the revenue recovered from users. If anything, in 1968 the social passenger services were operated at lower real cost than at the time of nationalisation. Many routes had been closed to passenger traffic, and the former steam locomotives and coaches had been replaced in most cases by electric or diesel multiple-unit trains. Although we have neither cost nor revenue data for these services in 1948, if they were losing £53 million, before interest, on revenue of £80 million in 1966,[4] having fallen from a much higher loss in 1961,[5] it seems reasonable to assume that they were not profitable at any time since nationalisation. Of course, we cannot be sure of this; even BR did not know for certain.[6]

In 1968 the Government decided to pay specific subsidies for these services on grounds of 'social need'. This social need had been declining over time, with the increasing private car ownership, availability of other alternatives, etc, and it is therefore likely that if BR could have confronted previous Governments with a 'subsidise or we close' ultimatum, a subsidy would have been forthcoming. One of the biggest failures of both the Transport Act, 1962 and the Beeching Report,[7] was their broad-brush approach to the means of treating the *causes* of the railway deficits. The 1962 Act, by suspending £705 million of the capital debt, and providing for a succession of deficit grants, in effect, 'changed the scale on the thermometer'[8] without actually diagnosing and treating the malady. In contrast, the Beeching Report's analysis was more detailed, if not always correct.[9] The Appendix which appeared in the Board's Annual Reports from the year 1965[10] showed a new awareness of the causes of the railways deficit. But the Beeching Report's expected savings from the withdrawal of unprofitable passenger services, £34–41 million per annum,[11] obviously did not cover the whole of the losses on these services, because by 1966 the Board claimed that, after withdrawing passenger services from 2,750 miles of route, a loss of £60 million per annum remained on stopping and suburban services, plus (and this was ominous) £16 million on 'fast and semi-fast' services.[12]

It was by then clear that a very large number of loss-making services had not been nominated for closure in the Beeching Report's Appendix 2. The report had suggested that some of these, the suburban services outside London, should be studied in conjunction with the competing bus services, and decisions taken on their futures in terms of the net social cost of retention. (This idea came to fruition with the new Transport Act, which set up Passenger Transport Authorities in the conurbations, to have responsibility for all passenger transport within their areas.) Other possible reasons for BR's failure to propose more loss-making passenger services for withdrawal may have been that they were profitable in the short-run, ie, until assets required replacement, or that their contribution to the revenue of connecting services exceeded their specific losses.

The first of these reasons is implausible as a basis for policy making in the long term. The rolling stock used in these services had already been replaced twice since nationalisation (with loco-hauled coaches, and then with multiple-units), and on non-electrified lines would require replacement again as the existing lightweight diesel multiple-units wore out. Of course, at that time BR top management incorrectly believed that track costs were fixed in the long run and therefore irrelevant to a profitability analysis of any particular service. The validity of the second reason (contributory revenue), depends upon the profitability of the recipient passenger services, and as passenger services were unprofitable overall this reason for retention of a particular service begged the question of the retention of the recipient services. Finally, there remained the true reason for accepting the continuation of these services: that BR did not believe that Government permission for withdrawal would be forthcoming. The tortuous process of obtaining approval for the services actually closed, and the reasons advanced by the Government for refusing closure in certain cases, formed a guide to the Government's likely view of other closure proposals.

If the preceding paragraphs have persuaded the reader that BR was in receipt of implicit approval for the running of loss-making services remaining at that time, we are justified in 'adding back' to its net cash flows an amount representing the subsidy which *should* have been paid directly and not through deficit grants, or, in the early years, from profits on freight traffic. The difficulty is that we have no precise data on the size of the necessary 'subsidy' in each year, with the exception of 1961,[13] 1966, and from 1969 onwards. We shall not be very far out by interpolating to find the 'subsidies' for the years 1962 1965, and 1967–1968, and in the absence of contrary information, we assume that the 1961 figure, estimated at £71 million, was the highest recorded. Now, on varying assumptions about the level of the 'subsidy' at 1948 and assuming:

(i)   Linear growth in the 'subsidy' to 1961.
(ii) No interest paid on original capital.
(iii) Positive or [negative] balances earning [paying] interest at six per cent per annum, cumulative.

We find:

	Nil	£20m	£40m
Assumed level of loss on suburban and stopping passenger trains in 1948	Nil	£20m	£40m
Year that the Railways would have passed into net cash deficit	1958	1960	1962
Total cash deficit end 1968 assuming subsidies had been paid. (calculations rounded)	£1,026m	£696m	£411m

Three immediate conclusions flow from this. First, the railways' initial total stock of assets had negligible value for their profit(?)—earning capability. Secondly, separating railway operations from the remainder of the British Transport Commission's activities, and adjusting their financial commitments to this much more realistic basis, BR's performance up to the late Fifties was much more creditable than hitherto supposed. But, thirdly, the burst of investment in the late Fifties and early Sixties was a massive misapplication of resources. This can be seen from column 5 of the Table on page 15, which shows, on the above assumption, the probable spread of net cash flows (before interest) adjusted for the imputed subsidy for passenger services.

From 1956 to 1968, between £776 million and £1,143 million (the precise figure depends on our assumption about the passenger service subsidy) was invested in what should have been the commercial part of the railways for no commercial return. In fact, the losses had mounted *despite* this injection of capital, and the Board could not even pay the interest on it. This was clear because, even if subsidy had been paid for the Government-imposed obligations, BR would still have been making a massive loss on its commercial operations.[14]

There are two possible explanations for this poor financial performance which we can consider quickly and discard. First, it might be suggested that the cost of the other obligations, museums, bridge maintenance, etc, which the Joint Steering Group enquired into, had been an important factor. But the Joint Steering Group found eventually that these amounted to only about £8 million per annum.[15] Secondly, it is sometimes argued that if only the Board had not been subjected to Government restraint on its proposed price increases over the years, it might have been able to recover these large sums from its customers. Note that this argument can apply only to BR's *commercial* traffic: freight and Inter-City passengers. Any losses thus caused on the stopping and suburban passenger services have already been taken into account in our imputed subsidy calculations. For the commercial services, we cannot measure the precise cost, if any, of Government restraint, but we can infer from the Board's normal pricing actions that it had no great complaint about the general levels of its charges, at least in the later years. On freight, the Board had complete pricing freedom from about 1958, and any pricing restraints imposed, for example, by reference to the National Board for Prices & Incomes applied only to a small proportion of the traffic. On commercial passenger traffic, the Board's own actions display its satisfaction with the position. It had complete pricing freedom from the Transport Act 1962, but it was not until the PIB figuratively twisted its arm in 1968[16] that it abandoned the inefficient 'standard rate-per-mile' basis of passenger fares. Even when instructed to adopt a market pricing approach, BR refused to exploit this fully. These were not the acts of an organisation which believed its fares had been constrained unduly by the Government. In fact, most of the constraint in recent years was a self-inflicted wound.[17]

So much for the excuses; a more important question to ask concerns the *social* value of the return on the £1,000-odd million the nation invested in the 'commercial' railway. That is, was the community better off because of the investment, even though, because of imperfections in the circumstances of charging for its services, BR could not recover the full costs from users of the railway? We will take up this point in detail later, because it is highly relevant to current problems. It can be argued that up to the passing of the Transport Act of 1968, the Government's preparedness to underwrite the deficits implied a belief that the total operations of BR produced a net *social* return, but this was not the result of any positive action to identify the respective benefits and costs. The truth was that the Government had not thought in these terms at all. Until the issue of the White Paper on Transport Policy,[18] Government policy on BR treated the deficit grants as a temporary expedient, necessary to tide the railways over a difficult period. Back in 1964, the Board had submitted to the framers of the ill-fated National Plan its estimate that the then working deficit on railway operations (before interest) of £67 million would be eliminated by 1970. There were only three provisos to this ambitious projection:

'(a) Substantial progress continues to be made in implementing closure proposals.
(b) A start is made within the period with the process of concentrating on selected trunk routes.
(c) Co-operation of the unions is secured in increasing productivity and in particular on the question of train manning.'[19]

Of these, (b) was wholly within the control of the Board, and (c) was in the main achieved, but at a high cost.[20] Only the closures were behind schedule, but the total savings the Board was expecting in this field were only £34–41 million: hardly enough to bridge the gap even if achieved in full. But the projected improvement was not being obtained. The £67 million of 1964 rose to £73 million the following year, and then fell slightly to £71 million for 1966.

The Government had this gloomy picture before it when it set up the Joint Steering Group in late 1966. By the time the Group got to work it was already clear that the railway deficit was out of control, and the Board itself was warning of worse to come.[21] (This was one of the Board's predictions which did come true; in 1967 the railway operating deficit rose to £86.5 million.) It was obvious to the Government that neither the 1962 Act nor the Beeching Report had attacked the fundamental problems of BR. It was clear that, even making allowances for the spurious capital debts and the costs of meeting BR's social obligations, there must have been wasted investment on a massive scale. The Government already knew from the report of the Select Committee in 1960[22] that much of the railway modernisation plan investment had been misapplied. But it was now clear that the Ministry of Transport's own detailed checks on investment, which were causing great ill-feeling on BR,[23] were having no observable effect; the Board was continuing to invest large sums in projects which were claimed to be 'profitable', yet the deficits were steadily increasing. Since 1955, BR had invested more than the net book value of Imperial Chemical Industries Ltd yet, even making allowance for the investments in soon-to-be-subsidised passenger services, it still could not manage to make a profit. Over the years the Board had always been ready to forcast a return to profits 'soon', but these forecasts had always been superseded by yet more forecasts; the profits never came.

Obviously the Board's capital debt had to be adjusted, and something had to be done about the social obligations to run passenger services. But otherwise the Board claimed that its businesses were in a healthy state, apart from the red herring of the 'stand-by' issue. The Board claimed that even in its commercial services it was maintaining a 'stand-by' capability which the nation required on social grounds, and that this should be subsidised.[24]

It was obvious that the enquiries of a prestigious committee, and the legislation which followed, were not going to produce an overnight improvement in BR's performance. Where the Stedeford Committee, the Transport Act of 1962 *and* Dr Beeching had failed, it was unrealistic to expect quick improvement now. After the committees and the acts of Parliament were done and gone the same railway management would be carrying on. So we must now look back in a little detail at the history of the British Railways Board and its hapless predecessor, the British Transport Commission. Between them, they had managed to spend some £1,000 million in rebuilding a commercial railway system. But there were just not enough rail users to justify this scale of investment.

1 *British Transport Commission: Annual Report and Accounts,* 1948, paragraph 79.

2 *Report from the Select Committee on Nationalised Industries: British Railways,* 1960, questions 858 − 861.

3 We also include collection and delivery by road of railway consignments for the years in which this activity was separately recorded.

4 *Railway Policy,* Cmnd. 3439, London, HMSO, 1967, paragraph 2.12 (includes losses on lines then expected to be closed).

5 See *British Railways: Annual Report and Accounts,* 1965, paragraph 8. It is not known if 1961 was the peak loss — it was the year used in the Beeching Report analysis.

6 See *Report from the Select Committee on Nationalised Industries: British Railways,* 1960, questions 1933−4, 1816, 1824, for the vagueness with which questions on the profitability of services were answered.

7 British Railways Board: *The Reshaping of British Railways,* London, HMSO, 1963. Afterwards referred to as the 'Beeching Report'.

8 An expression coined by Mr Julian Amery at the time he, as Minister for Aviation, was writing down the capital debt of British Overseas Airways Corporation.

9 If not always correct. See, eg, D.L.Munby: 'The Reshaping of British Railways', *Journal of Industrial Economics,* July, 1963, and Stewart Joy: 'British Railways Track Costs', *Journal of Industrial Economics,* November 1964.

10 *British Railways Board, Annual Report and Accounts 1965, 1966, 1967. Appendix I.*

11 Beeching Report, p. 54.

12 *British Railways Board: Annual Report and Accounts,* 1966. Appendix I.

13 The 1961 figure is available only on a 'replacement cost plus interest' basis. I have converted it to an estimated historical cost basis on the assumption that the 1961 relationship between the two was similar to that in 1966.

14 For example, given the most generous subsidy assumption, no initial capital debt, and 6% interest paid on accumulated profits or charged on accumulated losses, the deficit in 1968 would have been £37 million.

15 Cmnd 3439, *op cit,* paragraph 2.16.

16 See *National Board for Prices and Incomes Report No 72. Proposed Increases by British Railways Board in Certain Country-Wide Fares & Charges.* Cmnd 3656, London, HMSO, 1968.

17 In making its first 'market pricing' increase, BR reduced certain proposed increases from what they would have been under its standard fare proposals, in order to derive the same total revenue increase as its standard fares proposal would have produced. It took two more years before the market pricing was really exploited properly.

18 Cmnd 3057, London, HMSO, 1965, p.129.

19 *The National Plan,* Cmnd 2764, London, HMSO, 1965, p.129.

20 See Chapters 6 and 7.

21 See *British Railways Board: Annual Report & Accounts 1966,* London 1967, paragraph 7.

22 *Report from the Select Committee on the Nationalised Industries: British Railways,* London, HMSO, 1960. (Afterwards shown as *SCNI: BR 1960*).

23 See Sir Stanley Raymond's evidence to the Select Committee in 1967: *First Report from the Select Committee on Nationalised Industries: Ministerial Control of the Nationalised Industries,* London, HMSO, 1968 (afterwards shown as *SCNI/Ministerial Control, 1968.*) Vol.II, p.167, paragraphs 3.9 and 3.10, questions 584 to 597, and appendix 34: 'Relations between the Ministry of Transport and the British Railways Board on capital investment matters'.

24 See S.E.Raymond: 'British Railways — Towards a Solution and a Modern Railway', *Institute of Transport Journal,* Vol.31, No 10, May 1966, page 365 and A.V.Barker: 'Costs of Social Service and Standby Capacity', *Modern Railways,* XXIII 221, February 1967, page 64–5.

2 | The Background to Nationalisation

'It is the social duty of a Railway Company to concentrate upon
those transport services in which it enjoys the greatest advantage
over other means of transport, for the same reason that a
country's industries should concentrate on those in which it excels
over its neighbours.'
C.E.R.Sherrington: The Economics of Rail Transport in
Great Britain. 2nd Edition, London, 1937, p.101

Nationalisation of the main line railway companies was inevitable. The Transport Act, 1947 was the crossroads at which a number of irresistible forces met, and all of them were for taking the railways into public ownership.

The railway industry in Britain had been in economic difficulty since World War I. Even before the spread of motor vehicles, there had been, in aggregate, too much railway capacity, but the competitive structure of the industry prevented anything being done about it. Although a reduction in capacity was needed, as late as 1899 there was a major duplication of capacity, when the Great Central Railway built a main line to London which added nothing of significance to the nation's transport capability, but abstracted vital traffic from parallel lines.[1] Then there were the branch lines to everywhere, built during one or other of the railway manias of the mid-19th century, profitless appendages of the main line routes from which they absorbed far more resources than they contributed in traffics. Over 120 separate companies competed more with each other than with the then rail rivals: coastal shipping, the canals and, in the conurbations, the municipal tramway systems. Relations between railway companies were regulated through the Railway Clearing House, and their relations with users and competitors were regulated by the Railway Rates Tribunal. Although the railway system was physically integrated, in that a common track and loading gauge permitted the inter-running of rolling stock, in operating and commercial terms the integration left much to be desired. This became obvious during World War I, when Government control obtained significant improvements in efficiency. Such improvements were due mainly to the elimination of company boundaries, and the exploitation of possibilities for inter-railway co-operation which had just not been feasible when the separate companies had been competitors as well as co-operators. Of course, there was little effective competition during the war, either between the railway companies or with the railways' competitors, and this helped to hide the reductions in the quality of service which accompanied many of the improvements in operating efficiency. It was widely assumed at the time that such efficiency improvements could be sustained by unified operation of the railway companies in peacetime. Even without the new-found competition from motor cars, lorries and buses, this was not possible. But more importantly, it was assumed that the financial benefits of unification, derived principally on the main lines, would be sufficient to sustain the ubiquitous network of branch lines and their services. With the motor age upon them, there was never any hope of this. The real question was 'how much rail service does the nation need?', not 'is it nationalisation or just large scale mergers which are needed to produce the economies necessary to sustain the *present* scale of services?'.

The fact that grouping into four large, geographically distinct systems was preferred to nationalisation is irrelevant. Neither could have succeeded. But it is important to remember that the community was unlikely to have accepted any more drastic alternative. The fact that in the USA the railways are still organised and regulated in the manner of pre-grouping in Britain, and legislators (and railroad managements) are unwilling to seek a freely competitive solution to the industry's problems, suggests that Britain in 1921 was unlikely to have been willing to take such a bold step. The main problem was that Britain's railways, like those in the USA, were overbuilt. This was the price of competitive development of the systems. Most other countries had seen the error of 19th century Britain's policy and had exercised strict control over the construction of railways. Elsewhere, either regional or national monopolies had been created, and in many cases the marginal routes had been built on the cheap, under separate, local managements, and often with subsidies from local authorities. But in Britain, in addition to the weak and unprofitable railway companies, whose lack of success was due largely to the light traffic volumes they handled, each of the profitable companies had a large mileage of loss-making branch lines. It was already the implicit Government policy that the loss-making routes of the strong companies should be cross-subsidised, through the refusal to entertain closure applications. It was therefore a seemingly just solution to ask the profitable (or potentially profitable) companies to take all of the weak companies into the fold. fold.

Railways had been regulated for many years, both on the services they had to provide, and on the prices they could charge. The first type of regulation, which imposed the 'common carrier' obligation, was really a *quid pro quo* for the right to operate, while the second was aimed primarily at preventing the exploitation of monopolies.[2] Consider carefully the stranglehold that such 'product-plus-price' regulation places on a railway. For a given technology and level of operating efficiency, the arbitrarily fixed levels of prices will determine both the amount of traffic which is offered and, of course, the total revenue. But the amount of traffic offered also determines the railway's costs. The problem is that there is no necessary relationship between the revenue and the costs. Provided that it is working as efficiently as possible, whether a railway makes a profit or a loss under these conditions is entirely outside its control. It all depends on the relationship between revenue and costs at the time the regulation is imposed, and whether the regulatory authority allows prices to be increased in line with cost increases thereafter. Adding the further complication that the same mileage revenue scales were applied regardless of route or company, it becomes obvious that railway profits were almost wholly dependent upon the mix of traffic of each company.

Some recent writers have argued that the most damaging (to the railways) feature of this control of the industry arose because the freight charges were based, in a very crude way, on the values of the respective commodities carried.[3] But this is to misunderstand what the railways were trying to do. The common term for the railways' pricing principle was 'what the traffic will bear', and this was (and is) the optimal way of setting prices for railway service. The way in which this principle was applied, by using discriminatory rates based on the commodity carried, was often excused by railway managements as a socially desirable form of cross-subsidisation. But the pricing of traffics according to their respective values does not constitute evidence of 'cross-subsidisation', either attempted or achieved. For this to have occurred it must be shown that the railway would have been better off without its low-rated traffics, and there has never been any evidence of this.

A dangerous myth created by railway economics writings of the last forty years has been that a 'cost-based' charging system would have been preferable to charging what the traffic would bear. Both theory and experience disprove this assertion, however closely it may appear to match text-book notions of optimal pricing rules for public utilities. If these critics, at leisure and with hindsight, could not get the economics of the problem right, it is hardly fair to expect that the railway managers of the Thirties would have attained technically elegant solutions to their pricing problems.[4] In fact, the railwaymen's intuition had more validity than their critics' misplaced use of the theory.

It is difficult to find where all this confusion originated. Perhaps it was with Sir William Acworth, the grand old man of modern railway economics, who here and there stated the theory clearly enough, but insisted on dissipating its force with some of the apologia he offered in support.[5] His justifying statements that 'railway charges are fixed, not according to an estimated cost of service, but roughly on the principle of equality of sacrifice by the payer', and 'what the traffic will bear is a principle, not of extortion, but of equitable concession to the weaker members of the community', are completely misplaced. If the railway industry had at that time been earning super-profits there may have been some call for pricing restraint, but it had not, was not, and was not likely in the near future to be in that happy position. Thus any rate which was restrained on the grounds Acworth cited represented a simple transfer of wealth from the railway shareholders to the user who was prepared to pay more. This may have been a case of the academic supporter of the railways offering a spurious justification for the practice because he did not think that rail users, regulators and legislators would accept the true explanation. Many of them still will not, particularly in the USA. But the railway managers knew what they were doing, even if they may not have been doing it very well.

C.E.R.Sherrington, the railways' spokesman on economic affairs in the inter-war years, showed that he understood fully the difference between what the railways were really trying to do, and what they admitted to be trying to do. In listing the important factors in determining the freight rate classification of a particular commodity, although he managed to exclude all reference to demand, he was quite adamant that the aim of railway pricing was 'to yield the maximum net value'.[6] Sherrington was clear that every traffic must bear a rate which fell between the direct (ie, out of pocket) costs of its carriage, and the 'added value' induced by the transit. Although he admitted that '. . . in practice it is impossible for a rates expert to know what any individual traffic can bear.' he implied that they should make a pretty good effort to find out by opening the bargaining as high as possible.

There are two inter-related problems here, and a third which depends on the results of the first two. The first two are: (i) what should the railways have been trying to do; and (ii) how well were they doing it? The third is: if they failed at (i), what next? If the law prescribes that the railways shall carry all traffics offered, at rates not exceeding laid-down maxima, their optimum course is to try to charge as must as possible for each traffic, and to attempt to minimise the costs of handling the traffics.

That it what the railways were trying to do. They charged more to carry high-value commodities than, say, coal, because that was the way in which they thought they could maximise their revenue for a given mix of traffic and level of costs. The fact that their basic charging method appeared to tie charges to values of commodities has caused writers to think that questions of who *should*, rather than *could* pay, were a keystone of railway ratemaking. But the value of the commodity was used only as a quick, publicly acceptable, but crude alternative to making individual decisions about the ability to pay of each shipper in respect of each traffic.

The widespread use of 'exceptional' rates (and 'cheap' fares for passengers) shows that the railways were not unresponsive to competitive factors.[7] Where the value of the commodity was not a good representation of the shipper's preparedness to pay, ie, where he had a cheaper alternative (usually road) available, the railways were quick to quote him an exceptional rate. It is quite possible that particular railway commercial agents were not very good at extracting from shippers the highest possible 'exceptional' rate for each traffic, but even when the railways tried a supposed cost-based pricing system in the late Fifties and early Sixties, this difficulty was still present.[8] It is not an argument against attempting to maximise revenue in this way. The problem was not that the railways could not quote rates low enough to gain profitable traffic in competition; it was that the maximum rates permitted were not high enough to turn unprofitable traffics away to their competitors.

It was here that cost analysis was required, but even here the railways were inhibited by the public climate in which they had to exist. As C.D.Foster has pointed out, any success in maximising profits would have resulted in the imposition of further regulation.[9] And any concerted pressure to be relieved of passenger obligations (or to withdraw unprofitable services) might have jeopardised other railway initiatives in the field of regulation, such as attempts to have road haulage regulated.

Although the railways in the Thirties have been criticised for placing too rigid an interpretation on their obligations, they cannot be blamed for trying to observe the spirit of the 1921 Act. Their fault was that they kept on trying for too long. The public service obligation, however voluntarily accepted, dies very hard. Secondly, it was a valid tactic to try first to make a success of the competitive option which maximised the physical size and activity of their systems. The higher the level of profitable activity they could sustain, the better for themselves, their shareholders, their employees, and the nation at large. (This endeavour, to maximise the size and volume of the railway system, will recur in our narrative. The only trouble has been that the railway managers have tended to forget the crucial condition: that the system they retain should be profitable.) When, at long last, the managements of the four companies realised that their passive acceptance of the 'public service' obligations had failed to elicit from the Government the regulation of road haulage necessary to ensure railway profits, they took the only alternative route and opened their 'Square Deal' campaign.

The 'Square Deal' campaign sought the complete freeing of the railways from pricing and product constraints. Their competitors, the road hauliers, already had this freedom, although freedom of entry to the road haulage business had been severely curtailed by the Road Traffic Act of 1930. The railways wanted to be able either to obtain an economic price for each service, or to abandon it. They no longer had significant and widespread monopoly powers, and there was no possibility of their cross-subsidising any traffics. In fact, they were arguing that even some of their supposed 'monopoly' traffics were unprofitable and should be repriced. Had the 'Square Deal' proposals been accepted, even with some residual constraints on the exercise of local monopoly powers, the physical restructuring of the national railway network and its pattern of services would have been the inevitable outcome. But the nation was ill-prepared for such a climactic change. Although the Government accepted the principle of the 'Square Deal' proposals, the outbreak of war made the whole issue redundant as the railways were again taken into Government control.

The inevitable outcome of a vigorous implementation of the 'Square Deal', the pricing of unprofitable traffics off the railway and the consequent closure of routes, had of course always been available in a more crude form. Whole lines, or stations, *could* have been closed at any time, but the railways were very slow to use this power. In opting for the right to get rid of particular traffics, for that is what pricing freedom would have meant in most cases, they were still in the grip of some myths of the past. Certainly, there must have been traffics whose revenues failed to cover even their short run marginal costs,[10] and these were obvious candidates for abandonment. But the guts of the railways' problem was that there were many lines and stations which cost more to operate than they generated in revenue. This was the part of the railways' activity which needed to be cross-subsidised if it was to continue. Of all the unprofitable companies, ie, unprofitable routes and stations, which were taken into the grouping, only 800 route miles (out of 20,000) were closed between 1923 and 1939. It is obvious that the managements were unwilling to atempt the necessary restructuring of their systems away from the geographical ubiquity which had been justified in the horse and cart age. Of course, it can be argued that they had more important things to do, but seventeen years is a long time, and there is not really much else to show for the peacetime activities of the four companies. Apart from the publicity feats of some express passenger trains in the late Thirties, by 1939 railway technology, whether engineering operating or commercial, showed very little, if any, advance over the best practices of the pre-grouping companies.

Then came the war, and it can fairly be said that the railways did Britain proud. But it was inevitable that the conditions under which they had to do so, particularly with passengers, cost them incalculable goodwill when peace was restored. The restriction of all other forms of inland transport returned to the railways much higher levels of traffic for which, to their shareholders' cost, they had retained the capacity in the inter-war years. But the methods of financing railway operations through the war meant that no adequate reward went to the companies for this fortuitous providence. That was to be settled, after a fashion, by nationalisation. So too was the fact that the railways came out of the war with their physical plant reduced and in far worse condition than in 1939. But apart from these immediate financial handicaps imposed upon the companies by the war, a massive future burden was imposed because of the fact that, even with the continuation of motor fuel rationing, the railways' competitors would inevitably be able to restore their services to peacetime qualities faster than the run-down railways. All of these factors pointed to nationalisation as a means of softening the blow. Then the first post-war general election returned a Labour government, committed to the 'integration' of inland transport.[11]

Quite apart from any doctrinaire preference of the new Government for state control of the transport sector, the nationalisation of most of the industry was a logical development of transport policy between the wars. Almost every change had been a move away from the allocative efficiency of a free market. All the participants in the industry (but not potential participants) were for integration by regulation. Their minds had been closed on this for years. Back in 1931 Professor (later Sir) Arnold Plant had had the temerity to suggest in a paper read to the Institute of Transport that a competitive solution was more likely to give the same results, and at far less cost. But he was met with what can only be described as sneering condescension by people such as Lord Ashfield and Sir Osborne Mance.[12] The tenor of their criticism was that academics should address themselves to solving the problems of the 'real world' in which the 'practical men' had to survive. But their problems arose because of the inevitable shortcomings of regulations, and they could not see that Plant was proposing that they should avoid the problems altogether. 'Stability', at the expense of the users, and primarily for the benefit of the participants, was the basic aim.

The regulation of the road haulage industry, the brain-child of the Salter Conference in 1932, was a case in point. A committee of railway managers and established road hauliers concluded that 'stability' would be best obtained by denying access to the industry to any entrants who would entice traffic away from established operators.[13] Similarly with buses, the Road Traffic Act of 1930 favoured the large regional operators by restricting new entrants, and reduced competition with the railways, which were in any case substantial shareholders in regional bus companies.[14] In London, the creation of a monopoly of all public transport (except that provided by taxis and the main line railways) was supported by all three major political parties.[15] Now, if the railways' competitors were unwilling to compete with each other, and the railways were certainly unwilling to compete with them, if it could be avoided, we can understand the widespread belief that common ownership and total integration would be an improvement over the 'regulated competition' of the Thirties.

The notion of cross-subsidy was supported everywhere but in the road haulage industry. In the public eye, the railways provided a perfect mechanism for the maintenance of a 'national' and comprehensive transport service for freight and passengers. It was not so clearly recognised on the part of transport users that effective 'integration' and 'cross-subsidy' implied that more users would have either to pay higher prices, or suffer inferior service, or both, than would be the case under free competition. This is because 'cross-subsidy' is a tax on some users, for the benefit of others. Many railwaymen and busmen were happy to act as a *de facto* branch of the Inland Revenue in this way, because it meant that their own particular organisations would in consequence be larger. But they did not foresee that many of the users they were 'taxing' would eventually rebel and buy their own transport facilities. 'Cross-subsidy' depends upon the exploitation of a monopoly, and if the exploited user can find a way to profitably free himself of that monopoly, he will do so. As the private car could not be included in a national transport monopoly, and as the 'own account' lorry was deliberately excluded, the eventual destruction of much of the monopoly was inevitable.

The favourite phrase of the transport integrators was 'economies of scale'. It was expected that, in addition to savings derived from power effectively to direct traffic to its lowest-cost mode, by restricting services on the competitive modes, a national transport monopoly would achieve further economies solely by virtue of its large size. (In passing, we should note that the first-mentioned source of savings the ability to direct traffic against users' wishes, will almost inevitably impose higher costs (or worse service, which is the same thing) on the user. The monopoly's costs may be lowered, but total transport costs will be raised. We will come back to this point later.) Beyond a single, integrated process, economies of scale can be very elusive. Some firms, with good managements, achieve them; but others, which presumably have poor quality managements, find that increased size leads to less efficient operations, and *dis*economies of scale.

The nationalisation proposals of the Government envisaged an organisation of over 900,000 employees, comprising the main line railways, their docks, harbours, shipping services, hotels and their interests in bus companies and travel agents, the London Passenger Transport Board, the for-hire sector of the long distance (over 25 miles) road haulage industry, and most of the inland waterways. What was it that led people to expect that such an administrative juggernaut would produce economies of scale?

Firstly, it must be remembered that such a monster had already been created and, in its special role, had performed with merit. This was the Ministry of War Transport, which had been managed at its upper levels by a mixture of civil servants and men from the industry. And the head of that wartime organisation, Lord Hurcomb, was to be the first chairman of the new monolith, the British Transport Commission. Therein lay the seeds of failure, because neither customers nor managers (nor Parliament for that matter) are prepared to act in peacetime as they will in war. Secondly, a previous experiment in 'integration', the London Passenger Transport Board, had managed to reduce many fares on taking over from the small bus operators. But this was a benefit of its total *control* of public transport, not an economy of the scale of its organisation *per se.* In fact, the users of the bus services which had been 'rationalised' were probably worse off. Thirdly, there *should* be some savings to be made in 'overheads', in the provision of central services to the various operating parts of the organisation. Of course, the installation of an additional level of management above those who formerly ran their business on their own, means that the new superior level will wish to make decisions which were previously made lower down, and this opportunity for discord must be balanced with any savings from the provision of 'central services'. But the Ministry of War Transport had been making such decisions for a few years, and there was little cause for doubt on that score. Or was there?

1 See George Dow: *Great Central,* Volume III, London. Although this particular route, and its demise, have generated great emotions, it was a total irrelevancy. Only a few miles of it survive today. As an example of the lengths to which the more extreme railway 'enthusiasts' will pursue their causes, as late as 1966 the Great Central Association was asking the Government to instruct BR to divert traffic from its recently electrified North Western main line to the Great Central route, for which there were 'plans' to form a company to carry on its operation. The notion that BR should be instructed to 'short-haul' itself in the cause of railway romanticism did not excite much interest in Whitehall.

2 For a succinct account of the development of railway regulation in Britain, see Alistair M. Milne and Austen Laing: *The Obligation to Carry,* London, 1956, Chapters I and II. The common carrier obligation was the promoters in return for protection against competition. See H. Parris: *Government and the Railways in Nineteenth Century Britain,* London 1965. Parris found the idea of the doctrine of equivalents in an unpublished essay by J. Harold Wilson.

3 See, for example: Graham L. Reid and Kevin Allen: *Nationalised Industries,* Harmondsworth, Middlesex, 1970, p.114; K.M.Gwilliam: *Transport and Public Policy,* London, 1964, pp.90 and 98, and see the next footnote.

4 For example, one recent writer, Derek H. Aldcroft, contradicts himself in this area within seven lines in one book *(British Railways in Transition,* London, 1968, p 64, where at line 8 he wants demand-based rates and at line 15 he wants cost-based rates). The same writer provided an equally confusing treatment of this topic in the following year in H.J.Dyos & D.H.Aldcroft: *British Transport. An economic survey from the seventeenth century to the twentieth,* Leicester, 1969.

5 See Sir William M. Acworth and W.T.Stephenson: *The Elements of Railway Economics,* New Edition, Oxford, 1924, Chapter VIII and IX.

6 See C.E.R.Sherrington: *Economics of Railway Transport,* Second Edition, London, 1937. The factors listed (pp. 86—7) were: Exchange value: Cost (which depended upon loadability); Volume and weight; Perishability; Method of packing; Regularity; Consignment size: Owners' or Company's Risk; Dangerous goods. It will be noted that all but the first factor are cost determinants.

7 In 1935. 84% of the rail tonnage was moving at exceptional rates -- quoted in Gilbert Walker: *Road and Rail, and enquiry into the economics of competition and state control.* London, 1942, p.63.

8 See Chapter 5 where the flaws in any system of 'cost-based' pricing for railways are described.

9 See *The Transport Problem,* London, 1963, pp. 73, 74.

10 That is, the costs which would be saved *automatically* by the absence of the traffic, those which required no subsequent management and action. Examples are claims expenses, wear and tear on rolling stock.

11 For a general account of the railways' contribution to the war effort, see C.I.Savage: *History of the Second World War: Inland Transport,* London 1957. For a good account of the difficulties of securing an equitable financial arrangement, see O.S.Nock. *History of the Great Western Railway,* London 1967, pp. 167 – 175.

12 Competition and co-operation in transport', *Journal of the Institute of Transport*, January 1932, pp. 127 – 136. See particularly Lord Ashfield's comments following the reading of the paper, and Sir H. Osborne Mauce's letter to the editor (same volume, p.159.)
13 See, for example, G.J.Ponsonby: 'The new Conditions of Entry into the Road Haulage Business'. *Economica*, May 1937.
14 See John Hibbs: *Transport for Passengers*, Second Edition, London, 1967.
15 For a comprehensive account of the movement towards 'giantism' in British Transport, see G.J.Ponsonby: 'The Structure and organisation of the transport system', *Journal of the Royal Society of Arts*, October 1960, pp. 782 – 795.

3 | Nationalisation

'In setting up its organisation the executive endeavoured
particularly to avoid the creation of an over-centralised
organisation at the top and equally to avoid unduly drastic
changes at the outset, since the sudden disruption of the
well-tried organisations and long-established practices
and methods of the former railway companies might easily
have led to serious working difficulties.'
*British Transport Commission Report and Accounts for 1948,
para 140.*

On the first day of 1948, the process of railway unification, commenced in 1923, was completed. The assets of the four main line companies were taken over by the British Transport Commission, to be operated by a subsidiary appointive body, the Railway Executive. The motto at the head of this page is the creed promulgated by the Railway Executive. We will find that, to the peril of the railway industry; the Executive failed miserably in its first aim: to avoid excessive centralisation, and it succeeded only too well in the second: to avoid change. The backwash of these two failures of the Railway Executive is still being felt 25 years later. It was the RE which set the pattern, unfettered by its supposed master, the BTC, of British railway managements' 20 years of trying to solve yesterday's problems with tomorrow's money. The fact that these two rarely coincided is the fault of the railway managers; the fact that they were not stopped from playing this expensive charade was the fault of the BTC and the Minstry of Transport.

For a better understanding of the events following nationalisation we have to look closely at the backgrounds and experience of the men concerned. The main line railway companies, and in particular the LNER and LMS with their formal development programmes for junior management, provided some of the most interesting and exciting employment opportunities in Britain. To match them, a man would have needed to join the armed forces or the colonial service. With the possible exception of steelmaking, no industry provided the range of activity and satisfying man-management relationships of the railways.

A railway in operation is a living thing, dependent, like a fighting ship, on every man doing precisely what is expected of him. And, again like a fighting ship, when things go wrong (such as a wreck) those same men whose normal role is to observe a rule book to the letter must become instant innovators, responding to each unique emergency in a way which restores normality in the minimum of time and with a minimum of disturbance to the other parts of the operation. Although railway accidents represent a failure of management in some way, clearing the wreck and getting the traffic moving again provide the kind of challenge which gives great satisfaction to a particular type of manager. For (admittedly casual) evidence of this one has only to read the biography of G.F.Fiennes,[1] noting the way he was able to assuage some of his chagrin that an accident had occurred by his satisfaction at the professional way in which it had been cleared up. Even when he was general manager of a railway region, he still went to the scene of major accidents to express his involvement with the men actually doing the work.[2]

Similarly, many railway engineers develop an abiding interest in the physical aspects of railway operations. The many photographs in locomotive books of dust-coated or overalled senior engineers in steam locomotive cabs testifies to their continuing involvement with the basic mechanical details of their profession. The way in which the biographer of R.A.Riddles, the designer of the last BR steam locomotives, described his sensations on having a last drive of a locomotive before retirement suggests an almost orgiastic relationship between man and machine.

The successful wartime resistance efforts of the SNCF in France were possible only because, even in peacetime, railway operations are managed as a para-military organisation. There is really no alternative on the operating and engineering side. Railways may be the safest means of earth travel, but this depends upon an observance of rules and co-operative effort on the part of all workers which is not found on the same scale anywhere else outside the armed forces. If a worker on a car-assembly line does something wrong, the chances are that it will be detected on inspection. But even if the man-caused fault escapes detection, the worst that can happen is that some buyer has a 'rogue' car. In similar circumstances on a railway, a momentary lapse by one man can endanger himself, his mates, and the general public (in order of proximity, not necessarily importance!). Of course, the satisfactions of railway work are by no means limited to the management levels. Apart from the security of railway work before the war, to be a servant of one of the railway companies carried with it pride and romance which, for some companies, has as yet still not disappeared.

Under these circumstances, just as in the armed forces, a high quality of man-management ability is demanded of the successful railway manager at the operating level. But I will argue that, unlike the armed forces, the way in which the better railways developed their operating managers was not guaranteed to provide the necessary qualities at the highest levels. For our basic clues we must return to Fiennes' autobiography. He was one of the most successful railway managers, rising from what he himself admits was a barely earned fourth class degree in Greats at Oxford to be general manager of the Eastern Region, successor to the LNER he had joined 36 years earlier. Had it not been for a little peccadillo concerning the publication of his autobiography, he would probably have risen higher (in BR terms, but perhaps not in his own) to a position on the Board. But if we look at the pattern of his progress through the levels of operating management, and this was typical of what was expected of a man of his way to the top, two disturbing factors emerge.

The LNER's traffic apprentice scheme and the subsequent pattern of promotion were designed to provide men with an accumulation of experience in railway operation and man-management. It also, incidentally but importantly, closed the upper levels of the company to men who were unprepared to move house every four or five years. For example, in 10 years Fiennes moved house 11 times to take up new jobs.[3] The important question is: if the way to the top was open only to those who were prepared to pay the price in terms of family upheavals etc, did that cause an undesirable narrowing of the range of choice from which those top jobs had to be filled? Then there was the frequency of job rotation and its special effects. After ceasing to be a traffic apprentice, Fiennes had 15 different jobs before he became general manager of the Eastern Region; an average of one every two years. Such wide experience in the field is characteristic of senior railwaymen.

Whilst it makes for eminently capable operating managers, it has definite disadvantages at the highest levels, where memories of Whitemoor Yard, Bradford Valley Goods Depot or Crewe Works impose an unnecessary brake on thoughts of grand strategy. This path of management progression created other problems too. On the way up, especially in the inter-war years, men were plentiful but equipment was old and scarce. Hence the fetish, once in power, for solving yesterday's problems. Even when managers have made a complete change of function at the top, they find it hard to restrain a wish to see the ills they suffered put right. Hence a personnel chief arguing passionately for a particular signalling project because of his memory of difficulties as line operating manager in the past. Or the building of unnecessary wagons to relieve shortages of distant memory. Or the building of an unnecessary generation of easily maintainable steam locomotives by a man who had sweated with non standard, inside-cylindered, locomotives before the war. (But more of this shortly.)

It will help to expose this problem if we return for a moment to our analogy of the armed forces. Of course, they too are strong on preparing to fight yesterday's wars. But as an officer moves up through the ranks a clear distinction is made between tactical and strategic command. To move from one to the other an officer undergoes an intensive didactic period at the Imperial Defence College, where he is prepared for the much different scale and scope of problem in strategic command. The railways have never provided for this, and the period since nationalisation is littered with debacles caused by a failure to respond adequately to problems a little above the plane of simply keeping the trains running.

This was the background of the men who, having joined the GWR, LMS, LNER or SR straight from school or university, found themselves working in 1948 for the Railways Executive of the British Transport Commission. Apart from such horrors as the *Railway Magazine's* suggestion (with coloured illustration) that under the Government's ownership their beloved steam locomotives might be painted pillar-box red, the managers of the former main line companies had much to worry them. For a variety of reasons, they had nearly all opposed nationalisation. In many instances this was due to misapprehensions about working for the Government. They had been led to believe that the 1923 grouping, for the success of which they had been working hard before the war, was an alternative to nationalisation. Did nationalisation signify failure? The changes they had argued for before the war affected mainly their competitive relations with the road hauliers and bus companies. But the biggest change sought by nationalisation was the unification of the railways. It was to take the railway managers so long to come to terms with each other that, in the event, they never really got around to the co-ordination with road which they had so earnestly sought in the Thirties.

Unifying the railways was obviously not going to be easy. 25 years after the grouping, there were still stresses and strains in the LMS caused by Midland/ LNWR antagonisms.[4] Many were concerned that the loss of the old company identities would lose more in morale and public acceptance than it gained in savings of paint. Much of the dynamic of railway management followed, for good or ill, from the chauvinism of the managers and the men of the old companies. Now the traditions of over a hundred years were to be submerged as four of the biggest joint stock companies in the land were turned into the railway operating department of an unseen beaurocracy, the BTC. Worse was to come, when the railwaymen learned of the austere personal styles of the BTC members, so unlike the grand manner of the chairmen and general managers of the companies. The tone was set by Lord Hurcomb, whose published salary details read: '£8,500 (of which £7,000 taken)'. This nominal salary was below that of the general managers of the old companies, and the fact that Hurcomb was foregoing part of it was ominous indeed. Of course, BTC salaries determined RE salaries, although one member of the railway executive was able to retain his former salary on a personal basis (as were others lower down).

The fact that jobs demonstrably four times as large as those on the old companies were not considered to be worth any more salary added insult to the injury suffered by those whose chances of paramount office had been rudely quartered by nationalisation. But that was not all. The combined efforts of the BTC and RE to centralise control meant the stripping of authority from men down the line. The machinations at the highest levels are described in Michael R. Bonavia's book *The Organisation of British Railways*,[5] but it is probably too late now to provide a full analysis of the demoralising effects lower down. To give just one example: in the old LMS and LNER a crucial level of management had been the District, with its operating manager, passenger manager and goods manager, posts which represented the height of aspiration for most operating and commercial men. In particular, the district goods manager was a post of important status with customers and in community affairs; it represented the first level of top management, one which freight customers would approach to 'get something done'. In its haste to suck power upwards into the vacuum created by its own existence, the Railway Executive stripped these posts of nearly all their authority. If the RE was going to make all the big decisions, the little ones had to be left to regional officers, not the men in the districts who were in actual contact with most of BR's customers. Henceforth the RE wanted to control the whole railway, through its functional men at regional headquarters. The derisory authorities delegated to the 'chief regional officers',[6] suggest that these men, the inheritors of the general managers of the old companies, had no real authority at all.

Of course, the Railway Executive had its own struggle for authority with the BTC, and some of the delegated authorities it had were insults to reasonable men. With the exception of the industrial relations man, all the members of the RE were eminent railwaymen, and they believed that the Government had appointed them to run the railways, not the BTC. But the BTC did not accept this view, and Bonavia documents some of the undignified wrangling which characterised relations between the two bodies supposedly bringing about the Utopian dream of transport integration. If this kind of acrimony went down on paper, it does not require a brilliant imagination to sense the tone of oral communication between the two bodies. One trouble was that until the BTC had completed the purchase and organisation of the road haulage companies, there was nothing to integrate. And even when it had established control over the road haulage industry, the BTC had no clear idea on how the integration was to be effected. The Government had had a vague notion that integration would follow naturally from a 'rational' charges scheme, and had made the production of such a scheme a statutory requirement. The task of preparing this charges scheme was the responsibility of the BTC, and it was at this point that the rot set in. Although the RE was responsible for the cost of running the railways, the major responsibility for their financial performance lay elsewhere, because the revenue was in other hands. The failure to take full account of the financial implications of their actions was a habit of senior railway managers which would take twenty years to eradicate.

The nationalisation of the for-hire long distance road haulage industry brought an important change in the requirements of the railway freight pricing principles. 'What the traffic would bear' was no longer an equitable method because it was within the powers of the BTC to determine what many rail traffics would bear, simply by withdrawing road services. In fact, this did not happen, and the Road Haulage Executive competed with the railways as of old. It had to, because on its other flank it was competing with the 'C' licence, own-account, lorry operators. Thus the railways got the worst of all worlds: the continuance of competition *and* their traditional obligation to carry all traffic offering. The BTC's commitment to produce a new charges scheme was of academic interest to the RE. In the meantime, the old mixture of classification and exceptional rates continued. Even if the BTC had any ideas of how to achieve integration by a published charging scheme, a task not achieved before or since, most of its efforts had to be applied to obtain approval for general rate increases from the Transport Tribunal. As expected, costs were rising fast. It is difficult to see how the Government could expect even the BTC to be responsible for its financial performance. The revenue was determined by an independent, quasi-judicial body which took as its remit the protection of consumers, and the costs were determined either by the Railway Executive or the Government.

The most important Government-determined cost was interest on capital. It was widely agreed at the time that the old railway shareholders had been paid far too much for the railways. We can now see, of course, that the railway assets were worthless in terms of their earning power.[6] But this was not the basis on which the shareholders should have been paid. There were really two separate transactions. One was to compensate the shareholders, and this had to include a large element of belated reward for the running-down of their assets in the war. The second transaction should have been the transfer of those assets to the BTC, and this should have been in the form of equity capital, on which interest would be paid only if earned. Between them, the Government and the Transport

Tribunal ensured that BR could barely pay interest on its inflated capital debt, and in the eyes of both public and staff it looked like a lossmaker from its inception. This brought immediate difficulties because, if it is impossible to succeed, the gradations of inevitable failure have little meaning as a motivator of management and staff. The circumstances of the nationalisation were disastrous to morale, and the impossible financial target only made things worse. Before nationalisation, it had suited Labour politicians to vilify the railways as part of their claim that state ownership would improve matters. In rebuttal, Conservatives had argued that nationalisation would make matters worse, and the Government's confusion of a just reward to shareholders with a reasonable financial target ensured the truth of this prophecy. One trouble was that nobody knew quite what to expect of nationalisation. The frequency of newspaper cartoons of passengers proclaiming to railwaymen that the public were now their bosses was indicative of the general mood, but most peoples' dreams remained unfulfilled.

Some dreams were realised, however, at great cost to the nation and succeeding railway operating men. One supposed fruit of railway unification was the opportunity to standardise locomotive construction. In every sense but that of prolonging the romance of the steam locomotive, the way in which this was managed was a disaster of the first order. No one but the BTC seemed to notice this at the time, and they stood by impotent as the future was mortgaged. The apparent independence which Ministerial appointment imparted to the Railway Executive was to extract its greatest cost on this issue.

At the time of the grouping in 1923 the chief mechanical engineers of the constituent companies ranked second only to their general managers, and locomotive engineering had a very high standing indeed. Although there was a thriving commercial locomotive building industry in Britain, most of its production went for export because most railway companies constructed their own locomotives. This meant that in addition to designing the rolling stock, the chief mechanical engineer controlled a large manufacturing organisation. The reason for this particular form of vertical integration is difficult to understand. It placed the companies totally in the hands of their CME's designing skills and in practice denied them access to competitive bids for building. This practice continued in each of the four main line companies. Gradually each of them established standard locomotive policies, even though the financial stringency of the Thirties limited the amount of new locomotive building. Although coal and labour were cheap, each of the main line companies studied other forms of traction.

The Southern, with its particular London suburban problems, invested heavily in electrification. Of the others, the GWR introduced a number of diesel railcars from 1933 and carried out a study of total electrification of a main line in the West of England.[7] The LMS had been pioneers in the use of diesel shunting locomotives, and had experimented with diesel railcars. The LNER had preferred steam railcars, and up to the outbreak of war its nearest brush with main line diesel traction had been Sir Nigel Gresley's comparison of the economics of the German 'Flying Hamburger' trains with his own, steam-hauled, East Coast main line expresses. His successors had increased the LNER's interest in the new form of traction, and at nationalisation 'schemes were maturing . . . for a fairly large scale exercise on the East Coast Line with 2,000hp diesel units.'[8] There was more action elsewhere, for in the eight months before nationalisation the LMS had actually built a prototype main line diesel-electric locomotive, and had two more on the way, while the Southern Railway had already authorised the construction of prototypes. The Great Western Railway had commenced an experiment on different lines, ordering two gas turbine-electric locomotives of different powers and manufacturers.

All but one of the prototype diesel-electric locomotives which BR inherited from the LMS and Southern used the English Electric Company's generating and traction equipment, which was already being supplied to overseas railways in complete locomotives. Interest in the new form of traction in Britain had been sufficient for years to justify a specialist monthly journal *Diesel Railway Traction,* and at the end of 1947 the president of the Institution of Locomotive Engineers had devoted most of his presidential address to extolling its virtues.[9]

The idea of using an internal combustion engine to develop electric power for rail traction was not new. Such locomotives had been in series production for shunting and transfer work in the USA since 1925, and by 1948 the US railroad industry was committed to complete dieselisation. In France, high-horsepower prototypes had been in service before the war. All of this was obvious to the BTC, and in April of 1948 Lord Hurcomb suggested the creation of an 'impartial committee' to consider the relative merits of diesel traction. The word 'impartial' was ominous; why should a committee of professionals be anything else? Either diesel traction was better than steam or it was not. The indications from North America were that it was far better, so why could not Hurcomb just ask the member of the Railway Executive for mechanical engineering matters, R.A.Riddles, to advise him? Did he not trust Riddles' judgement? Or was the committee a way of trying to circumvent Riddles' obsession with steam? Whatever were the machinations between the BTC and the RE, Hurcomb had not counted on the strength of the personal ambitions of the successor to Stephenson, Webb, Churchward, Gresley and Stainer, who wished to design *his* own fleet of steam locomotives.

So the prototype diesel-electrics were left to chug in splendid isolation, and the impartial committee finally managed to report in October 1951 after work was well underway on twelve classes of BR standard steam locomotives of Riddles' design. Not surprisingly, the committee's recommendation, after three and a half years' deliberation, was that there should be large scale experiments in diesel traction and main line electrification.[10] This was after three years of large scale experimentation with an obsolete form of motive power, and of design and construction of new classes of locomotive on an extravagant scale not seen before or since. It is perhaps indicative of the gentlemanly leisure with which RE and BTC business was conducted that, although the committee reported in October 1951,[11] the BTC 'received' the report three months later in January 1952. The BTC's difficulties with its railway 'experts' are disclosed by a paragraph in the 1952 Annual Report, more for the Railway Executive eyes than for the general public:

'The object must be to provide or introduce on each section of British Railways those forms of motive power which by reason of their inherent compliance with fundamental operational requirements and their economic characteristic are likely to give the most efficient and economical service.'[12]

There were two points at issue: whether BR should have been building steam locomotives at all, and whether the experimentation and construction of new classes was justified. Subsequent attempts to explain this waste have hinged upon the underlying preference for main line electrification, which was itself no more than a guess, and a desire to use indigenous fuels.

Concern, both from a private BR viewpoint and nationally, about the security of fuel supplies is quite understandable. Britain was only three years out of a war in which the supply of petroleum products had been a critical factor. But the diesel oil equivalent of BR's total 1948 coal consumption of 14 million tons was only 220 tanker loads with the small vessels then in use. In any case, the country was short of coal at the time.

The argument about waiting for electrification is far less strong. If capital spending restrictions were going to defer electrification, it was argued, it would be better to have one more generation of steam locomotives in the interim.[13] But even if electrification were the ultimate objective, the advantages of diesel traction made it preferable to steam even as an interim solution. As we now know, had diesels been chosen their relative advantages over main line electrification would probably have made them the permanent solution, because a large part of the case for main line electrification, even as late as 1968, rested on the 'unreliability' of diesels. Had diesels been developed at a deliberate pace from nationalisation, their reliability would have been much greater in later years. This was only an indirect effect of the determination of the Railway Executive to ignore diesel traction in 1948. The most costly effect was to defer for nearly ten years the most important single technological advance in railway history.

While BR was developing its obsolete fleet of standard steam locomotives, the only development work in progress on diesels was by the commercial locomotive builders, in conjunction with their export business. With no home market, the British locomotive builders found difficulty in competing with the American producers in export markets. Then, in 1954 when BR belatedly recognised the advantages of diesel traction, it found its own design staffs and the commercial locomotive building industry unable to meet its demands. Even the report of the 'impartial committee' in 1951 had not led to any experimentation in addition to the running of the five pre-nationalisation protypes. This brings us back to the second question which was more immediate for the Railway Executive: whether new steam designs were justified for an admittedly interim requirement. After the 1923 grouping, the chief mechanical engineers of the new companies had met their locomotive needs in the early years by carrying on with construction of the best of the designs of the constituent companies. Even if they gave their personal designs the benefit of any doubts, it was at least a consistent and economical policy. By nationalisation, each company had developed its locomotives further, and one, the LMS, had announced a complete range of 11 standard types.[14] Naturally, building to each company's design continued after nationalisation. In fact the last steam locomotive to a former company design was out-shopped as late as 1956. But the determination of 'The Last Steam Locomotive Engineer', as his biography was named, to leave his aesthetic imprint on the rails of Britain meant that four drawing offices were engaged on the design of a new range of locomotives, the maximum life of which was 17 years, and the minimum, a scandalous 7 years.

In another field of rail traction, diesel railcars, the story is only a little better. These had been in use in small numbers on the Great Western Railway since 1933, and both the LNER and the LMS had tried them. In heavy-weight (usually petrol-electric) form, such self-propelled passenger coaches had been in use on US railroads since before World War I, although their main success only came after about 1925. The attractions of the railcar were obvious: the two-man crew, obviating the need for a fireman, the economy of the lightweight diesel (bus type) engines over the steam locomotive, the faster turnrounds in terminals, and the ability to operate all day without refuelling, taking water, or cleaning grates. Britain was the world's biggest exporter of these machines. Even if some of the mechanical arrangements employed looked as if they were by Heath Robinson, it was clearly the solution for branch line passenger operation. But this potential economy did not attract the attention of the Railway Executive until 1952, when a working party reported that the costs of operating lightweight diesel trains would be 26d/mile, compared with 87d/mile for steam. By then virtually all of the BR standard steam locomotives for branch line working were designed and under construction. It is pertinent to note that there was still no unseemly haste. Although the first LMS diesel-electric locomotive had been designed and built between April and December of 1947, it took two years to get the first trial DMUs on to the rails.[15]

In all 1,403 steam locomotives were built by BR in the years 1948 - 1960.

Year	Company Design	BR Standard	Totals
1948	410		410
1949	391		391
1950	411		411
1951	208	89	297
1952	114	97	211
1953	28	123	151
1954	24	184	208
1955	18	156	174
1956	9	129	138
1957	3	141	144
1958	—	62	62
1959	—	15	15
1960	—	3	3
	1,616	999	2,615

The last locomotive built had only seven years of useful life. Even in the one area in which the advantages of diesel traction were accepted from the start, shunting, one of the regions was allowed to go on building steam shunting engines. 'The advantages of 350 hp diesel-electric locomotives for shunting duties are now established, and a specification for a British Railways standard locomotive is being prepared,' said the BTC in its 1949 Annual Report,[16] yet only four months earlier the Western Region had the first of 200 new steam shunting locomotives delivered. These deliveries carried on until 1956.

Within two years of nationalisation it was clear that the British Transport Commission was not working to anyone's satisfaction. It had been forced to ask for additional time to produce its freight charges scheme (a task which finally took six years). In the meantime, 'integration' consisted of a BTC policy statement describing traffics which were 'specially suitable' for rail and road respectively, and which asked all Executives and their staffs to act as a total transport team.[17] Its agent, the Railway Executive, was under severe criticism from above and below and outside. The RE's treatment of the railway regions, and the railways' failure to satisfy their customers, led to a powerful pressure for the restoration of the structure of the old companies. The presence among Conservative shadow ministers of men (or relatives of men) who had been directors of the main line companies added fuel to the fires of nostalgia.

The Labour Government had acted irresponsibly in assuming that all it need do was to group all the services under the one management and all would be well. It had set the BTC financial targets so severe that no possible amount of 'integration' could have maintained profits. Perhaps because of this, the BTC did not even try. By denying the BTC control over its own charges, the Government had denied itself the right to expect the BTC to be accountable for its financial performance. In these circumstances it was inevitable that the BTC should act primarily as a spending agent, with some revenue raising powers. It took its own idea of 'the public interest' as a reason for failure, for example, to try to rationalise rail services. Not that, given the intransigence of the Railway Executive, it could have done very much had it wanted to. But the combination of BTC resentment at the RE's inactivity in coming to grips with pressing railway problems, and the new Conservative Government's resentment at the RE's hyper-centralist activity, meant that the Railway Executive had to go. So, too, did nationalised road haulage and the railways' common carrier obligation, and under the Transport Act of 1953 the railways could at last look forward to the 'Square Deal' their predecessors had requested before the war.

1 G.F.Fiennes: *I Tried to Run a Railway*, London, 1967.
2 See *Modern Railways*, London, May 1967.
3 See Fiennes, *op cit*, p.28.
4 One of the attractions to the LMS in hiring W.A.Stainier chief mechanical engineer in 1931 was that he 'had the advantage of not belonging to one of the constituent companies of the LMS and therefore would be in a neutral position to sort out the differences between rival practices.' See Harold Hartley: 'William Arthur Stanier', *Biographical Memoirs of Fellows of the Royal Society*, Vol.12, November 1966, p. 492. Similarly 25 years after

nationalisation, managers main line railway antecedents are still sometimes adduced in explanation of particular acts.

5 London, 1971, Part 2.

6 See Chapter 1.

7 See O.S.Nock: *History of the Great Western Railway*, London, 1967, pp.111 and 152–156.

8 E.S.Cox: *British Railways Standard Steam Locomotives*, London, 1966, p.210.

9 See 'The Challenge to Steam', *Diesel Railway Traction*, January 1948, p.10.

10 See E.S.Cox: *Locomotive Panorama*, Vol.2, London, 1966, p.2.

11 *ibid*.

12 BTC Annual Report & Accounts, 1952, para.7.

13 See *Railway Gazette*, 18.4.47.

14 See E.S.Cox: *Locomotive Panorama*, Vol.2, London 1966, pp.117–118. Cox notes that construction was 'pushed through' by a man who had experience of DMU's in Ulster. In fact both the Irish systems were years ahead of BR in this field.

15 Paragraph 254.

16 See *Railway Gazette*, 4 August 1950.

4 | The Railway Modernisation Plan and the Select Committee

'. . . I find it difficult to understand how the whole of
the modernisation scheme could have the economic results
forecast by the BTC in their last appraisal.'

'. . . we find one of the most difficult things in the
Ministry is to discover where the money is being lost.
It is very difficult to get an answer to that. Most
of the loss is taking place on the busier traffic routes,
I think.'
*Replies of Sir James Dunnet, Permanent Secretary,
Ministry of Transport, to the Select Committee on
Nationalised Industries, 1960*

In abolishing the Railway Executive and denationalising the road haulage, the Transport Act of 1953 left the management of BR as the main activity of the BTC. London Transport remained a separate executive of the BTC and the bus, ports, hotels and other activities were in effect subsidiaries, but the main task of the commission was to try to succeed where the Railway Executive had failed. At the same time, the Act had required the setting up of 'areas', ie, railway regions, with a substantial degree of autonomy. Such autonomy had to be limited, because in financial terms BR was still to be treated as a whole. Bonavia's book describes the organisational difficulties of the BTC in this period.[1] The excessive centralisation of the Railway Executive was replaced with excessive regional autonomy, with the BTC wavering between its proper role of policy formulation and an abdication of its responsibilities to the Regions. The situation can best be described as one where the Regions played the strokes and the BTC kept the score. But in the end, even the score-keeping role proved to be beyond it.[2] The BTC rarely showed any idea of how it might exploit the freedoms provided by the 1953 Act which gave to the railways virtually all of the powers they had sought in the Square Deal campaign before the war. Just before the Act was implemented, Sir Reginald Wilson, the comptroller of the BTC, argued for the introduction of total regulation on the USA scale, when the intention of the Government was to have minimum regulation.[3] In 1959, Wilson, who had been elevated to membership of the BTC on the demise of the Railway Executive, was still arguing for an 'administered' solution to the problem of road/rail competition. In a paper to the British Association, which was subsequently published by the BTC,[4] he suggested the creation of a new, independent body, which might give further study to the problem, in particular to the track 'problem'.[5] Thus 20 years after the railways had asked for their

Square Deal, all the BTC could suggest was further study. The commercial freedom of the 1953 Act was obviously *not* what the BTC wanted, because it had patently refused to exercise it. Between the passing of the 1953 Act and 1962, the BTC, deliberately or through ineptitude, voluntarily painted itself into a corner from which there was no escape but subsidy. Or, to be more precise, the BTC obtained the paint from an indulgent Government and railway managers weilded the brushes.

It is vital characteristic of railwaymen that despite almost any amount of indecision at the top, the men down the line keep on running the trains. In the policy vacuum created by the BTC they did even more than that: they embarked simultaneously on the greatest shopping spree and began the greatest bargain sale in railway history. The first was the railway modernisation plan, and the second was the pricing and control of freight services, which we will consider in the next chapter.

The railway modernisation plan[4] provided for the spending of £1,240 million over fifteen years. In presenting it, the Commission compared this sum with 'about £600 million which would in any event have had to be spent over the period of the plan merely to maintain the existing equipment.'[5] These words were to excuse many bad investments over the succeeding 15 years; they indicate the false premise on which so much railway investment has been based.

Before the advent of serious competition, it must have seemed to railwaymen that there would be a demand for all of their services for ever. But all the trends in rail carryings since the first world war had suggested that this happy situation had ended. The primary task of railway management in the 1950s should have been to engineer a strategic retreat from those traffics and geographic areas in which rail could no longer compete with road. Albeit on a minor scale, the Railway Executive had commenced this rask in 1949, but in the intervening years progress had been very slow:

	1948	1953	% Change
Passenger stations	6,686	5,867	12%
Freight stations	5,395	3,985	−26%
Route mileage (standard gauge)	19,630	19,222	− 2%

In framing the modernisation plan the BTC knew there were further potential economies from passenger service withdrawals, but they were hopelessly wrong on the extent of these. In 1956 they thought that by 1962, after saving a further £3 million, 'the process will be more or less complete.'[6] Perhaps the BTC was just optimistic about the traffic-generating powers of the diesel multiple-unit trains it was introducing. But a more plausible explanation is that 1962 was the year in which the modernisation plan investments were expected to have returned BR to profits. If that happened, there would be no need to withdraw more services. But there was no chance of reaching that desirable situation.

Two golden opportunities to carry out a major re-structuring of BR had been missed: one at the end of the war, and the other in 1954. At both these times it was open to the BTC to decide *not* to rebuild all of the railway system (a decision which had been taken by the Dutch railways at the end of the war). But, following nationalisation, the BTC (and the Railway Executive) took a course which gave Britain the worst of all possible worlds. The Government decided to help its own management of the economy by severely limiting investment in the transport sector and in particular in BR. Then the BTC used these limited funds to patch the whole railway system, instead of concentrating investment where its long run prospects were brightest. It took, for example, until the mid-Fifties to restore pre-war qualities of service on the main line passenger services, yet meanwhile funds were being squandered on steam locomotives and coaches for branch line services.[7] Nothing in the 1948 Act had altered the economics of providing this type of service, and 'integration' must have meant transfer of much of this traffic to road. But the BTC persisted. Then, when the 1953 Act denationalised road haulage, it was obvious that BR freight traffic would come under new competitive pressures and be even less able to support loss-making activities. This was the second chance for a major restructuring. The 1953 Act expressly provided for BR to abandon loss-making activities and to cease trying to support them through inflated prices elsewhere.

But apart from the modest proposals for passenger withdrawals mentioned above, and the closure of a number of goods depots, the modernisation plan set out to rebuild the existing railway, whether there was a demand for its services or not. It has been estimated that the net disinvestment in railway assets between 1937 and 1953 amounted to about £400 million (at 1948 prices).[8] That was not necessarily a bad thing. Disinvestment on such a scale meant simply that the nation had been using up its railway assets faster than it replaced them. As it was generally conceded that, except in wartime, Britain had far more railway capacity than it needed, the disinvestment really meant that capacity had been reduced toward the level which could be supported commercially by the traffics carried. By 1953 it was widely accepted that BR had been run down too far, and that an increased rate of investment was necessary. To know how much investment was needed was the responsibility of the BTC, and this is where the waste began. For the proposals of the railway regions which were packaged into the modernisation plan provided for the restoration of virtually the whole of BR's assets at a time when the traffics carried quite clearly could not support renewals on this scale. The proposals looked innocuous enough at that time[9] (*see Table opposite*).

Apart from the £125 million for main line diesel locomotives, which was to rectify the mistakes of the Railway Executive, all of the remainder looked eminently reasonable provided profits did not matter. In 1954, the year in which the plan was prepared, BR had a surplus, before interest, of only £15.8 million. Adding in the depreciation provision of £19 million meant that, even without paying interest on the capital debt, BR was unable to finance all of the £62 million it invested that year and that the remainder had to be borrowed. But the modernisation plan envisaged investment at more than double this rate, with no immediate improvement in the operating surplus. Then, almost before the plan was properly under way, BR had two successively worse years. At this stage, the Government called for a review of the modernisation plan.

It is significant that in its reply[10] the BTC referred only to its total working

	£m	£m
FREIGHT SERVICES		
Construction and re-construction of some 55 marshalling yards, resulting in the total or partial closure of about 150 existing yards	80	
Reconstruction and mechanisation of freight terminals while closing various old depots, so as to improve transits and speed up exchange of full-load traffic between road and rail	50	
Associated expenditure on handling equipment and road vehicles	10	
Provision of continuous brakes on freight stock, thus securing best results from new forms of motive power	75	
New and improved wagon stock	150	
		365
PASSENGER CARRIAGES AND STATIONS		
New passenger carriages, including electric and diesel multiple-unit vehicles and refreshment cars	230	
Improvements to passenger and parcels stations, and carriage-cleaning and servicing depots	55	
		285
TRACK AND SIGNALLING		
Improvements to make possible higher speeds (of at least 100mph on the main lines) and better use of track capacity		210
MOTIVE POWER		
Electrification:		
Main lines	120	
Suburban lines (including schemes already planned)	65	
	185	
Dieselisation:	£m	
Main lines	125	
Shunting and trip locomotives	25	
	150	
Steam motive power depots	10	
		345
ANCILLARY ITEMS		
Improvements at Commission's packet ports	12	
Research and development work	10	
Offices and equipment, and staff welfare	13	
		35
Total envisaged cost of the Plan		£1,240m

surpluses, and not to the progressively worsening results of BR alone. Most of the setback was ascribed to the difficulty of obtaining approval for fare and freight rate increases to keep pace with inflation. This had been a recurrent problem since the war, but the statistics conveyed an even more alarming message than the fact that BR was missing out on some revenue. Delayed fare and freight rate increases meant that BR prices were falling in real terms; this should have resulted in the attraction of traffic from its road and air competitors. But such a shift of traffic had not been observed; either rival modes' prices were not rising any faster than BR's or their quality of service was improving much faster. In fact, it was some of each, and they conveyed most dangerous implications for BR. For example, BR freight rates had fallen in real terms between 1939 and 1956 by 22½%[11] yet rail traffic was falling both absolutely and relatively to other modes. This should have been disturbing news about the declining competitive attractions of rail freight. Actually, the more recent picture was not quite so gloomy, and failed to support the BTC's claims that interference by governments and the Transport Tribunal was costing it revenue. A series of diagrams in the BTC's 1956 annual report suggested that after 1951 BR freight receipts per net ton mile were keeping pace with the wholesale prices of the commodities moved.[12]

A similar picture existed on the passenger side. The decline in the average receipts per passenger mile (in real terms), accompanied by a persistent decline in the BR share of the total market,[13] showed that the passenger business was, as a whole, in secular decline. But the total passenger business contained some specialised areas of great promise, which were to be exploited fully only when railwaymen had confidence in their product. This was to take much longer to obtain than the physical equipment.

Instead of drawing lessons from these facts, the BTC chose to argue that the secular decline in rail carryings could be arrested and reversed with higher qualities of service, and that the failure to raise prices in line with inflation was the fault of the Government, anyway.

The guts of the BTC's pricing complaint was that it had got behind in its pricing increases up to 1951, and that this explained the deficit. But the major shortfall due to disallowed price increases was a once-for-all affair which had a constant money effect on each year's results after 1951, and this could not explain an increasing deficit. At the time the modernisation plan was prepared the BTC was unwilling to do anything on the pricing front which might expedite the traffic loss.[14] So it was proposing to carry on attracting traffics at subnormal prices, and to invest in the facilities those traffics would require for the next 20 years or so. The expected deficits to be incurred in the interim, of which the Board made no secret, were as much a part of the cost of carrying those traffics in the future as the investments in the plan. The Government agreed with this course, and obtained legislative power to make up the annual deficits.

It is clear from the BTC's financial justification of the plan that it had no idea whether the investment would be profitable. For example, it argued that its assets had a written-down book value of over £1,500 million but admitted disarmingly that 'their real value today is dependent on their earning power, no doubt, and this must depend mainly on the fares and charges which are permitted, and on the burdens of public obligation which are carried.' Of course, taking all these into account it was obvious that on their earning prospects, the existing assets were, in total, worthless. The BTC showed no preparedness to consider them in this way. But from this dead end, it turned and marched right over a precipice by claiming that the replacement value of the assets, which if their earning power was zero, did not need replacing, was over £4,000 million; and as this sum was three times as large as the BTC's capital debt, effectively to double that capital debt in order to stay in business was claimed to be justified.[15] Replacement values are relevant only if, in the absence of the present assets, they would require replacement. But as the whole tenor of the modernisation plan was that the present assets would only have required replacement if a further sum, far greater than the current capital debt, were to be invested to work with them, their value was dependent solely on the net financial effect of the new investment. And that, believe it or not, was bound to be negative.

The BTC provided a sketchy tabulation of the expected financial results, as follows:[16]

	December 1956 £m	*1961 or 1962 £m*	*1970 £m*
Annual rate of deficit at starting point (excluding interest on deficits and finance of Modernisation Plan)	−40	−40	−40
Improved contributions from Activities other than BR		+ 5	+ 5
Improved contribution from BR			
(*a*) Modernisation	—	+ 35	+ 85
(*b*) Pruning Services	—	+ 3	+ 3
(*c*) Productivity	—	+ 5	+ 10
(*d*) Freedom	—	+ 20	+ 25
		+ 63	+ 123
Less: Interest on Modernisation Loans	− 2	−25	− 40
	− 2	+ 38	+ 83
Total	−42	+ 3	+ 48
		Say, Balanced	Say, + 50

Naturally, the achievement of this was subject to many provisos, which we can summarise as:

   (i)   No further delay to price increase proposals.

  (ii) Freedom on structure of charges and services provided.

 (iii) No resource shortages.

 (iv) No further change in regulatory framework.

  (v) 'Financial targets must be set which are reasonably possible of achievement in the circumstances, *but which contain no element of subsidy.'* (emphasis added.)[17]

It can only be assumed that the BTC expected the indefinite continuance of the precise level and mix of traffics (or their equivalent) which was experienced in 1956. This implied that the quality of service improvements to be obtained from the new investments would be sufficient to arrest the secular decline being experienced in all traffics. At the same time, prices were going to be raised slightly faster than inflation, under the new charging freedoms. The prospect of doing all this was slender enough, but there remained a catastrophic omission in all the published calculations. The financial forecasts had been made at constant (December 1956) prices; that is, they assumed that inflation of costs would be matched by inflation of revenues. For most costs and revenues this is quite unexceptionable, but for labour costs special provision must be made. This is because, to attract and hold the necessary manpower, every industry has to offer money wage increases at a greater rate than general inflation. Railwaymen are no different from any other workers, and if their real wages (ie, their standard of living) do not keep pace with those in other industries, they will leave the industry.

Over the years 1948–1956 inclusive, railwaymen's earnings in real terms had risen at only 2.8%[18] per annum, compared with a national average rate of increase of 3.3%. Even if the future rate of increase could have been held to the 1948–56 trend, BR costs would have risen at an alarming rate from this cause alone. It is quite evident that the BTC took no account of this in its published forecasts for the period of the plan. By this omission, the BTC overstated the profits by over £50 million per annum. But worse was in store. Look back at the comparison between the rate of increase in BR and national average earnings: 2.8% and 3.3% per annum, respectively. This meant that over the first eight years of nationalisation, annual increases in railwaymen's earnings had slipped behind the national trend by half a percentage point each year. If the railway unions were to realise this and demand wage increases in line with past national trends, the financial future of BR looked very bleak indeed. This is clear if we correct the BTC's financial forecasts to take account of the inevitable real wage increases:

	December 1956	*1961 or 1962*	*1968*
Claimed by BTC	[42]	3	48
Adjusted for real wage growth			
(i) minimum (past BR trend)	[42]	[33]	[28]
(ii) realistic (past national trend)	[42]	[49]	[66]

(All figures £ millions of profit/[loss])

We now know, of course, that the rail unions finally realised that they had slipped far behind other industries; the outcome was the Guilleband Report in 1960 which recommended substantial increases in rail pay to restore 'comparabilities'.[19]

It must have been as clear then as it is now that even if all of the modernisation plan improvements had been obtained in full, there was no hope of BR returning to profitable operation. This simple arithmetic could have told the BTC and the Government, before one penny was spent, that investing £1,400 million was not going to cure BR's financial ills. Perhaps these sums were done in both places, but there was blind-eye-turning on a grand scale. Maybe the Government's approach was tempered by an element of guilt about the previous period of capital starvation. But that could not alter the fact that there was no justification either for investment on the scale proposed, or for continued operation of the current scale of railway services. To have embarked upon such a massive programme of investment without recognising the realities of the wage-setting process was grossly negligent. Even three years later the BTC was either unaware of, or still hiding this error,[20] and the Ministry of Transport could not, or would not, pick it up. All that Sir Reginald Wilson, the BTC member for finance matters who was responsible for the calculations in the plan, could say was: 'We are assuming a stable currency.'[21] Only access to internal BTC records will establish whether he was ever told that it is not the rate of increase in general prices but the rate of increase in railway rates of pay which determines the total labour cost.

Of course, had the true prognosis been admitted, the modernisation plan would need to have been greatly reduced and many later difficulties would have been avoided. But in producing its plan on such a superficial basis, the BTC was taking it upon itself to tell the nation, in defiance of the intentions of the 1953 Act, how much railway service it should have. Five years later, when confronted by the Select Committee with the fact that there was no economic justification for much of the programme, the Chairman of the BTC blandly admitted that although the 1953 Act had deliberately terminated the Commission's responsibility to provide 'adequate' service, it continued to attempt to do so, even though his only definition of 'adequate' was that the expression ' . . . conveys a certain impression to my mind. I feel I know roughly what is meant, but I could not go further than that.'[22] As Humpty Dumpty said in *Alice Through the Looking Glass:* 'When *I* use a word, it means just what I choose it to mean — neither more nor less.'

This was the major flaw in the modernisation plan. But even without it, there were other flaws a-plenty. Many of these were elicited by the questioning of the Select Committee, and were summarised by C.D.Foster in *The Transport Problem*.[23] They relate mainly to the logic of the investment appraisal methods employed. The first, and potentially most dangerous, was to consider only the expenditure *in excess* of the cost of 'essential renewals', (a practice which was to persist for at least another 15 years).[24] This 'essential renewals' assertion begged the vital question, because the purpose of investment appraisal is to determine whether renewals are essential. Many railway managers still make a mental distinction between 'renewal' and 'development' expenditure, on the assumption that the 'renewal' is to meet some immutable demand and therefore having an infinite return. But any 'renewal' is the same in concept as any development investment; it is a purchase of future capacity. The fact that the traffic concerned is already moving by rail may make the investment's outcome easier to judge, but it does not obviate the requirement to ensure that deploying resources in the proposed way *will increase the net revenue of a profitable business.* Note the qualification: that the business must either be already profitable or capable of being made so by the investment. Investing just to reduce a loss is unprofitable investment; if losses will continue it is *disinvestment* which is indicated. It was on this point that conventional railway appraisal processes, such as they were, broke down, for they assumed the indefinite operation of all railway services other than those identified for abandonment in 1954. (These were the £3 million worth of annual savings, ie, about one percent of railway operations.) With this brief (or was it lack of a brief?) from the top, it is little wonder that the men on the ground went off and bought themselves what was virtually a new railway. We will see in the next chapter that in the freight business this was due to a fundamental misunderstanding by the BTC about the nature of a railway's costs and the problem of managing them. Correct decisions could only have been made at the BTC level, ie, headquarters, because it was not possible for a railway region or division to see enough of the process. In setting up its Traffic Costing Service in 1949, the BTC had not geared it to answer the kinds of strategic questions the BTC should have been asking. From the answers given both to the Transport Tribunal[25] and the Select Committee it is clear that the assumption of inevitability pervaded the whole process, based on some corporate 'feeling' that the level of railway service being provided was the level of railway service the nation wanted. The nation did not really get a chance to say that some other level was all it was prepared to pay for, and the Ministry of Transport did not think it worthwhile to ask itself if there might have been a difference between these two levels.

There were other, more technical flaws in the BTC's analysis, and these are discussed in full in Foster's book[26]. But there are two other lines of inquiry worth pursuing before we leave the modernisation plan: (i) the legacy of the Railway Executive, and (ii) the plain bad judgements.

The most obvious legacy of the Railway Executive was the fleet of obsolete steam locomotives, many of which were still under construction, and the negligible rate of development of the diesel locomotive between 1948 and 1953. By the time the BTC had overthrown the Railway Executive, the need for diesel locomotives was so urgent that the development was forced on an ill-prepared loco-building industry and on an inexperienced BR design staff. In its haste to go diesel, the BTC commissioned too many locomotives, of too many classes, and to too many designs. There was an urge to allow every loco-builder to experiment at BR's expense, even though only two or three had the kind of experience which justified their being entrusted with this work. Significantly, the firms with the greatest experience in building diesel-electric locomotives — the Americans — were expressly excluded by the BTC on chauvinistic grounds. The explanations offered by the Chairman of the BTC to the Select Committee can only be described as lacking in logic and fact :

. . . 'It is probably correct that we could have bought in the United States of America: there was certainly a very reliable diesel locomotive being built there. But when I say it is probably correct, I do so because those firms, and one in particular, were very fully booked up at the time, and it is questionable whether we could have drawn large numbers from there. . . . we were anxious to give British manufacturers a chance before we committed British Railways almost indefinitely to locomotives of foreign manufacture, and there was at that time no question of those American locomotives being built anywhere but America.'[27]

The American firm in question, the Electromotive Division of General Motors, had already licensed the production of its locomotives in Canada, Australia, Belgium and Denmark (using US–built engines and electrical equipment), and it is interesting to note that BR was prepared to order locomotives with Swiss and German engines and German hydraulic transmissions. Readers must judge for themselves whether the most experienced diesel-electric locomotive builder in the world was excluded on any grounds other than its nationality. In all, 41 different types of diesel locomotive were purchased between 1954 and 1962. Although the wide and thin spread of these orders gave every British man-ufacturer a belated bite of the cake, it is significant that by 1970 the only firms remaining in the business were those already pre-eminent in the mid-Fifties. None of the smaller firms and novel designs which were given an opportunity by the BTC's largesse had managed to produce locomotives good enough to keep them in the business of supplying BR. Many of these diesel locomotives had a useful life of less than ten years, mostly because they were surplus to requirements (capital cost: up to £100,000 each), but many because they were poor designs, and in too small numbers to make maintenance worthwhile.[28] Had development of diesel locomotives proceeded gradually from 1948, most of this wasted design (but not the building of excessive numbers) would have been avoided. This would have been a much more profitable use of the engineering resources devoted to the abortive production of the BR standard steam locomotives. But it must be said that even after the BTC reversed the Railway Executive's all-steam policy, it did not stop construction of steam locomotives. As a casual indication of the ruinous financial legacy of this infatuation with steam, in 1967, when only a few hundred steam locomotives remained in operation, their elimination promised the greatest single economy then in sight.

In passing, it is worth noting that the same famine-feast cycle added great cost to the electrification programme, especially on the North Western main line. The over-generous provision of electrified trackage, and the over-building of physical plant (particularly the catenary and its support structure) would have been much reduced if electrification had proceeded at a slower pace from nationalisation.

Then there were the errors of judgment made after the departure of the Railway Executive. These fell into three main categories:

(i) Too much construction,
(ii) of the wrong assets,
(iii) to the wrong technical standards.

Some projects, such as the diesel locomotive programme, combined all three. Although the BTC proclaimed its determination 'to exploit the opportunities for re-equipment which modern science and techniques present,'[29] many of the projects fell far short of this ideal. In far too many cases old techniques were employed to resolve old problems, where the problems themselves were about to disappear. The construction of locomotives and multiple-unit trains for service which in a few years would be proposed for closure is an extreme example of this. Some of the marshalling yards, built to solve problems which by then existed only in the memories of senior managers, were symptomatic of a tunnel-vision in the freight field.[30] Travellers on the North Western main line will have seen a massive concrete flyover built at Bletchley, which carries the Oxford-Bedford route over the main line. They will rarely see a train on it because its purpose, to be part of an outer London avoiding line, disappeared before its completion as a result of modern methods of working and the fall in freight traffic.[31]

On the rolling stock side, the tragedy was that the new-found spending power was dissipated on the production of great numbers of replicas of the obsolescent stock inherited at nationalisation. Perhaps the wierdest example was the proud announcement of the development of a BR standard horsebox.[32] In loco-hauled coaches, passengers had to wait until the Mark II stock in 1964 to get new coaches which offered any significant advance on the company designs; in the meantime some 7,000 had been built to obsolescent designs. Non corridor loco-hauled coaches for suburban services were still under construction in 1956; the first of these was scrapped in 1960. Of freight wagons, it had been recognised for years that BR's unbraked, short wheelbase, low capacity designs were obsolete. But the new builds under the modernisation plan were mostly repetitions of the same types, although, being of steel construction, of higher capacities. With coal wagons, this was dictated by the need to match existing loading and unloading facilities; it was not until the Beeching era that the 19th century methods of the coal trade were seriously questioned. For merchandise wagons, there was no excuse at all for building great numbers of pallet vans, which carried less than a motor lorry. Again it was a question of looking back to see what BR had been short of, rather than looking forward to see what BR would need in the future.

Early in the programme, two vital decisions were made which since then have had to be reversed at great cost. The first was to standardise on vacuum brakes, rather than the Westinghouse air brake which most other railways use. From the time the original decisions were made to standardise on vacuum brakes, at the grouping in 1923, there had been powerful pressures for a change to the Westinghouse system. Obviously, an important reason for avoiding changing the system was the heavy task of converting existing locomotives and rolling stock. The time to do it was when most existing locos and rolling stock had only a limited remaining life, and it was envisaged that in the near future most rolling stock would be of comparatively recent build. *The only time in British railway history when that condition was met was at the inception of the railway modernisation plan,* but the preference for vacuum brakes was confirmed. Certainly, the immediate cost of fitting Westinghouse brakes would have been higher, but the long term benefit outweighed this. In 1965 BR announced that henceforth it was adopting the Westinghouse air brake as standard.

On a smaller scale, a similar blunder was made with train heating for passenger trains. With steam locomotives it had been a simple matter to pipe steam back into the train for heating. But with a diesel-electric locomotive, steam heating required the installation of a special oil-fired boiler on the loco., and the attendance of a second man to operate it. But there was an alternative: to tap the main generator of the locomotive to feed electric radiators in the coaches. Early in the diesel-building programme, a few locomotives were fitted for this method, but the experiment was dropped and steam heat remained standard. But with the spread of electric traction, a large fleet of dual steam/electrically heated coaches was needed, and to carry a man on the locomotive just to tend the train heating boiler was an expensive nonsense. So in 1968, BR decided to standardise on electric heating of loco-hauled coaches. With the exception of the electrification works, in which some path-breaking technical advances had to be made to fit the overhead wiring into the tight physical limits of the routes concerned, it was not a happy period for British railway engineering. The task of making good, under great pressure, the technological lag created by the Railway Executive's obsession with steam traction, added to the greatly increased rate of spending, was not conducive to elegant engineering. At a time when, ten years after the war had ended, things should have become easy, the opposite was the case. But the biggest wastes occurred not in projects the engineers were hurried into doing wrong, but in projects which railway operators and commercial men should have seen were either unwarranted by future traffics, or unnecessary because of altered operating patterns.

There was clearly no case for rebuilding the whole of the railway, fixed plant and rolling stock, but that was what the BTC and the railway regions tried to do. When the Select Committee confronted the BTC with the error of this, they could only say that they had spent the money in fulfilment of an obligation, which no longer applied in statutory form, to provide *adequate* services. But these need not necessarily have been *rail* services. Indeed, a primary aim of the creation of the BTC in 1948 was that it would seek some optimal distribution of traffic between the modes. But hardly anything was done in this direction. We will leave the freight question for the next chapter.

In the passenger field, it inherited interests in a number of bus companies from the main line railway companies, and subsequently it bought control of them. It had close working relationships with the other large bus companies. Even between 1948 and 1953, when it was obliged to provide *adequate* service, it should have been transferring traffic to buses on many low density routes. Then, when the 1953 Act deleted the *adequate* requirement, and put pressure on the total economics of many railway routes by denationalising road haulage, the BTC went ahead and invested in local diesel trains on a scale which could have been explicable only if the motorbus had not existed. Its obsession with keeping the traffic on rails even went to the extreme of building rail vehicles which were, apart from the track, little different from buses, but which must inevitably have been much more expensive to run. In partial justification of this, it must be explained that the railbus had many vocal supporters among railway enthusiasts, who saw similar vehicles operating on the Deutsche Bundesbahn[33]. It was necessary to try them out on BR to satisfy this lay pressure, but *five* separate designs were hardly necessary, especially when similar experiments had been conducted before the war by the LMS.[34] Only a fraction less futile than the railbuses were the single unit railcars of conventional size..[35] They still only carried the load (seated) of a double-decker bus, but cost more to build and run.

But the greatest mistakes arose on routes of even heavier traffic, where at least two-car trains were thought to be justified. For evidence of this we need only to look ahead a little to the Beeching Report,[36] which in 1963 listed 376 services which should be closed. If they should have been closed in 1963, and their passengers diverted to buses, they should equally have been closed in 1954, *before* the BTC re-equipped them all. Although the BTC had high hopes for the diesel multi-unit trains, these were justified only on clearly identifiable routes, where the combination of heavy peak loadings and speed advantage over buses together generated adequate loads. If there were only bus loads, the bus was the optimal vehicle. In the Beeching Report, savings from withdrawing the 376 services (and modifying 102 others) were estimated at £34—41 million (1963 prices)[37], but in the modernisation plan only £3 million (1954 prices) was obtainable from this source.

There are a number of explanations for this apparent failure of the BTC to face reality in preparing the modernisation plan, but most of them evaporate when it is found that even in the Reappraisal they were still not admitted. Certainly, that document admitted that something was wrong: 'In the days when the railways enjoyed a virtual monopoly of freight traffic they could perhaps afford a lower return from their passenger traffic. Now that the position of the freight traffics is keenly competitive it is essential that the passenger traffics should make their full and proper contribution.'[38] But what was the BTC intending to do about those which were not making 'their full and proper contribution'? The Reappraisal was very guarded on this. Although it was claimed that by 1958 £1.3 million of the 1954 estimate of £3 million annual savings had been achieved, the forecasts of future savings from this source were either mixed up with freight service savings or just not quantified. The nearest the BTC came to a categorical statement was to say (emphasis added): 'By 1963, the total number of passenger and goods station *may* have to be reduced by over 1,000 compared with 1958, and some 1,800 route miles *may* have to be closed unless improvements in traffic justify *some retention.*'[39]

Of course, in having to write the Reappraisal of the modernisation plan and then to explain themselves before the Select Committee, the BTC were in an embarrassing situation (of a type which was to recur in 1967). If they were to admit that their 1954 plan was as wrong as events were proving it to be, they would have been admitting that they were either knaves or fools, or a bit of both. So they tried to brazen it out, claiming that their plan and its financial appraisal were 'soundly based,' and that 'where the financial forecasts made in 1956 have not been realised, the causes lie predominantly in factors which were expressly excluded from the forecasts as being outside the control of the Commission.'[40] Everyone was out of step but the good old BTC. If only the following were done everything would be all right:

- The Government and the Transport Tribunal had not held up fare increases.
- Industry would burn more coal.
- Railway workers would put up with a stagnant standard of living while that of all other workers improved.
- The national economy could attain consistent steady growth.
- The Government would continue to bear the mounting deficits.

There was, of course, the risk that the Government would decide that these factors were likely to be harder to change than to change the BTC.

While the Parliamentary Select Committee was deliberating, the Government appointed a private inquiry into the management of the BTC, known (after its chairman) as the Stedeford Committee. Out of that came the dismemberment of the Commission, and the appointment of one of the members of the Stedeford committee, Dr Richard Beeching, as the first chairman of the new British Railways Board. The great experiment of 1948 had failed. Far from having co-ordinated the various modes of transport under its control, the British Transport Commission was finally adjudged incapable of managing even its major constituent, British Railways. In fact, it is likely that the other activities, London Transport, the bus companies, the docks and inland waterways, and the road haulage and travel subsidiaries, performed *better* because the BTC parent had its hands full in trying to manage BR.[41] The Stedeford Committee's report to the Minister remained unpublished, but it clearly carried more weight with the Government than the report of the Select Committee. Perhaps the Select Committee's optimism about BR's future, on the lines already laid by the BTC was demolished by the much more critical report of the Stedeford Committee, and this deflected the Government's attention from the sound recommendations of the Select Committee. Whatever the reasons for the view of the Government that appointing a super-manager and suspending some capital debt would allow it to ignore the urgent need to reform its own relations with BR, this was to cost the Nation (and BR) dearly in the following six years. Using the Select Committee's own words, its main points were:

* What size and shape should British Railways be? The first consideration must be financial; the size and shape must be such as can enable the Commission to carry out their statutory task of balancing their accounts, taking one year with another. But if the Commission are to know which of their services are justifiable on grounds of direct financial return, they must first have some form of accounts by which the profitability of Regions and services can be judged

* However, the consideration of direct profitability is not the only one which applies in this case. Because of the cost of the roads, and of the congestion on them, the national interest may require railway services which do not in fact directly pay for themselves, but which may cost the nation less than the alternatives.

* In some cases, there may be a third and different consideration — one of social need. A service may be justified on other than economic grounds, because

for example the less populous parts of Britian might otherwise be left without a railway service. Account may, in other words, need to be taken of social considerations.

* The consideration of profitability, mentioned above, should be left to the Commission. But if decisions are to be taken on grounds of the national economy or of social needs, then they must be taken by the Minister, and submitted by him for the approval of Parliament.

* Furthermore, if Parliament is to specify that certain services should be undertaken, despite the fact that the Commission cannot profitably undertake them, then the additional cost of them should be provided, in advance, out of public funds.

* If subsidies of this kind are to be paid to the Commission, then they should be paid for specific purposes, and they should be paid openly. They should not be disguised as, for instance, a payment of the track costs (which are an integral part of railway operations), nor as the writing-off of the burden of interest; and they should not be hidden away in the Commission's accounts.

* This need for clarity in the accounts is important. Your Committee have suggested, at various points in this Report, that payments should be made to the Commission of appropriate sums from public funds. Provided that these payments relate to specific services dictated by the Minister, or are compensation for specific losses incurred by his actions, the Commission would be able to publish accounts for British Railways which would reflect only the matters within their control.

* If this were done, there would be one important consequential advantage — the advantage that both the Commission and the Minister would become much more clearly accountable to Parliament for their separate railway responsibilities.[41]

Before going on to the Beeching era, we must retrace our steps to look more closely at the development of BR thinking on the economics of the freight service. Although this was to bedevil BR right through the sixties, its disastrous foundations were laid by the BTC.

1 See M.R.Bonavia, *The Organisation of British Railways*, London, 1971.
2 *Ibid*, Part Two, chapters 4 and 5.
3 See his 'The Framework of Public Transport', *Journal of the Institute of Transport*, July 1953, pp. 145 − 185.
4 *Modernisation and Re-equipment of British Railways*, British Transport Commission, London, 1955. (Hereafter: Modernisation Plan, 1955.)
5 BTC Annual Report and Accounts, 1954, para. 117.
6 *The British Transport Commission: Proposals for the Railways*, Command 9880, London, HMSO, 1956, para. 57. Henceforth cited as 'the Proposals (1956)'.
7 BR was still building non-gangwayed loco-hauled coaches as late as 1956.
8 See P. Redfern, 'Net Investment in Fixed Assets in the United Kingdom', *Journal of the Royal Statistical Society*, Series A, Vol. 118, No 2, 1955.

9 From *BTC: AR & C*, 1954.

10 'The Proposals (1956)', *op cit*, para. 6.

11 Calculated from Annexes 4 and 5 to Appendix 3, *Report from the Select Committee on Nationalised Industries, British Railways*, London, HMSO 1960. (Henceforth cited as SCNI:BR.)

12 *BTC: Annual Report & Accounts*, 1956, diagrams 5(a), (b) and (c), pp. 62, 3.

13 See *ibid*, diagram 4; and Ministry of Transport: *The Transport Needs of Great Britain in the Next Twenty Years*, London, HMSO, 1963, p.25.

14 See 'The Proposals (1956)', para. 86.

15 *Ibid*, para. 100.

16 *Ibid*, para. 101.

17 *Ibid*, para. 1.

18 Calculated from staff census data in BTC Annual Reports. This data omits 'senior officers', but they were a very small component of the total.

19 *Report of Railway Pay Committee of Inquiry*, London 1960.

20 See *The British Transport Commission: Re-appraisal of the Plan for the Modernisation and Re-equipment of British Railways*, Cmnd. 813, London, HMSO, 1959.

21 *SCNI:BR*, Q.1153.

22 Evidence of Sir Brian Robertson, *SCNI:BR*, Q.269.

23 London, 1963. Chapter 5.

24 See, eg, *SCNI:BR*, Q.1690; evidence of H.E.Osborne. Proposals based on the 'return on outlays in excess of minimum renewals' were still being made in 1970.

25 See next chapter.

26 *The Transport Problem, Op cit*.

27 *SCNI:BR*, Q.1122.

28 For a 'catalogue of miscalculations and subsequent changes . . . (which were) the inevitable outcome of tackling the world's most intensive railway dieselisation so precipitately,' see G.Freeman Allen: *British Rail after Beeching*, London 1966, Chapter 4. It is only fair to point out that the greatest single debacle, the diesel hydraulic shunting locomotives built in 1964 at £50,000 each and sold at scrap prices of less than £1,000 each in 1968, were designed and built by BR itself. (See 'Four-year-old diesels go for scrap', *Daily Mail*, 24 June 1968).

29 The proposals, (1956), para. 24.

30 See Fiennes, *op cit*, pp. 77—78. Apart from Perth marshalling yard, which was closed on completion of construction, the worst example was Carlisle Kingmoor yard, built to solve the problems of interchanging traffics between the old Maryport & Carlisle, Glasgow & South Western, Caledonian, North British, North Eastern, Midland & London & North Western Railways. The fact that in 1923 five of these railways had been grouped into the LMS, thus shifting the optimal marshalling locations to points far to the North and South of Carlisle, had apparently gone unnoticed.

31 See *Railway Gazette*, 31/1/58, and Fiennes, *op cit*, p.78.

32 See *Railway Gazette*, 28/2/58.

33 See, eg, Roger Calvert. *The Future of Britain's Railways*. London.

34 See Essery and Jenkinson: *The LMS Coach*, 1923—1957, London, 1969, p.12.

35 See *Railway Gazette*, 10.8.51.

36 British Railways Board: *Reshaping British Railways*, London, HMSO, 1963, Appendix 2, Section 1. Henceforth cited as the Beeching Report.

37 *Ibid*, p.54.

38 The Reappraisal, *op cit*, para. 83.

39 *Ibid*, Appendix B, p.43.

40 *Ibid*, para. 110.

41 *SCNI:BR*, Paras. 420—427.

5 | When the British Transport Commission Lost Control of its Freight Business

'Without freight the main railway network could not exist.'
Beeching Report, p.24

The public debate on the way in which railways should set their freight rates has ebbed and flowed over the past fifty years without diverting rail commercial men from their time-honoured practice of charging what they think the traffic will bear. They have always had sufficient intuitive grasp of railway economics to ignore pressures from academics, their own financial colleagues, the Transport Tribunal and any other expert who has proposed an alternative solution. The greatest expert in this field in recent years, A.A.Harrison, has shown how he and his predecessors accepted as much of the current arguments circulating as was necessary to justify their practices, and quite rightly ignored the rest.[2] The theorists who argued for a cost-based pricing system based their arguments on an invalid appreciation of the economics and cost-escapability of railway freight operations. In trying to meet the textbook requirements for an optimal solution, without really understanding them, the BTC traffic costing men and the higher management at the BTC (and later BRB) level, allowed themselves to be deflected far from the paths of profitability.

As suggested in Chapter Two, the difficulties can be traced back to Sir William Acworth, who argued that costs are relevant only for constructing the profit and loss account. Because it was impossible to measure the cost of a particular transit, he argued, revenue maximising rates should be charged, with the hope that the sum of the rates exceeded the sum of the costs. Such an argument assumed implicitly that provided a railway was working as efficiently as possible, nothing could be done about the level of total costs. As long as the railways had the common carrier obligation and no real competition, this may have been true. But it was then a tautology to argue that because the railways costs did not obviously respond to variations in their traffics, it did not matter how much traffic and of what kinds of it they were asked to carry. The reason the railways' total costs did not respond to variations in traffic was simply that railway managements chose not to make them do so. Before the 1923 grouping, this was because a unilateral reduction in capacity by any railway company would mean a reduction in its competitive power since capacity and quality of service (ie, speed of transit and reliability) tend to go together. With over 100 companies, each of whose services were at least partial substitutes for those of others, they were in a 'competitive lock-in', to use the very descriptive American jargon. Every company had more capacity than its traffics required, but none was prepared to act because of fear that its competitors would thereby gain an advantage. In these circumstances it was right to ignore costs in setting prices, and to charge as much as possible for every traffic in the hope that total costs would thereby be covered.

Although the grouping in 1923 relaxed the 'lock-in' by creating large regional rail monopolies, we have already noted the unwillingness of the main line companies to withdraw services. They too, tried to maximise revenues and hoped that the costs would look after themselves, but the increasing competition from road hauliers set strict limits to the rates the railways could obtain for directly competitive traffics. The widespread allegation that hauliers were thereby 'skimming the cream' of railway traffics implied that the railways themselves could tell cream from water, and that the loss of these traffics took away 'profits' which were needed if the railways were to survive to carry all their other traffics. The 'other traffics' were of two distinct types. There were some, such as bulk traffics in heavy flows, whose cost on rail was low and which would be profitable to the railways at any rate which a road haulier could quote. But there were also the atomistic flows — small consignments using low volume facilities — whose cost on rail would inevitably be high relative to the rate maxima then in force. It was to meet losses on this latter category that the 'cream', if any really existed, was required. Before the 1953 Act, the railways could avoid making a loss from carrying such traffics only by closing the stations at which they were consigned. This could only be a partial solution, because similar traffics would still enter the system at other stations, which were profitable for the other traffics they generated.

In these circumstances, the only effective solution open to the railways was to seek rates for those traffics high enough either to make them profitable or to divert them to road. But they were averse to upsetting the whole structure of rates to resolve what they still thought to be a small problem. Here it must be borne in mind that the rail *users* were happy with existing rates, otherwise they would not have been users. The railways' dilemma was that if they had tried to raise rate maxima to eliminate the losses caused by their common carrier obligations they would have had a terrific fight on their hands at the Transport Tribunal. Instead, as we have seen, they accepted their 'obligations', and hoped in return to obtain equivalent regulation of their road competitors. The proposals produced by the road haulage industry for regulating its rates would have been quite unworkable, as they relied on the use of statutory powers to raise road rates to 'protect' the railways.[3] This would have given 'stability', ie, greater profits, to the established hauliers, who would have been the main beneficiaries. There were no benefits in the proposals for the users, and the railways would have been left with their unprofitable traffics. So the railways asked for the 'Square Deal', which would have given them the freedom to quit traffics that they could not make profitable by pricing action.

The railways were under pressure from two directions: (1) the freight rates they were having to reduce to retain traffics; and (ii) the rates they could not increase so as to make non-competitive traffics profitable. For the first category, to attempt to cover the railways' costs by charging, however imperfectly, what each traffic would bear, was the optimal solution provided that no traffic was attracted from road at a rate lower than the costs which would be saved by not carrying it. Here was the rub, because the man quoting a keen price to keep a particular traffic was not the man who might save some cost if it was lost to road. In practice these two men never met. The commercial man, sensing that any particular traffic would not affect the total cost of operating the railway by very much, would know that the railways would be better off with the revenue than without it.

In some other office, perhaps in another city, the operating man would not know the rates obtained for the various traffics he was handling. There was no facility for deciding that, at a rate low enough to retain a traffic, it was not profitable to keep it. And anyway, was not this traffic which was vulnerable to road competition the 'cream' of the railways' business, to be retained at all costs? Few noticed that in reducing rail rates to meet road competition the 'cream' had become skim milk; the cream was the price differential brought about by the competition, and once that was gone the traffics should have lost their attraction.

The difficulty, as the commercial men (but not their masters) perceived, was that if a railway's total cost was going to be unresponsive to the size of any traffic variations, upward and downward, which their efforts could produce, it was always going to be better to keep or gain traffic than to lose it. An unthinkably large amount of traffic would need to be lost before train miles, engine hours, etc would be significantly reduced. Much has been written about the limited 'escapability' of railway costs; that most costs are fixed for a long period, and that it is very difficult to transfer manpower and rolling stock at short notice. My own view is that the most crucial factor in this cost escapability question is the time it takes a railway management to *recognise the possibility* of profitably escaping particular costs. This usually takes far longer than the elimination of the cost itself. This is partly due to the complexity of railway operations, but it is mainly a result of the inherent optimism which drives managers who have spent their careers in what is, in many parts of its operations, a declining industry. If a manager is not under powerful pressure from his superior, it is personally easier on himself and all of his subordinates to adopt a Micawberish attitude, and to avoid reducing his capacity in the hopes that traffic will grow again to fully utilise it.

To the enduring benefit of Britain during the war, the whole railway industry did just this through the Thirties, although much of the retained capacity, eg, many rural branch lines, was totally irrelevant, if not an actual drain, on the war effort. Unfortunately, the BTC carried on the practice between 1948 and 1953, when it was hoped that 'integration' would redirect traffic from road to rail. After 1953 there could be no rational explanation for the practice, except, perhaps, that a big railway is nicer to work in than a small one.

One of the most important aims of nationalisation was to secure a split of traffic between rail and road which would minimise the total national transport costs, and by 'total' in this context we mean all costs which are determined by the choice of modes. Broadly, the theory on this dictated that optimal resource allocation will be effected only if prices reflect the costs of service.[4] Users, confronted with prices for competing modes which reflected their respective costs, would be able to make a choice between modes which was optimal from the user's, the modes', and the national viewpoint. Cost-based prices, it was argued, would work as an automatic allocator of traffic to the optimal mode. But neither Parliament nor rail-user groups were prepared to take the word of the BTC on what was cost-based charges; a draft charges scheme had to be prepared for consideration by the Transport Tribunal. This proved a very difficult task; it was not until 1955, after the passage of the new Act which denationalised much of the BTC's road haulage interests, that the scheme was ready.

The primary purpose of the draft charges scheme was to raise the rates maxima on traffics which caused high costs on rail. Obviously, the shippers of such traffics were going to have to pay much higher rates, either to keep their traffics on rail or to switch to a road alternative, and such a big change in the rates structure required that the Tribunal be convinced of its 'fairness'. This would depend upon the relationship between the costs and rates for the affected traffics, and those for all the other traffics which the BTC was happy to retain at the rates they were already 'bearing'. To satisfy the Tribunal that the affected rates were not being raised to levels which were 'too high', the BTC was required to prove that all of the other rates were not 'too low'. This was because the main complaint of the affected users, some of whom had been cross-subsidised for years, was that the new charges scheme might make *them* cross-subsidise the other users, whose rates were being determined by the competitive road haulage prices. Over the years since nationalisation, the BTC had developed a most elegant scheme of maximum rates, simple to apply, and related broadly to costs. It was based on the 'loadability' of traffic, aiming to obtain the same revenue from wagonloads of traffics of different densities. Naturally, the costs used in compiling the scheme were 'adverse' levels, ie, in low volume situations, because it was these which the maxima were intended to cover. They were not the extreme 'adverse' level. Whilst it met some of the requirements of the BTC's critics, particularly in the way it grappled with the loadability issue[5], the new scheme did not, as had widely been suggested, apply a published, *cost-based* rate to every traffic.[6] Clearly the maxima in the charges scheme were going to apply only to a small proportion of the traffic, because most traffics were moving at competitive rates below the current, much lower, maxima.

The BTC had clearly decided that a comprehensive cost-based rate system was not feasible. But the arguments it used, correctly, to establish this point before the Transport Tribunal were then used in a quite invalid manner for the next ten years to excuse the BTC's and the British Railways Board's failure to take adequate control of their freight operations. Much of the detail of the costings arguments need not concern us here; they have been described adequately elsewhere.[7] Our concern is the BTC's attitude to costs it claimed were 'fixed', and therefore (it argued) 'joint', and the erroneous policy which flowed from this.

The issue which concerns us centred around the recovery of what the BTC argued were 'joint' costs. In its calculations of adverse cost levels for determination of rate maxima the BTC had distinguished between 'direct' and 'indirect' costs. It explained to the Tribunal that 'direct costs cover all those items, the cost of which, taking a sufficiently large volume of traffic and a sufficiently long term view, may be expected to vary with changes in the volume of traffic: indirect costs cover items, which, in general, do not so vary.'[8] Although the BTC used average values of all items of both 'direct' and 'indirect' costs in calculating its maximum rates, it argued that only the direct costs were relevant for determining the rates for competitive traffics. Its reasoning was impeccable, provided its facts were correct, ie, provided that the indirect costs could not be varied with changes in output. These costs were track and signalling expense (about 38% of total rail freight expenditure), and general administration costs (about 5%).[9] It was argued before the Tribunal that these costs were 'joint' to all traffics, and therefore it would be an 'economic nonsense' to try to recover them arbitrarily from particular traffics. The argument was that as these costs did not vary with changes in traffic — ie, that they were fixed provided — they were recovered from all traffics together, the fact that particular traffics made very little contribution to the total was irrelevant. Because, it was asserted, no part of these costs would be saved by losing the particular traffic, it was better to keep the traffic for any 'contribution to indirect costs', however small, it was able to make. The whole argument here depended upon the testable hypothesis that, in particular, the track and signalling costs concerned could not be varied with changes in the traffic volume. Of course, for the time which would elapse until it was seen that the costs could be varied, the argument was valid. But this was not the 'length of run' the BTC had adopted for its costing exercises.[10]

Although this categorical assertion of the fixedness of track and signalling costs remained the official line of the BTC's and the BRB's costing experts, it was completely wrong. Constant reiteration of this assertion led to its adoption as a foundation of BR policy, with distressing results. As Foster pointed out in the article already cited, the use of an arbitrary split of costs into 'direct' and 'indirect' begged far more questions than it answered. This was because the BTC and its successors convinced themselves that costs which they erroneously claimed to be 'fixed' were therefore 'joint' and thus 'indirect', and need not be covered by any particular traffic. This confusion, based in the case of track and signalling costs upon muddled thinking which could have been detected by a boy with a Hornby trainset, occurred repeatedly in BR writings. Any boy, playing trains on the parlour floor, would know that the more trains he wanted to run, the more tracks and signals he would need, and *vice versa*. It was the reversibility of this proposition which baffled the railway costing experts and policy makers. But I have never met a railway civil engineer or signal engineer who did not accept that if you run fewer (or slower) trains, the track and signalling cost can be reduced.[11] 'Indirect costs' became a euphemism either for costs which BR did not know how to allocate, or those which, for a variety of reasons, they were not prepared to consider avoiding. For examples:

'. . . costs incurred jointly in the provision of two or more services cannot be saved, or cannot be proportionately reduced, by curtailing or withdrawing one of them.'[12]

'Certain of the resources and facilities employed in rail transport are not directly related to any particular operation or transit and their cost does not vary significantly with the work done . . . In such circumstances there is no factual basis on which cost can be apportioned.'[13]

'So long as railways carry their own track financially, instead of "paying as you go" like the road users, their fixed cost is very high, and the additional cost which is caused by additional business is very low. This is a benefit which the railways should share with their customers wherever possible . . .'[14]

'The total cost of providing the route system . . . amounts to nearly a quarter of the railways' total revenue. This is a fixed cost, in the full sense of the term, all the while the route system remains unchanged . . .'[15]

'The system cost of routes used by all types of services are joint and can only be apportioned to selected operations on an arbitrary basis.'[16]

This was the position of the BTC and the Board right up to 1967, when the Joint Steering Group set up a special committee on the 'Standby' issue finally to demolish it. Earlier discussions of my own 80,000 word thesis which disproved the BR assertions led only to suggestions that it was a complex matter unlikely to be resolved by an outsider. An article in an academic journal on the same theme was ignored.[17]

All of the BTC and BRB quotations which I have cited were saying, in effect, that on the railway track the production of A and B was carried on in conjunction, and as the railways were not prepared to consider stopping the production of B, it was redundant to talk about saving cost by ceasing production of A. We will defer consideration of why these assertions of the fixity of railway track costs were wrong, and how much of the cost *can* be allocated to traffics, until Chapter 9, when we discuss the track cost problem in greater depth. For our present discussion, even if all of the quotations above had been correct, they do not support the BR's subsequent actions. The argument before the Tribunal in 1955-56 was that, because the BTC thought the track and signalling costs were fixed, the optimal course was to attempt to recover them commercially. Thus the traffic costing service would advise the freight marketing men the 'direct' costs of a proposed flow, and this would be the charging 'floor', below which a rate could not be quoted. Salesmen were expected to obtain the highest possible rate in excess of that direct cost 'floor', so as to maximise the 'contribution' toward the indirect costs.

There are two perils in such a system, and both quickly became evident on BR. The first is that if salesmen are given a 'floor' below which they cannot negotiate a price, there is a strong temptation for them to allow themselves to be bargained down to this price to secure the traffic. In a situation where the BR official line was that any traffic whose rate exceeded the 'direct' costs was worth accepting, it was to be expected that salesmen would emphasise 'acceptance' at the expense of the rate. This obviously happened on a wide scale in the years following the 1953 Act. It may, of course, have been happening on a minor scale for many years before that; before the creation of the traffic costing service it would never have been known whether the competively determined rates exceeded the 'direct' costs.[18] But once the new system was introduced, the pricing floors specified by the traffic costing service were just invitations to cut rates down to those levels. One of the few public indications of this problem arose through two complaints of the coastal shipping industry that rail rates for china clay and gasworks coal were 'under cost'.[19] When, after enquiries by an independent accountant, the rail rates were raised, the fact that BR retained the businesses showed that the original rates were lower than they needed to be for competitive reasons.

In 1968, a report of the Prices & Incomes Board based on extensive enquiries into BR's freight marketing practices suggested that underpricing was still widespread.[20] The rate reductions offered over the years in the competitive traffics may be seen in the traffics other than coal and coke, and iron and steel:

Average Receipts per net ton mile (£)*

	1953	1958	1963
Actual	.0161	.0176	.0187
Adjusted to constant 1953 price basis	.0161	.0150	.0145

In a period in which there was very little change in the mix of traffics, the length of haul or the load per wagon, BR virtually held its freight prices constant. In ten years in which consumer prices rose by 28%, BR receipts per net ton mile for these traffics rose only 16%, that is, in real terms effective BR freight rates for road-competitive traffics fell through the period. Presumably these rates were all at the levels thought necessary to secure the traffics from road, but there is no evidence that road rates were themselves falling in real terms over the same period.[21]

So far, so bad, but worse is yet to come, for the events following the downturn in freight volume in 1958 showed there was a negligible connection between changes in the cost 'floors' and changes in the rates themselves. The 'cost' for any particular transit was supposed to be synthesised from average cost values for all the facilities, terminals, yards, trains, etc through which the transit passed. Now it so happened that, in 1958, coal and steel traffic fell disastrously, and total freight traffic continued to fall until 1963. It was the BTC's inability to make any significant decrease in its total costs to match this decline in traffic which caused the explosive growth in its deficit. Coming back to our problem of the costing 'floor', below which rates cannot be set, we can see that this 'floor' must have been rising continuously through the period 1958-63. This is because, if the throughput of a facility is reduced, but the total cost remains unchanged, the *average* cost for the remaining traffic must have risen substantially. As all of the cost 'floors' for pricing the remaining traffic were comprised of a combination of such averages, they, too, must have been rising. But we have just seen that in traffics other than coal or minerals average rates did not even keep up with inflation, let alone adjust to the altered cost conditions on the railway.

Of course, there could have been a very good, short-run reason why BR did not get its prices up; they may then have been uncompetitive, thus losing the business. But if that was the case, only one conclusion can follow: that large parts of the freight business should have been closed down. If costing information was really used as a pricing floor, that is the only conclusion available —

*Taken from *BTC & BRB: Annual Report & Accounts*, 1963, actual data from 1964 Accounts due to break in series. 'Constant price' values calculated by consumer price index.

that the BTC deliberately carried on into the hopelessly unprofitable state which Beeching found. This really *is* one of those 'knaves or fools' situations; if the BTC were religiously applying their proclaimed price-setting criteria, they would (and should) have priced themselves out of many markets. But clearly they did not do so. Was it because the whole question of an automatic pricing 'floor' was a myth, or did the BTC deliberately retain uneconomic traffic just to bolster its own corporate ego?

The proof was not long in coming that the BTC had been highly irresponsible in its management and control of the freight business. If we look at BR freight revenues in relation to aggregate costs a more alarming picture emerges. We have already seen that the ostensible aim of freight pricing was at least to cover direct costs, and, hopefully, in aggregate to cover the indirect costs. Provided the rates still exceeded direct costs, the salesmen would have achieved their objective. It is possible that they were too hungry for traffic at any price, and did not bargain hard enough, but provided they had been obtaining rates which made some contribution to 'indirect' costs, we might just say 'too bad', and look elsewhere for solutions to BR's freight problems. In fact, that was precisely how the BTC saw the issue. In 1960, Sir Brian Robertson claimed that: 'The full load (merchandise) traffic on the whole is unquestionably profitable in the sense that it makes a contribution to the central charges.' That is, covering track costs, and normal overheads.[22] Yet within two years it was clear to his successor that hardly any rates for road-competitive traffics could have been covering 'direct' costs. The Beeching report blandly admitted that the 'direct' costs of wagon-load general merchandise traffics were £96.6 million, while the revenues were only £64.8 million![23] So even if the rates negotiated were the best that BR salesmen could bargain, it was obvious that most of the traffics should have been rejected as costing more to carry than they earned! Something was drastically wrong with either:

(i) The validity of the traffic costing methods,
(ii) The control of the freight salesmen's traffic acceptance criteria, or
(iii) The ability of top management to react to a situation where, on its own admission, every £1 of merchandise traffic revenue was costing £1.49 in 'direct' (ie, claimed to be controllable) cost to earn, *plus* an unspecified amount of indirect cost.

Four years later, this apparent waste of national resources had only been reduced to £1.25 of direct cost for every £1 of revenue, with still nothing contributed to the 'indirect' costs.[24] When BR was failing by such a massive margin even to cover its direct costs, it is not hard to see why there was a pronounced official indifference to suggestions that important 'indirect' costs such as track and signalling cost should either be recovered from users, or the traffic causing them abandoned. With the publication of this data in 1963 it became clear that competitive rail freight traffics were not being subsidised by those users paying the published maximum rates, but by the community in general through the deficit grants. If the costing calculations were accurate it is obvious that the acceptance criteria must have been ignored on an almost universal scale.

It is easy to see why, at the salesmen's level, this was allowed to happen. Faced with a customer's claim that a road haulier had offered a lower rate, in the salesman's mind the discussion would have been about a piece of truly marginal business. On the assumption that his operating colleagues would be unable to make any cost savings if that particular traffic were lost, the salesman would be justified in quoting virtually any price low enough to secure it. But over time, all traffics come up for review in a similar way, and the 'no-cost-savings' assumption cannot be valid for them all. It was clear from the way in which freight rate increases were lagging behind prices generally (and railway wages in particular) that even if rates were covering 'direct' costs in 1953, they must have slipped well below them by the end of the decade. It was the same traffic costing service which told Dr Beeching he was spending half as much again in 'direct' costs as he was taking in revenue for the wagon load merchandise traffic, as had led Sir Brian Robertson to believe these traffics were contributing to 'central charges'. It is hardly credible that Dr Beeching was able to teach the traffic costing service some sophisticated new methods; more likely he was interested in having information which the BTC did not wish to know about.

Thus between 1953 and 1961 the BTC had allowed BR's freight business to get completely out of control. In a period in which the Government wished to bring about a reallocation of inland freight traffic based on the actual comparative costs of road and rail, the BTC deliberately retained traffics at rates far below the costs of carrying them and managed to make the Government pay for its defiance through the deficit grants. Right through the period (and for a long time afterwards), BR and its senior managers were to make claims of how low total rail freight costs *could* be, provided traffic volumes were high enough. But such arguments related to the use of fixed plant, the cost of which was claimed (erroneously) to be unresponsive to charges in output. If low rates, which were below even those costs which were admitted to vary directly with output, could not attract traffic to fully use the capacity provided, the only logical course was to abandon traffic and save those costs. It is clear that for all the lofty talk about pricing 'floor' based on 'direct costs', at the salesmen's level no one could have been taking any notice of them. But then, it seems, neither did anyone take notice at any other level. The BTC just sat on its hands and said, in effect, that there was no connection between the prices it could obtain for traffics and the quantity of those traffics it could profitably carry. The doublethink about 'contributions to indirect costs', espoused to the Transport Tribunal for one purpose, became a dual justification, first, for doing nothing about those 'indirect' costs when the competitively determined rates failed to cover them, and then, for doing nothing about the 'direct' costs when they, too, failed to be covered.

The BTC's analysts were led up this blind alley by their need, in the Transport Tribunal, to rebut the suggestions of academics and others that rail rates should be based on costs. On a railway, this was never possible, but the success of their rebuttal in the Tribunal blinded them to the much more important dictum that, for commercial viability *and* in the national interest, the costs which are incurred should be based on the prices at which traffics can be obtained. If prices could not be based on costs, costs should have been used to tell whether, and for how long, BR could profitably accept traffic at prices determined in the market. Costing information was thus needed for two types of decisions: (i) whether or not to accept a particular traffic; (ii) whether or not to replace a particular asset being used as a whole variety of traffics of varying levels of long run profitability. From the evidence cited above, it appears to have been used for neither purpose.

BR's operating objectives should have been to carry only those traffics whose rates exceeded their short-run (ie, until investment was needed) marginal costs, and its investment strategy should have been to replace assets only to the capacity which was justified by traffics which were able to bear long run marginal costs. Now all of this may appear a bit too sophisticated for an organisation which could not even understand which costs could be varied with output,[25] but it is clear from its actions, in the investment proposals of the modernisation plan and in its day-to-day control of the business, that the BTC was not even interested in the corner shop maxim that if you spend more on a product than the customer pays you, you will go bankrupt. The BTC always felt that its interpretation of 'the national interest' justified it in defying the expressed wishes of the Government to try to break even. Unfortunately, as we shall see, the bad habits which grew up in the period of irresponsibility, 1953-61, took many years to eradicate. The great freight bargain sale was to run, at the community's expense, for many years.

We have seen that, by a combination of under-pricing and over-providing merchandise freight services, the BTC managed to defy the Government's intention that inland freight traffic should be allocated according to the costs of the respective modes. It does not matter much now whether this occurred through the BTC's incompetence (in that it did not even know what it was doing), or because of a deliberate decision that it thought it knew better than the Government what was best for the Nation (in which case it was incompetent of the civil servants to let the BTC get away with it). There is one further possible explanation, which, if valid, reflects even more damagingly on the BTC and the railway managers. Because it will recur, as a justification of inaction in the face of unprofitability in a much more recent episode, it will suffice if we just note it for the present. This possible explanation, which we will treat fully in Chapter 14, is to the effect that any attempt to have controlled capacity and costs to match the level of demand might have worsened the financial results even more, because it would not have been possible to reduce administration costs in step with reductions in the level of output. Not to put too fine a point on it, this is really suggesting that one objective of railway activity is to make jobs for managers and clerks. Not even the BTC was brash enough to claim this at that time, but as it has been asserted rather forcibly more recently, it is worth mentioning at this stage.

---

1 For a more technical discussion of the issues involved here, see my *Railway Economics*, (forthcoming).

2 See 'Railway Freight Charges', *Journal of the Institute of Transport*, July 1967, pp.143–169.

3 See Gilbert Walker: *Road and Rail*, London, 1942, pp. 188 191.

4 We will go into varieties of 'cost' in a moment.

5 As early as 1950, Professor Gilbert Walker had suggested that a classification of terminals might be as important as loadability. (see *Railway Gazette*, 1/12/1950, p.481) This was subsequently incorporated in the BR maximum rates schedule which is still in use today.

6 See, for example, Gilbert J. Ponsonby: 'Towards a New Railway Charges Policy', *Journal of the Institute of Transport*, September 1954, pp. 427–433; and A.G.Pool: 'The Basis of Transport Charges', *Journal of the Institute of Transport*, Jan. 1955, pp.45–48.

7 See C.D.Foster: 'Some notes on railway costs and costing', *Bulletin of the Oxford University Institute of Statistics*, February 1962, pp. 73–103. The following analysis is at variance with Foster's arguments in this article and in his subsequent book (*The Transport Problem*, London, 1962), which were over-reliant on railway assertions of the inescapability of costs. But it owes much to a very helpful exposition of the problem in a letter Foster wrote to me in response to criticisms of his book.

8 *In the Court of the Transport Tribunal, Transport Acts, 1947, and 1953, In the Matter of the Application of the British Transport Commission (1955 No.2) To confirm the British Transport Commission (Railway Merchandise) Charges Scheme*, London, HMSO, 1955 & 1956, Question 826. Afterwards cited as 'Transport Tribunal 1955-6'.

9 See Foster, *op cit*, Table A1. It is significant that these data, offered in evidence to the Tribunal in 1955/6, suggest that the track and signalling cost allocated to freight for this purpose was at a much higher rate than the proportion of total track and signalling cost to total railway cost. See the Beeching Report (1963), p.6, which shows track and signalling cost to be less than 20% of total expenses.

10 See footnote 7, above. Foster has pointed out that for a *shorter* time period, the BTC's criteria *overstated* the relevant costs.

11 See, eg, the motto at the head of Chapter 9.

12 H.E.Osborne: 'Transport Charging Policies', *British Transport Review* April 1957, p.11.

13 *SCNI : BR* Appendix 39, para. 10.

14 *SCNI : BR* Appendix 9, para. 58. The notion that 'who pays' the track costs determined how fixed it is, is certainly a novel approach. It is none-the-less invalid.

15 Beeching Report 1963, p.9.

16 British Railways Board. *A Study of the Relative True costs of Rail and Road Freight Transport over Trunk Routes*. London, 1964, p. 12.

17 See my 'British Railways Track Costs', *Journal of Industrial Economics*, November 1969, pp. 74–89.

18 The limited scale of the practice before 1953 is indicated by BR's ability to break-even overall.

19 Under S.53 of the Transport Act, 1962.

20 See *National Board for Prices and Incomes Report No.72. Proposed Increased by British Railways Board in Certain Country-wide Fares and Charges*. Cmnd. 3656, London, HMSO, 1968, paras. 51–53.

21 Because road hauliers must either cover costs or go out of business and because most of their costs are labour costs (which rise faster than inflation), without a significant change in technology or labour produtivity in the period, hauliers' prices would have been rising in real terms, 1953–1968.

22 *SCNI : BR (1960)* Q.1816, 1818.

23 Beeching Report (1963), p.8. These costs included interest on capital and provision for depreciation.

24 *BTC : Annual Report & Accounts*, 1967, Appendix 1.

25 I did not expound it myself in this form until 1968, when I joined BR and found the head of the freight costing section busy trying to work out the long run marginal costs of traffics in accordance with the Government's directive in its White Paper: *Nationalised Industries: A review of the economic and financial objectives*, Cmnd.3437, London, HMSO, 1967, pp. 8–10.

6 | The Beeching Years

If the whole plan is implemented with vigour, . . . , much
(though not necessarily all) of the Railways' deficit should be
eliminated by 1970'.

Beeching Report, p.60

British Railways Board deficits for the years 1963 - 1968 were as follows:

1963	£134m	1966	£134m
1964	£121m	1967	£153m
1965	£132m	1968	£147m

BRB: Annual Report & Accounts, 1963-68

To use a simile from military history, Dr (subsequently Lord) Beeching was a Montgomery to Sir Brian Robertson's Auchinleck. By the time Beeching took over in June 1961, the old BTC had been through the Select Committee and Stedeford Committee mills, and had at last been confronted with the error of its efforts to pursue a line contrary to the Government's wishes, but financed by Government grants. The better investments of the modernisation plan, such as diesel locomotives, were starting to pay off. Many of the management initiatives of the last years of the BTC were, if mis-aimed, at least pointed in the right direction. There was to be hardly a technical or operating development of the Beeching era which did not have its roots back in the BTC years. But the new, highly-paid manager from Imperial Chemical Industries supplied the vital new persona which signified to all, community, Government and railwaymen alike, that further change was in store. The community was the last of these to know the precise form of that change; at the beginning it was widely expected that Beeching would simply make the railways more 'efficient', whatever that might mean. For the Government, which had stood idly by while the BTC poured national resources into lost causes, it was inevitable that it would exercise its right to name a culprit and eliminate it. Perhaps the Government did accept some of the blame, for it eliminated only the British Transport Commission *organisation*: most of the individuals who had been concerned with its downfall survived. To make way for Beeching, Sir Brian Robertson was replaced as Chairman of the BTC a couple of years before the normal expiry of his appointment. But Sir Reginald Wilson, former comptroller and then the finance expert on the Commission itself,[1] went on to become Managing Director of the Transport Holding Company, and subsequently Chairman of the National Freight Corporation. The other full-time members of the BTC remained for the time being, although one, K.W.C.Grand, left before the formation of the British Railways Board.

In the new capital debt burden it set for the British Railways Board, the Government displayed its unwillingness to admit that it could have been the modernisation plan itself which lay at the root of BR's troubles. The new capital debt was set as an amount which roughly approximated the gross investment which had been made in BR since the inception of the modernisation plan. It was as if all the pre-1954 assets were given free to BR and it was only expected to earn a return on money spent on new assets since that time. But, at current interest rates, even that was too much, and £705 million of the new capital debt was 'suspended' indefinitely. Even then, BR could not pay interest on the remainder and the 1962 Transport Act had to continue powers to make good the annual deficits. Although the Government appeared to be adopting a realistic stance on BR's immediate financial prospects, in the back of the first BRB Annual Report there appeared a piece of comic nonsense which showed the Utopian performance which was expected of the new management. It was a schedule of required debt repayments,[2] starting at £45 million per annum at the end of 1964, and tapering slightly until the whole of the £857 million of active debt was to have been paid off by January 1st, 1985. This was 'expected' of an organisation which in its first full year of operation was to lose £76 million *before interest.* There had been plenty of time to get these things right; the Government's White Paper[3] outlining its proposals was published in December 1960, Dr Beeching joined the BTC in June 1961, and the new British Railways Board was not to be created until January 1963. But the capital debt arrangements with which the British Railways Board had to commence operations can only be explained in terms of a determination on the part of the Government to punish it for the sins of the BTC. By 1963 it was quite irrelevant that the BTC had wasted all those millions. It should have been clear that there was no chance of returning to profitable operation; not even Dr Beeching could manage that.

Further indications of the Government's cynicism in its treatment of the new BR were to be found in the new arrangements to constrain the closure of passenger services. By 1963, the BTC's early optimism (that only £3 million might be saved in this way) was completely deflated, and it was obvious that these services were a prime cause of the deficit. But the 1962 Act maintained the Government's powers to refuse or amend the passenger service closure proposals of BR. Admittedly, even then the full cost to BR of these services was not realised, mainly because of BR's invalid approach to the track cost issue, but it was clear that much of the working deficit was caused in this way. The Government could have no right to expect BR to restore overall profitability, let alone refund some of the capital debt, if it was going to constrain the railways' freedom of action in this way. It is greatly to the credit of some of the railway managers of the Beeching era that they set about such a hopeless task as if total success was possible, and out of this vain attempt Britain achieved improvements in railway operating efficiency and product quality on a major scale.[4]

Two years after Beeching joined BR, the famous Reshaping report was published, known ever afterward as the Beeching Report. It is no accident that this report and its chief author are best known for the attack on the branch line passenger services. This, in the public mind, is what Beeching's 'plan' for the railways was all about. Having failed to secure an equitable or workable capital structure and basis for financing the provision of loss-making services, the Beeching administration set about axing them with an obvious relish. The whole tone of the report suggested that the rapid elimination of loss-making activities would be the fastest route to profitability. This had been Beeching's experience when chairman of ICI's Metals Division, but there the central activity had been profitable. With BR there was the risk that the unprofitable activities were in fact all leaning on each other, and an attempt to eradicate some would just disclose losses elsewhere. Although the BTC had been wrong to persist for so long with activities which could better have been served by other modes, the Government and the community had rather liked its failure to face reality in this way. It was only when the bills had to be paid that anyone really objected. And just as there was an administrative hiatus between the BR commercial men who accepted traffic at rates below costs, and the operating men whose financial responsibility it was to carry the traffic, so there was a similar gap in the mind of any Minister of Transport, who could force BR to continue uneconomic services, but who would complain about the size of the railway deficit. True, not all of the working deficit could be explained in this way; despite the massive investments in the modernisation plan, the BTC still managed to hand over to its successors a very inefficient railway.

It will help to set the scene for this discussion if we summarise the proposals of the Beeching report, with some quick comments (*see page 72*).

It was perhaps not entirely coincidental that the postulated range of improvement neatly blanketed the 1963 deficit (after interest) of £134 million. An ominous omission was any estimate of savings from the main line electrification programme then in progress: that was one thing on which Dr Beeching seemed to differ from the railway managers. There were even two classes of passenger trains, London and provincial suburban services, on which BR was not proposing significant withdrawals, thus implying that the losses on these would adequately be carried by the remaining services.

With this optimistic prospectus, Dr Beeching was to deliver himself and his successor into the hands of the Government and public opinion — hostages to various claims of financial improvement which either the Government was unprepared to countenance or the management was incapable of achieving. Having made such grandiose claims and then failing abysmally to achieve them, BR was denied adequate credit even for the workmanlike progress it did achieve. But then, Dr Beeching was Lord Beeching, safe back at ICI, and it was his successor who had to try to explain BR's hitherto hidden problems to the government.

There were obvious and serious flaws in the Beeching prospectus for the railways; often adverse effects were to pop up as an indirect result of an eminently justifiable, but ill-thought out initiative elsewhere. We have already touched upon the absurdity of leaving BR with a burden of fixed interest debt which it had no hope of servicing. The mere fact that continuing deficit grants were required even to cover *working* deficits showed that BR was hopelessly over-capitalised in having any fixed interest commitment at all. Possibly it was due to a refusal by a Conservative government to let a public corporation 'get away with it', but the 'getting away' had been going on, with the overt approval of the Government, for years. If the BTC had got the railways into the deepest financial mess of any commercial organisation in British history, it had done so

Proposal	Estimated Financial Improvement, £m per annum	Comment
Passenger service withdrawals and station closures; subsequent line closures or reduction to freight standards.	29 — 32	Dependent wholly upon Government approval.
Freight service withdrawals.	5 — 10	Could have been achieved at any time since 1953.
Reduction in passenger coach fleet.	2 — 3	Savings overstated, but could have been achieved by BTC.
Reduction in freight wagon fleet.	10 — 12	Freight wagon fleet enlarged by BTC.
Workshops rationalisation.	4	Probably possible ever since regrouping in 1923.
Further dieselisation.	15 — 20	Wholly the fault of the BTC and Railway Executive that this had not been achieved before.
Coal concentration depots. Block coal trains.	7 — 10	Could have been done by BTC. Depended upon successful negotiation with National Coal Board. Technically feasible for at least 40 years.
Concentration of sundries traffic.	15 — 20	Should have been done by BTC after 1953 Act.
Introduction of Liner trains.	10 — 12	Groundwork laid by LM Region in BTC days.
Repricing of presently unprofitable freight traffics.	5 — 6	Always possible — continuing programme.
Additional freight traffic to be secured (net profit).	10 — 15	Implied approx. 15-20% increase in freight traffics — if valid, equally available to the BTC.
Reduction in general administration expenses.	3 — 4	About 7% of 1963 level; not a very demanding target, given planned reductions in level of BR activity — implied little, if any, improvement in actual efficiency.
Total	£115 — 148 million	

as agent for the same Government which was now determined to visit the sins of the BTC on the new management.

Of course, it must have been very difficult for civil servants and ministers to accept that, even after nearly all of the investment of the modernisation plan, BR was no nearer to profits. I remember the late O.F.Gingell, an under-secretary at the then Ministry of Transport, addressing a seminar at the London School of Economics in 1963 and arguing that even if the BTC was as incompetent as it appeared, he could not believe that, given the free use of pre-1955 assets, the new investments could not be made profitable. But right then, in 1963, they were obviously not profitable on this basis, because BR was failing by about £170 million per annum to cover a reasonable interest bill on its modernisation plan investments. That is why £705 million of the commencing capital debt had to be 'suspended'. The Government and the BR management were in a repetition of the dilemma which had faced the BTC in 1956; to have admitted to each other (and to the Treasury, Parliament and the general public) the impossibly bleak future facing BR with the proposed capital debt arrangements would have been to admit the massive scale of their own mistakes in the immediate past. To have done this would have taken all credibility from any new forecasts they might have made, so it was better for all of those directly concerned to brazen it out and hope that something would turn up.

The only way in which the new capital debt arrangements could have been accepted as even vaguely realistic was for Beeching and the remainder of the BR Board to accept fully the prognosis of the Reshaping Report, that savings could be achieved at the rate of about £20 million per annum for seven years. Even this required that no further misfortunes, such as the inevitable 'unstable currency' which Sir Reginald Wilson had offered as an excuse three years earlier, befell BR. It is worth noting that only about a quarter of the claimed improvement potential was subject to Government approval; the only difficulties in achieving the remainder could be BR's honesty in forecasting it, and its ability to carry it out. Looking back, it is amazing how quickly the lessons of the modernisation plan debacle had been forgotten, and the BR management was allowed to make the same glib claims of profits 'soon'. But once BR had made those claims, the responsibility of the Government for the realism of the new arrangement disappeared.

We turn now to some detailed aspects of the Beeching Report and its aftermath. It will be recalled that, in the 1962 Act, the Government rejected the Select Committee's proposal that specific subsidies should be paid for loss-making services run at the Government's request. BR was to propose some for closure, and eventually to support the others from profits earned elsewhere. In the meantime, deficit grants would cover the losses. The Government's decision to leave the arrangements for these services in such an unaccountable and vague form obviously satisfied BR. The comments of the BTC on the Select Committee's recommendations[5] displayed an unwillingness to submit to too close a level of Government surveillance in return for the chance to produce unambiguous accounts. Partly, they had no real choice, because as the Beeching Report was to show only too well, the mental blockage of the traffic costing service on the track costs issues would have prevented BR from making an adequate charge for the track costs caused by these services. This difficulty was to pursue BR for the next five years; because they had accepted the 'deal' offered by the 1962 Act they were never prepared to make a public issue of the effects of this on their deficit. The nearest they came to doing this was in the 'Appendix 1' published with the *Annual Report & Accounts* in 1965, 1966 and 1967, but because far more of the deficit was due to causes apparently within BR's control, not too many stones could be thrown from that particular glasshouse.

With the unthinking agreement of BR, the Government thus had the best of all worlds. The 1962 Act left the onus on BR to prove that particular loss-making services were not in the public interest. To save Government expenditure, in the form of deficit grants, all the initiatives had to be taken by the railway managers, and the Government could then act as the protector of the public interest by refusing the application. Then, at the end of each year, it was the railway managers who made the loss which the innocent Government had to make good. A more politically perceptive BR Chairman would have resisted such an arrangement.

Turning to the analysis of the report itself, the reader must inevitably be disappointed. It was lacking in arithmetic, logic and a sense of priorities.

It had all the marks of a rush job, based on 'facts' which were in many cases of doubtful value.[6] Having accepted the disadvantageous position of having to try to withdraw passenger and freight services to reduce its deficit, BR offered some dubious arguments in support of what were quite justifiable proposals. But the public were quick to claim the Jesuitical point that if the supporting arguments could be shaken the proposals were themselves invalid. The trouble was that Beeching, who was rumoured to have personally drafted much of the report himself, could only gain his understanding of the problem from the same managers and administrative machine which had been responsible for the debacle he was trying to rectify.

Right through the report, what we now know to have been broadly correct solutions were reached by what appeared to be very doubtful analysis. We have already mentioned the spectre of the 'necessarily high and fixed' track costs. It was as if Dr Beeching, looking for some magic key to the problem of the railways with the capital-intensive view of one experienced in the chemical industry, had lit upon the single most costly asset as the explanation. The report noted with concern that this item of expenditure 'amounts to nearly a quarter of the railways' total revenue'.[7] Of course, it amounted to only 20 per cent of total cost, because costs were a bigger total than revenue. The Board showed no concern for the fact that the same item comprised a different proportion of other comparable systems' total costs.[8] But if it was to be argued that this cost was 'fixed' in some meaningful sense, it is understandable that BR would not pay much regard to other systems' track and signalling costs and their implications, for by definition 'fixed' meant irreduceable (unless the route was to be closed).

If the reader looks very hard at the Beeching report he will see hints here and there as to the essential variability of this cost category, but this certainly ran counter to the analysis of the report. For example, the table on page 9 did concede that there were at least nine different categories of route (to four maintenance standards and with varying numbers of tracks), each with a different quality/capacity/cost value. And later, on page 17 it claimed that ' . . . the presence of a stopping passenger service on a main line adds appreciably to the system cost, by complicating the signalling, . . .' . But nowhere did the report suggest that savings could be made by finely tailoring the system capacity to the traffic, instead of just abandoning both traffic *and* system where current traffic could not support current facilities. The implicit assumption of the report was that every route already had the minimum capacity (and cost) for its particular traffic, and if, as was common at the time, the traffic could not pay for that capacity, both had to go. This partial treatment of the track and signalling cost problem was to freeze any constructive thinking for at least another five years: railway managers were perhaps entitled to believe that if the Doctor accepted this, it must be right.

From the 'necessarily high and fixed' dictum, Dr Beeching drew two far-too-simple conclusions. First, that there was substantial unused capacity on the main lines which could be used at negligible marginal cost.[9] True, but not very meaningful if that unused capacity could not be sold. Secondly, at the other end of the spectrum of traffic densities on many lightly loaded branch lines it stated that there was little hope of the traffics ever being sufficient to cover their track and signalling costs. Whilst no doubt true for many of the services concerned, this was a blind to cover up the fact that for many years the same services had failed hopelessly to cover even their movement costs, which were always easily reckonable, and were not bedevilled with 'cost-sharing' problems. On page 18, the report's own example, which presumably was typical, had uncovered direct costs double the indirect (ie, track and signalling) costs. These were the services for which the British Transport Commission had spent millions in re-equipment with diesel trains, to halve movement costs to a level where the fares still only met half of the direct costs.

The only reassuring feature of this depressing fact is that if so many services had such poor economics, it is hardly likely that any of the Beeching closure proposals actually completed included services which the later and more sophisticated cost-benefit analysis could have shown should have been retained. Having accepted a faulty recapitalisation, which put the responsibility for withdrawing services on to the Board,[10] the Beeching administration had no alternative but to use any available presentational points to secure public acceptance of its acts. If the high and fixed track cost argument was persuasive inside BR, it was obviously a strong candidate for the public presentation of the rationale for reshaping the network. At this stage, we can only regret that such a *simpliste* notion was accepted internally.[11]

What about the other items, which in aggregate were to return BR to profitable operation by 1970? The freight service withdrawals, comprising mainly the closure of low-volume depots which were relics of the horse and cart days, were so obvious that the only question is why it took so long to decide to do this. There was no reason why the BTC could not have achieved such a step ten years earlier.

In contrast the expected 'savings' from reducing the passenger coach fleet were quite illusory, being based upon an extremely crude average cost, when the marginal cost was appropriate. Similarly, with the proposed reduction in the freight wagon fleet, savings came from a reduction in repair costs, and as these were primarily related to the annual number of wagons loaded, reducing the stock of wagons used for a given volume of traffic would not make a significant cost reduction. But this whole question of the size of the wagon fleet was a sore point with BR, and it was a prime candidate for action. In 1959 the Select Committee had made a big issue of comparative statistics for wagon turnround for BR and Continental systems, and had concluded that BR was performing badly. Now the fastest way to improve wagon turnround statistics is to reduce the wagon stock to the barest minimum capable of handling the traffic, and this BR set out to do with great success.[12]

The workshops rationalisation, to save £4 million per annum, was a faltering start to a streamlining process which has continued ever since. The proposed changes in the scale of rail operations were to necessitate far greater changes than the initial adjustments to what was still virtually the pre-grouping pattern of workshops.

The need for the rapid elimination of steam traction needs no further comment here.

On reforming the archaic methods of working coal traffic, the report was rather pessimistic. There were two main problems. The most obvious of these to the public, but the less important to BR, was the way in which coal distributors' traffic was worked. For far too long BR had borne the expense of working small consignments of coal from particular mines to particular retail distributors. The distributors operated nearly 4,000 coal yards, 43 percent of which received less than 20 tons per week. Such arrangements were hardly appropriate for a country where the Clean Air Act and competition from other fuels were causing a sharp decline in domestic coal consumption. Quite apart from the inefficiencies of handling coal by rail for such a 'horse and cart' distribution network, the inefficiencies within the coal trade itself were enormous. BR had already had to take the initiative in streamlining this trade, but the only effective pressure it could exert was by arbirtarily withdrawing services from the smaller terminals, an unpopular step with the coal merchants who were thereby put out of business. The retail coal trade had benefited from real protection by the railways' inertia in adjusting coal rates. At the Transport Tribunal hearings in 1955-56 the coal merchants had rightly been concerned that commercial freedom for the railways would adversely affect their business. As it happened, BR struck a blow for total fuel distribution efficiency when it chose physical reshaping for the coal trade, rather than just squeezing its margins through rate increases.

The other BR coal problem was on the growth side of the business; coal for power stations. The growth in demand for electricity, and the trend toward much larger generating stations and technical advances in power transmission, combined to offer BR an important new market opportunity. Although coal remained coal it was clear to all that it could and should be moved between mine and power station in a completely new way. A revolution in railway methods of coal handling was required. Although the long distance movement between primary yards and power station of whole trains of conventional coal wagons was increasing, what was required was the use of:

> 'Large, braked, hopper wagons which have a better load/tare weight ratio, which can be drawn at high speed, and which can be unloaded very quickly at the receiving terminal.'[13]

There was nothing very new in this; a similar working had been established in 1929 to serve the LMS Railway Company's own power station at Stonebridge Park. It was a commonplace on the Continent, and in the USA the growth of similar methods had always held such promise for the railroads that the US Interstate Commerce Commission had virtually banned them *to protect* the rails' competitors. But British railway history was against such a development, from the earliest standardisation on a low capacity open, unbraked, box-on-wheels for the Railway Clearing House coal wagon, to the inexplicable decision of the British Transport Commission to buy the 544,000 private-owner coal wagons at nationalisation. These had been owned by either coal users or coal mines, both of whom had developed the practice of using their wagons as much for coal storage as for coal movement. The problem was that the movement of these private-owner wagons had been charged for only in the loaded direction, but the railways had to use just as much effort to get an empty wagon from its owner's yard to the nominated mine as they expended on returning it when loaded. During both world wars the wagons had been taken into a common pool, and being able to allocate the nearest empty wagon for every loading requirement, the railways made great savings in shunting and empty wagon miles.

The key to this major economy was *common* ownership of the wagons, not necessarily *railway* ownership. If the newly created National Coal Board had assumed ownership of the wagons, it would have built in a great incentive for efficient wagon utilisation, but the BTC was blind to this point. In its haste to retain the operating advantages of the wagon pool, the BTC paid £43 million for the fleet.[14] But the worst was yet to come. Having relieved the coal industry of the responsibility for providing and maintaining its wagons, it went on and allowed the Coal Board to continue to use the now BR-owned wagons as cheap storage.[15] That was the legacy of BTC (or Railway Executive) mismanagement out of which BR had to bargain its way with the Coal Board. Although the Beeching report offered some fighting talk, the end result of the demurrage issue was that Lord Robens proved more than a match for Dr Beeching.[16] And as long as the demurrage issue remained unsatisfactory to BR (ie, satisfactory to the NCB), there was no incentive for the NCB to install loading facilities for the new high-capacity wagons which BR wanted to introduce. Then there was another drag on this particular piece of railway progress. The necessary loading bunkers at the mines were costly (up to £250,000 per mine) but there were very few mines with a sufficient output of power-station coal to fully use the bunkers, if installed. Here was a case, if it is permissible to stretch the term in this way, of *tri*-lateral monopoly, where BR, the NCB, and the Central Electricity Board had to bargain a solution in which the role of each was irreplaceable, but only two parties, BR and the CEGB, stood to make significant economies.[17] So the new method, enthusiastically christened 'merry-go-round' working by BR, arrived too late and suffered too many railway-inflicted handicaps to permit its fullest exploration.

The remaining five items of Beeching improvements were :

- — Concentration of sundries,
- — Liner trains,
- — Repricing freight traffics,
- — Gaining new freight traffics,
- — Administrative economics,

These we will pick up as the narrative proceeds. For we must turn now to some vital matters the Beeching report did not mention.

It will be recalled that the fundamental flaw in the railway modernisation plan was the implicit assumption that increases in railway wages could be held down to the rate of general increase in prices. Just as the BTC's fixation on this impossible target led to the Guillebaud Report,[18] and a general restoration of comparability with the rates for non-rail jobs, so the Beeching era insistence that BR could not 'afford' increases greater than the rate of inflation was to lead to midnight trips to 10 Downing Street and the ridiculous and embarrassing attempt to break one such impasse during a television interview with Mr Ernest Marples. The report did not shrink from mentioning the run down in staff which would be the inevitable consequence of most of the projected improvements in efficiency. But with the exception of work study schemes and the need for a further bargain on locomotive manning,[19] the report was unduly silent about needing any other gains in labour productivity. And as the book by the principal industrial relations officer of the time shows, nothing was achieved in this field until 1965.[20] Right through the Beeching period, railwaymen's average *real* wages rose at over three percent per annum, and to the extent that this was compensated at all by increased productivity, that productivity was obtained by massive injections of labour-saving equipment, financed by interest-free deficit grants.

Most of the apparent gain in labour productivity in that period was quite spurious. The staff remaining were not necessarily working any harder; it was just that the staff displaced by service withdrawals and terminal closures had been much less productive than those who remained. Eliminating them automatically raised the apparent average productivity of those remaining. It should be remembered that the efficiency improvements outlined in the Beeching report were to restore BR to profitability in conditions of what Sir Reginald Wilson had called 'a stable currency', ie, where railway staff were expected to forego the increases in living standards which everyone else in the community obtains. Where 60 percent of your costs are labour costs, this is a crucial matter. In the event, the rises in real railway wages conceded between 1962 and 1970 meant that even if the Beeching report improvements had all been obtained as planned, it would still have been about £70m. (1962 prices) short of breaking even.

The true picture is that the Beeching report's prognoses were hopelessly optimistic, and failure to achieve them helped to cost Dr Beeching's successor his job. Even allowing for the 'real wage increase' error, and the Government's frequent refusals of BR proposals to withdraw passenger services, it is clear that there must have been many more things wrong with the railways than the writers of the Beeching report were aware of. Seeing that it was to take more than ten more years for the management to admit the existence of these more fundamental faults, Dr Beeching and his helpers perhaps cannot be blamed for not noticing them in 1961-2.

But the superficiality of the Beeching report was to cost BR and the country a lot in wasted resources in the following years. Prepared and presented with such a fanfare, it lulled the Government, the community and the railway management and staff into a completely false sense of security. At last, the famous report had told everybody what needed to be corrected on the railways. That was the trap; everybody thought it was an exhaustive list. Thus vital years were lost while the management shunted round looking for excuses when it became obvious that the Beeching prescriptions were not even relieving the symptoms, let alone curing the disease. Straight talk and analysis in 1962 could have saved much wasted effort later, by directing scarce management resources into areas of really high pay-off, instead of scratching for negligible returns in trying to close rural branch lines. By this I mean areas such as :

(i) *Maximising the profits from the Inter-City passenger business* — it was 1968 before the railway management was forced to admit to itself that it could profitably charge much higher fares on routes where it offered high class service.

(ii) *Obtaining continuous true improvement in labour productivity* — apart from loco-manning and work study schemes, this hardly began until L.F.Neal was hired, at the Minister's suggestion, in 1967.

(iii) *Demanding improved performance from the non-rail subsidiaries.*

(iv) *Commencing a fundamental analysis of the future of the freight business,* instead of just closing the obvious low volume terminals and leaving the future policymaking to the unsupportable (but equally untestable) assertions of one man. [22]

(v) *Getting the capital structure right,* even if it meant deflating a few unearned reputations by telling the truth about the debacle of the modernisation plan.

Together all of these were more important than the set of low level objectives postulated in the Beeching Report. And many of them were not achieved in total. Anyway, the enormity of the task confronting Beeching's successors can easily be imagined.

1 Although Sir Reginald Wilson later added an appointment as Chairman of an Area Board to his BTC duties, it is clear from the questions he was called upon to answer before the Select Committee Sir Brian Robertson still relied upon him on matters concerning the financial aspects of the modernisation plan.
2 *BR : Annual Reports & Accounts,* 1963. Direction D. pp. 75–6.
3 Command 1248, London, HMSO, 1960.
4 See next chapter: 'Some Results of Beeching'.
5 These were set out above, in Chapter Four.

6 Much of the difficulty arose from an over reliance on 'test-week' data. But see D.L.Munby: 'The Reshaping of British Railways', *Journal of Industrial Economics*, Vol.11, 1962—3.

7 Beeching Report, p.9.

8 In 1961, BR's track cost per unit of net output exceeded those of the DB, SNCF, NS, FS and SNCB, by a range of 2 per cent to 73 per cent.

9 Beeching Report, pp. 4, 9. This was to be reinforced in the two subsequent British Railways Board reports: *The Development of the Railway Trunk Routes*, London, 1965 and *A Study of the relative True Costs of Rail and Road Freight Transport over Trunk Routes*, London 1964.

10 It is interesting to speculate whether the Government of the day might have felt that the loss-making passenger services were really a self-inflicted burden on BR. After all, the BTC had willingly invested in new trains when it should have been closing routes on a widespread scale, thus raising public expectations on the 'permanence' of rural railway passenger services.

11 See Chapter Nine.

12 'Wagon turnround' is calculated by dividing the *number of wagons loaded* for the year into the *wagon stock* times 365 days, to find the mean period between successive loadings of each wagon.

13 Beeching Report, p. 31.

14 And immediately started scrapping many of the wagons which, with grease-filled axle boxes, were no longer suitable for operation on BR. See *BTC: AR&A* 1948, paras. 23 and 24.

15 *Ibid*, p. 31. 'The Coal Board have the use of (the wagons) as bunkers for about 22 million days a year, either at pits or washeries. This, with an allowance for coverage of peak demands, costs the railways about £1 for each wagon supplied, or about £11m per year. Under established practice, the Coal Board pay a total demurrage charge of only £1m per annum.'

16 See Fiennes, *op cit*, pp. 8—12, and Pryke, *op cit*, p. 72.

17 For the CEGB the proposed method offered big savings in construction cost of coal storage and handling areas at new power stations.

18 *Report of Railway Pay Committee of Enquiry*, London 1960.

19 *Ibid*, p. 49.

20 Charles McLeod: *All Change*, London, 1970, pp. 66—76.

21 This flaw in the plan was first noted by Richard Pryke in his *Public Enterprise in Practice*, London, 1971, p. 250.

22 See Chapters Twelve and Fourteen.

7 | Some Results of Beeching

'In no form of transport will change come as quickly and
as radically as on the railways.'
G.F.Fiennes (1963)

It is time to take stock; to discuss the achievements of the Beeching years, but
also to look at some of the less desirable features and to bring back into our
discussion the results of our analysis in Chapter Two. There, it will be
remembered, it was shown that for the years 1956 to 1968, and allowing for the
cost of the social passenger services which the Government now bears, BR
invested between £776 million and £1,133 million[1] for no commercial return.
That is, after all of that investment in its commercial services, and even if
subsidies had been paid for social services, BR could still not make a profit.
Looking back in 1968 it was hard to see where the money had gone, because so
much remained to be done. The continuously welded rail programme was only
half completed, the National Signalling Plan had barely begun, electrification of
the remainder of the West Coast Main Line was still only a project awaiting
approval, and so on. In Chapter Four I have offered some suggestions on where
the money did go. Remember that all of the investments in social passenger
services which survived beyond 1968 are covered by our imputed subsidy
calculations. Only investments in stopping passenger services closed by 1968 are
included in our reckoning of the waste. But waste it was, none-the-less. The
other chapters have sketched in some explanation of the way in which BR was
led to such a disastrous programme of investment, and much more importantly,
such a costly continuation of loss-making services, passenger and freight, which
should have been withdrawn gradually from 1948 onward.

Then there was the abysmal slowness with which the British Transport
Commission set about the general question of the efficiency of the rail services.
It has been suggested in a recent study[2] that rail productivity improvement was
not possible beyond 1951 due to shortage of capital. This is clearly not so, as we
saw in Chapter Six, where £43 - 59 million per year of the proposed Beeching
savings could have been achieved by the BTC. Examination of the projects will
show that little investment, only good management, was required to achieve
these. It is obvious that in its first ten years, the British Transport Commission
failed to exert effective control over BR. It was only when financial collapse was
upon it that the BTC realised the need to do better, and by then the obvious
mismanagement of its modernisation plan discredited it in the eyes of the
Government and community alike.

Dr Beeching, whom the Government hoped could rectify the BTC's mismanagement, inherited all the faults (and most of the management) of the BTC.
Its investments between 1948 and 1961 determined the physical shape of the
railway which Dr Beeching had to operate. The BTC's indolence in attacking the
loss-making passenger and freight services determined the service patterns which

Beeching had to rationalise. And, worst of all, the refusal of both the BTC and the Government to admit the depth of the financial disaster into which the former had taken BR left Beeching with a ludicrous capital structure. But even taking account of this, and despite all the trumpeting, after 1964 Beeching made no impression on the railway deficit. This fact, quickly obvious to the public, led to allegations that the implementation of the Beeching Plan was actually doing harm to the railways. Although slightly more plausible than the widespread claim among the railway enthusiasts that the scrapping of steam locomotives was the cause of the deficit, the suggestion that the closure of branch lines was denying the trunk routes vital traffic paid no regard to the economies of the operation of the branches themselves. The real trouble lay much deeper. The Beeching Report implied that those parts of the railways' operations which were not slated for improvement were already healthy. This prognosis was hopelessly optimistic. It was the worsening on the supposedly healthy services which swamped the effects of any Beeching Plan improvements. The concentration on the obvious loss-makers blinded the management to the increasingly unhealthy state of the whole railway.

It must all have been very difficult for the BR managers to understand. The Traffic Costing Service had been in existence since 1951, yet still it could not tell the management precisely why it was losing money. The typically pompous statement of the BTC in 1960, that it had instructed a firm of chartered accountants to advise it 'how, not whether,'[3] regional accounts could be prepared had come to nothing. The hiring-in of finance experts to new posts of Assistant General Manager (Finance) on each Region, whilst improving budgetary control and the speed of reporting, had not helped to answer the fundamental question: 'where are we losing all the money?' It was all the more disturbing because the few big schemes of the modernisation plan which should have been profitable were coming to fruition with obvious improvements in traffic, costs, and therefore, net revenue, but still the deficit climbed. That was the most demoralising part of it. The railwaymen knew they were running a generally more trim and taut railway, with service quality higher then ever before. What else did they need to do?

Ironically, it was some of the low-investment developments which were turning out the winners. For example, 22 Deltic locomotives and the charisma of G.F.Fiennes had given the East Coast Main Line a superlative passenger service while the West Coast Main Line was still littered with electrification works. Similar things had happened on the Western Region, although there the gloss was dulled a little due to locomotive reliability problems. Nowadays passengers take for granted the speed, frequency and quality of the Inter-City passenger services, but it came only recently, with diesel and electric traction. This improvement, commenced in the dying days of the BTC, has continued to the present without any particular achievement being attributable to the Beeching years. In contrast, it can be argued that the Inter-city business' contribution was unnecessarily constrained by the refusal, until pushed by the Prices & Incomes Board,[4] to break out of the standard fares barrier and charge, on the routes with high quality service, fares nearer to users' own valuation of the services.

Before leaving BR's financial performance of the period, there is one point which needs to be cleared up, because it was later to be the source of much confusion among senior railwaymen. One of the proud boasts of the period from Dr Beeching's arrival until the end of 1968 was that the Board was able to finance all of its massive investment 'internally' and had not needed to call on the Treasury for loans.[5] 'Internal' financing of investment means that a firm is able to pay for its new investments out of retained profits (of which BR had none) and from the cash generated in the form of depreciation provisions. A short explanation of the relationship between the depreciation provisions and a firm's 'cash flow' is necessary here. Let us take an imaginary railway, IR, and follow the process through. At the end of a year, IR finds that it has £10 million more in cash or bank deposits than it had at the beginning, ie, its revenues exceeded the cash it expended by that amount. But during the year another type of expenditure took place, even though it involved no cash payments. This was the wearing out of the assets. So IR's profits for the year were £10m, less the provision for depreciation of the assets. If IR's assets cost £100 million, and they were expected to last for 20 years, by the simplest method of calculation this provision for depreciation would be 1/20th of £100m, ie, £5 million. Thus the net profit would only be £5m, even though there was a *net cash flow* of £10m. Although the profit of £5m could be distributed to shareholders as dividends, the £5m of cash represented by the provision for depreciation would be available either for investment, or, in the case of a declining industry, to pay off debts.

The difference between our Imaginary Railway and the British Railways Board was that because BR was incurring an annual deficit greater than its interest bill *and* the provision for depreciation,[6] at the end of each year it finished up with far less cash than it started. It was only able to keep going because the Government wrote a cheque to cover its total deficit. To claim that investment was financed internally was a nonsense. What really happened was that BR failed even to take in enough cash to cover its normal expenditure, and the Government gave it enough extra cash to cover its depreciation provision and interest payments. But the situation was even more weird than that. Because the Government each year gave BR the cash to cover its depreciation provisions, it was in turn able to spend that cash on new investments which thereby created the need for increased provisions for depreciation in following years, which the Government again made up with cash, and so on.

This totally lax method of controlling BR's finances led to an irresponsible attitude on the part of the Board toward investment. As long as it was able to finance it with gifts of Government money it did not really have to worry whether the individual investment projects could produce a reasonable return or not. A secondary effect was that the availability of 'free' funds for investment in labour-saving equipment meant that the surviving labour could be given the whole of the original paybill, without the higher wages adding to the deficit. In 1968, after investing over £100m a year since 1962, and after running down staff by 200,000 BR was still just as labour-intensive. What had happened was that virtually the whole of the return on the new investment had been distributed to railway workers in the form of higher wages.

Throughout the period, as Bonavia describes in his book *The Organisation of British Railways,*[6] BR was reorganising itself, causing little apparent improvement in the profit and loss account but great upheaval among those affected. Some of the organisations dismantled in 1963/64 are now (1972) being recreated. BR cannot be criticised for trying to improve its organisation; improvement was clearly needed. But the short duration of many of the experiments was ludicrous.[7] G.F.Fiennes has made much of the turmoil created by the continual reorganisation, and it is clear that for much of the short life of BR too many people have had nthing more important to do with their time than to dream up changes which would have been laughable if they were not so tragic.[9] For far too long these armchair strategists concentrated on the *horizontal* dimension of the organisation — 'how many divisions, etc, should we have?' — without looking at the crucial *vertical* levels. Apart from Scotland, where the rapid run-down in the scale of activity was followed by a very neat contraction in the organisational lines, the rest of the railway had made little worthwhile progress by 1968. In fact, the big move planned in that year, the merging of the Eastern and North Eastern Regions, is now being undone at great cost.

Although BR was still in as deep trouble when Beeching left as when he arrived, clearly it would have been far worse if he had not been appointed. Richard Pryke has shown that, apart from the passenger closure programme, the other objectives of the Beeching Report were achieved.[10] And, looking at it another way, there was a marked improvement in all of those inter-system comparison statistics in which BR's tardy performance had so annoyed the Select Committee in 1960. Although of limited value in making judgements about railway efficiency, in view of the beating which BR took when inter-system comparisons were unfavourable, it is only right that we should give them the same prominence for a period when BR performed well in these terms.

All of the key British Rail physical efficiency ratios showed a sudden general improvement from about 1962.[11] Clearly the sudden improvement in the statistics coincided with the change in the top management of British Rail. But it is important to note that the quick improvements in the efficiency statistics at that time were due more to sudden reductions in the denominators of the ratios — route miles, track miles, total staff, locomotives, carriages and wagons. Whether these reductions in the numbers of assets were accompanied by proportionate reductions in the costs of providing and maintaining the various asset-groups cannot be disclosed by efficiency ratios. In fact, the 1962-4 trend in working expenses, adjusted for price level changes, disclosed no sudden improvement. It required some years of consistent improvement in the physical indicators before any effect was observable in the profit and loss account. But for those who wish to evaluate BR's performance in terms of inter-system productivity comparisons, the results were there to see.[12]

In surveying the improvement in terms of international comparisons, we must keep in mind that the improvement of its operating statistics is not the *raison d'etrê* of BR. This can only be a measure, and a partial one at that, of the railways' success in meeting other goals. At this stage, it is worth asking: 'What goals?' because whatever the explicit goals were, BR was demonstrably not meeting them. The Board's formal objective, laid down by Parliament, was to 'so conduct their business as to secure that their revenue is not less than sufficient for making provision for the charges properly chargeable to revenue, taking one year with another,'[13] but with the annual deficit hovering around £140 million, clearly neither BR nor the Government was taking that very seriously. In practice, BR was working to a whole range of sub-goals, some imposed by the Government, others voluntarily assumed by BR, and all of which were in conflict with the basic break-even objective laid down by Parliament. This in turn created great difficulties, because the purpose of a formal objective, which is accepted by the organisation concerned, is to have a benchmark by which to judge its subsequent performance. In the case of BR, the formal objective was always invalid because of the obligation to continue running certain passenger services at a loss. Add to that the impossible capital structure imposed by the 1962 Transport Act, and the financial objective in the same Act became a joke.

If only the BR management had seen the impossibility of this objective, clarification may have come sooner. To obtain this would have required a public confessional on the past sins of railway management, because the post-1962 capital structure of BR expressly denied the magnitude of the errors of the BTC. With these two crippling defects in BR's ability to meet the break-even objective, it was impossible to judge the performance of the Board from its profit and loss account. The next question, then, was 'how *could* BR be judged?' Putting it formally, the most generous interpretation of BR's general objective, as implied by continuing Government acceptance of the deficit, was that it existed to transport freight and passengers in such a way as to maximise the (positive) difference between the value of its services to users and the community, and the cost of providing those services. Or, putting it more simply, BR was possibly trying to maximise the net social profit, the excess of total benefits over total costs, of its operations. But even this stretched the credulity a little.

Take 1966 for example, which was the first full year of Sir Stanley Raymond's chairmanship. After nearly £1,400 million of net investment in the previous ten years which had not been paid for by users, the result in 1966 was that users paid only £464 million for output which cost £584 million to produce.[14] This takes no account of interest payments on past investments which, in so much as they represented an application of resources to railways that could have been used elsewhere, were as much a cost *(ex ante)* as the other expenditures. So the question is: were railway services which cost (in round terms) £584 million (plus interest) to provide, worth that much to the nation? We know that users only paid £464m for them; was the other £120m (plus interest) accounted for by social benefits which were not charged for? Note that these social benefits are of two kinds: those derived by the rail users, in that the rail service they consume is actually worth more to them than the charge the railways make; and benefits received by non-rail-users in the form of, for example, emptier roads, etc.

In his book, *Public Enterprise in Practice*[15] Richard Pryke deploys a rather doubtful argument to suggest that BR's services were actually worth much more to rail users than BR was able to recover in fares and charges, but a more realistic assessment will show that the 'consumer surplus' generated by BR is very small, relative to its revenues. Pryke argues that, assuming a general price elasticity of demand for rail traffic of two, had BR been a perfect price discriminator, able to set the marginal 40 percent of users' prices equal to the value of service to them, revenue could have been increased by about £73 million per year. There are a couple of factual flaws here. First, nearly all of BR's £250 million worth of freight traffic was already priced, in a myriad of individual contracts, at the maximum the user was prepared to pay. Secondly, even if Pryke's use of Mr Lecomber's calculations of BR passenger traffic price elasticity of 1.1 is valid at the margin, there is no evidence that an elasticity as great as two would apply generally over a 20 percent increase in fares. The net result would have been far less than Pryke's estimated £73m of extra revenue which could have been gained if BR had been perfect price discriminators, and whatever the true amount, it was obviously far below the £120 million-odd of difference between resources committed and *actual* BR revenues.[23] We are left with the second type of net social benefit: the value to non-rail-users of having all the rail traffic off the roads and the value, if any, of having the railways available for casual use. This was never evaluated in those days, but when it was done later (in 1971) the value of BR's operations (outside the London commuter area) in terms of road traffic avoidance was found to be far less than £120 million per annum.

The fact that the Government was prepared to go on paying deficit grants could be taken to infer that it considered that the value of the social benefits of having BR exceeded the cost. But this position could not last. Even without BR's recent history, it was unrealistic to expect Parliament to go on paying for the railways on this scale without requiring a detailed accounting of what the community was getting in return. With general government grants making up about 20 percent of BR's total revenue, it had virtually ceased to be a commercial organisation and had become, in effect, a branch of the industrial civil service. But BR was unwilling to be treated in this way, and wanted a return to the arm's length relationship which existed between other public corporations and their sponsoring departments. In 1966, the new Minister for Transport, Mrs Barbara Castle, was prepared to give the railway managers what they were asking for. But she also gave them quite a lot which they did not want, too, as we shall see in the next part of our study. For the first time since the railways were nationalised, a Minister was prepared to look right into the railway problem and to act to correct all of the ills she found. In particular, she sought a new framework of relations between Government and the railways in which, putting the past behind it, the management of BR would not be inhibited in exploiting its assets and techniques to find the optimum set of roles for BR in the future transport scene.

1 Depending on our assumption about the early results on what are now social passenger services.

2 Richard Pryke, *Public Enterprise in Practice*, London, 1971, p. 42.

3 SCNI : BR, Q. 1321.

4 See National Board for Prices and Incomes: *Report No. 72: Proposed Increases by British Railways Board in Certain Country-Wide Fares or Charges*. Cmnd. 3656, London, HMSO, 1968, pp. 23–4.

5 See, for example, *BRB : AR&A* 1963, paras. 11 and 140.

6 *Op cit.*

7 'The Eastern Region set up the GN, GE and LTS Lines in 1956/7. They abolished them in 1963/4. The London Midland set up their lines in 1961 and abolished them in 1966. The Western set up a Division at Plymouth in 1963 and abolished it in 1965'. G.F.Fiennes: 'The Eastern — North Eastern Merger', *Modern Railways,* January 1967, p.6.

8 See Fiennes, *ibid,* and in *I Tried to Run a Railway, op cit.*

9 Even M.R.Bonavia had time and space in his book for a long discussion of the problem of 'penetrating lines', a nonsense which occupied the RE and BTC for years, but which any other firm would have fixed in a few minutes discussion.

10 See his *Public Enterprise in Practice, op cit,* pp. 249—250.

11 For a fuller treatment of this issue, see my book: *Railway Economics.* (forthcoming).

12 See *European Council of Ministers of Transport Annual Report,* 1968.

13 Transport Act, 1962, Section 18.

14 Actual cash expenditure on operations, plus capital expenditure for that year.

15 *Op cit,* p. 397. Pryke used 1968 for his example but the principle remains the same. His use of the working deficit considerably understates the consumption of resource.

16 It was an unknown fraction of the *passenger* share of Pryke's £73m, ie, a fraction of £30m.

The Train
That Ran Away

Part Two

8 | The Joint Steering Group Studies

The objectives of the new enquiry into BR were set out in the White Paper on *Transport Policy:*[2]

(a) To establish an acceptable basis for costing and to identify those categories of services (both passenger and freight) which are not covering costs; to isolate those categories which are potentially viable; to examine the remaining loss-makers and to isolate those with no prospects of becoming viable; and to cost in detail the annual loss on each passenger service which is unlikely ever to become viable so that the Government can decide whether it should be grant-aided on broad social and economic grounds.

(b) To consider any steps in the field of pricing policy or elsewhere which may be necessary to improve the prospects of those services which are already remunerative and those which are potentially viable.

(c) To examine the Board's methods of costing and financial control in the light particularly of the new proposals for meeting the cost of essential but unremunerative services and of other changes proposed in the White Paper.

(d) To assess whether and, if so, to what extent the cost of the railway infrastructure includes an element of 'standby capacity'.

(e) To examine the Board s investment programmes and the criteria for investment appraisal.

(f) To examine the continuing obligations deriving from the past which rest on the Board, including those in respect of road bridges and level-crossings, of superannuation and pensions for past and present employees, and of the British Transport Police Force.

(g) To consider the suitability of the Board's management structure and procedures for the future operation of the system in the light of the contents of the White Paper and the changes which may stem therefrom.

(h) To make consequential recommendations, including suggestions for possible legislative changes.

The first objective represented a belated acceptance by the Government and BR that the Select Committee had been right in 1960 to recommend the payment of explicit subsidies for loss-making passenger services. The next two objectives, on pricing and financial control, supported the first. The Board's big hope, however, was objective (d), the 'standby capacity' issue. The Chairman of the BRB, Sir Stanley Raymond, had made his bid for financial support under this head in a speech to the Institute of Transport[3], and now it was to be given exhaustive study.

Unlike the previous enquiries of a similar kind, the Stedeford Committee and the Parliamentary Select Committee on the Nationalised Industries, the Joint Steering Group was intended to be exactly what its name implied: a group including full time members of the Board, to commission, oversee and report on a series of studies which it was hoped would plot a lasting solution to the railway problem. It was chaired by the Joint Parliamentary Secretary to the Minister for Transport, John Morris, 'MP. The Board appointed its Vice-Chairman, P.H.Shirley, and two other full time Board Members. For the Government, in addition to two Under Secretaries from the Ministry of Transport, there was one from the Treasury and one from the Department of Economic Affairs. It was unusual to have the Treasury (and its temporary *alter ego*) represented on such a group, and, presumably, committed to support its conclusions. The three independent members were Mr J.P.Berkin, recently retired as a Managing Director of Shell Oil; Mr John Cuckney, chairman of an industrial holding company; and Professor A.J.Merrett of the London Business School. Finally, there was a trade union representative, Mr J.W.Wardle.

From the outset the railway members seemed to attach less importance to the JSG's deliberations and supporting research than did the MoT. In part this was the expected reaction of a group of tired managers, feeling misunderstood, groggy with enquiry, and beyond embarrassment about the mounting and apparently uncontrollable deficit. In contrast, some of the men at the Ministry were more than ready for the chase. Bear in mind that the need for this enquiry signified the failure of their reorganisation of BR under the Transport Act of 1962, and the failure of the super-manager they had appointed at that time. And they too were tired of the railway 'problem', with its frequent and embarrassing need to approach Parliament for Supplementary Estimates because, yet again, BR was going to lose more in a year than it had forecast. Here was their problem child refusing to leave that disobedient adolescence so clearly documented by the Select Committee on the Nationalised Industries in 1960, when both the Ministry of Transport and the Treasury had been forced to admit that they had been completely in the hands of the railway management, with little or no power to restrain the grosser absurdities of the ill-fated Modernisation Plan. In answering the Select Committee, both the Ministry and the Treasury had been fulsome in their claims that everything in the house was now in order.

But, of course, a railway of half a million employees cannot be managed by an investment approval veto power alone. Nor could the appointment of a super-manager, aided by a large number of very temporary marketing and finance managers, provide lasting solutions when they had not even identified the primary problems. By 1966, it had been clear that Dr Beeching's route closure programme, which had brought on the Board more public opprobrium than any action since Nationalisation, would be only a minor part of the answer. And while managerial energy and public goodwill were being spent closing branch lines, the profitable parts of the railway were slipping. Beeching had departed just as the underlaying malaise, which he had failed to cure, showed through in the form of mounting deficits. The most serious reflection on his own term at the Board was that he left behind many problems and a top management apparently unable either to recognise them or to do anything about them. Beeching had failed to shake the belief of BR management that the Nation wanted to have a comprehensive railway service, regardless of its cost. From this came the notion that the railway managers were the only fit judges of the required scope and quality of service. This had already led to many years in which the signs of the market had been ignored. In effect, in 1967, the Board was again saying 'this is the railway the Nation wants, but our annual deficits show that they do not seem prepared to pay for it; if we can somehow put the deficit on a regular and more automatic basis, all will be well.' In brief, and this was the most common attitude of the BR representatives on the JSG, they thought its purpose was to 'whitewash the deficit'.

In contrast, the civil servants were now determined to act, belatedly, on the main recommendation of the Select Committee on the Nationalised Industries. This was to identify the causes of the railway deficit, eliminating those which had no public policy support, and to pay specific subsidies for the unprofitable activities which were imposed on BR by Government edict. The Ministry had to know what it was paying for, and this was going to require detailed analysis of BR activities. This was seen by the railway managers as 'interference', and inconsistent with the notion of managerial responsibility. But of course much of the responsibility for BR activities had already passed from the Board, but had not yet been assumed by the new decisionmaker. The Ministry of Transport was spending around £150 million per annum of public money without really knowing what it was getting in return. So while the Ministry assembled a team of economists to support its representatives on the JSG, the Board made no special arrangements for an inquiry which was fundamental to its future.

Perhaps if they had predicted that it would result in the firing of the Chairman and the non-renewal of appointments of most of the full-time Board members more would have been done. Significantly, the civil servants concerned did not take leave in the summer of 1967. But in June of that year, a BR Board Member pointed out that any further analyses requested could not be available until near Christmas because different peoples' annual leaves did not coincide, and there were Bank holidays and other distractions coming up. The low-key involvement of the railway representatives also reflected the vastly different approaches to the delegation of staff work in the Board. At one stage in the work of a subcommittee of the JSG, the BR representative, a Board Member with heavy functional responsibility, claimed that it would be some time before a paper he had promised could be ready, because he had 'lots of other things to do'. The amazement of the chairman of the sub-committee, one of the independent members of the JSG, turned quickly to annoyance at the realisation that Railway Board Members thought it a good use of their time to draft staff papers.

It was a constant claim of the BR representatives that, in addition to the work generated by the JSG, they 'had to run a railway'. This told much about their own notions of their role as Members of the Board, appointed by the Minister to look after the Nation's interest in the higher direction of a great State enterprise. The favourite diversion of one Board Member was to conduct tours of the York Way Freightliner depot. Another, asked in a meeting to say a few words about the function for which he was responsible, rambled for nearly twenty minutes about the modern equipment he had installed, and the proportion of his activities which had been work-studied, and the number of facilities he had closed. The first question from one of the independent members was: 'Yes, but what does your division *do*?' When a BR Board member seemed able to give a detailed answer to any question asked over the whole range of BR activities, the inevitable question arose as to whether he saw this to be his prime function.

If this was the level of detail at which he wished to manage, was there anything left for the levels beneath him to do? And strangely enough, it was the member appointed from outside who was most obsessed with railway detail as if, perhaps, denied a train-set in his youth, he was now determined to play trains in twelve-inches-to-the-foot scale. The professional railwaymen who made it to the upper levels had their own interests in detail, but in their cases it was a nostalgic interest in the fate of stations or yards which they had managed in their many-stepped climb to the top. (In contrast, the senior civil servant must deal with detail; the paramount objective of never exposing his Minister to embarrassment requires him to have the most meticulous grasp of every facet of a matter before him. But the important difference between civil servants and railway managers is that once consideration of a matter is finished the civil servant unconsciously cleanses his mind of that lot of detail in readiness for the next problem. Unlike the typical railway manager he does not accumulate a store of 'examples' which can be produced as required, with varying degrees of relevance, to support any point at issue.)

There is one more personal difference, which had a bearing on stances adopted within the JSG and its offshoot committees. Even if the railway manager is not explicitly empowered to act on behalf of his Board, civil servants dealing with him act as if that were the case. But of course the civil servant always needs his Minister's subsequent approval for his actions. Whereas the railwayman was expected to offer, the civil servant would only propose, subject to his own second thoughts and that of his superiors. An economist colleague and I were innocent participants in what culminated in a most embarrassing situation, due to our failure to comprehend this difference between the practices of the civil service and those generally accepted elsewhere. When the time came to sort out details of matters about to be enacted, on the question of the surplus capacity grants the two of us were the only people on the Ministry side who understood fully the intentions of the legislation and the railways' problems in meeting it. So we were despatched to a series of meetings with the senior railway managers concerned, at which we sorted out the detail, specifying documentation which would be required, giving interpretations on technical points, and generally facilitating the task which, once enacted, would have to be carried out very quickly. Having agreed all points, the BR men advised their masters of the terms of the agreement and the tyro (and in one case, very temporary) civil servants reported back to their Ministry colleagues with a draft letter to be sent to the Board to formalise the agreement. Oh, the naivety of the technicians! The administration grandly informed us and the Board that no agreement yet existed but the 'proposal' developed with the aid of the Ministry's economists could now be put by the Board to the Ministry, and if the Board could justify it, it might be accepted. The administrator was taking a proposal, itself the product of a series of compromises, as a starting point from which he expected BR to compromise even further. And right through the subsequent discussions the fact that the Ministry economists had suggested or agreed any point gave it no more weight with the Ministry than if it were a snap decision by the BR side. This unidirectional flexibility took another form which had serious effects on the work of the JSG.

The civil servants, through years of frustration at being unable to control the railway deficit, had developed the habit of trying to elicit quantitative targets from the railwaymen, on which they subsequently could be nagged if not achieved. By the time of the JSG, railwaymen were afraid to give figures on any topic without prior analysis. Often, on unfamiliar territory, the Ministry people would ask for some order of magnitude within which to frame their discussion, only to be refused. Not even undertakings not to repeat or otherwise hold some number against the Board would break the impasse. This groping by the Ministry for commitments to which the railwaymen could be held was an inevitable outcome of the consistent failure to meet targets. But it ended in a fiasco with the Board's financial forecasts for the basis of recapitalisation. By then, disillusioned with fifteen years of misplaced BR optimism, the Ministry side thought the Board's projections were too optimistic and screwed them down. When, in 1969, BR's financial performance met its own expectations and exceeded the Ministry's, there were murmurings from St Christopher House of BR having been 'set too easy a target'!

The lack of mutual confidence extracted its price in one quite unexpected way. The JSG appointed two firms of management consultants to investigate and advise on most aspects of the railways' business. But the Group quickly became dissatisfied with the performance of one of the consulting teams, and after a period of close surveillance this firm was dismissed. Inevitably, there were discussions as to why this firm had been appointed in the first place. It then transpired that the Railway representatives on the JSG had been in a position to have rebutted most of the sales pitch made by the consultants concerned, but had refrained from doing so in the fear that they would be accused of trying to 'rig the jury'. As the Ministry were taking the initiative on the appointment of consultants, the railway people laid low. This resulted in much irritating waste of time for the JSG, and, more importantly in the long run, much repetition of enquiries with an already harassed BR middle management. It is only fair to say that the other consultants fell short of perfection too. Perhaps it was because they had pushed into fields in which they had no real expertise, but a client has a right to expect that a consultant will know more than he does.

During the enquiries, 'corporate planning' became an in-phrase. When the consultants were asked by the JSG to report on the implementation of corporate planning in BR, the Board's Chief Planning Manager enrolled on a rather fundamental course on the subject. It is easy to imagine his mixture of surprise and disquiet to find the consultant's supposed expert enrolled on the same course! Then later, as this particular consultant's reports on various topics came in, it was noticed that they were strong on unsupported diagnosis but weak on solutions. One of the independent JSG members taxed the consultants on this point, that if they were going to say that something in their own field of expertise was bad, they should also be prepared to estimate the costs and benefits of improvement, with at least a hint of how the improvements could be obtained. This elicited the disarming reply that 'If you want us to do any work on this, we will need to quote you for an amount of extra time'. It requires an unique ability to be able to know that something is capable of improvement without being able to say how the improvement can be obtained.

Much of the early work of the JSG was absorbed by a variety of very minor matters, which, given the scale of the main problem, were not worth any effort at all. The Board had recently started giving in each annual report a list of its financial handicaps, and the JSG was asked to report on these. In the Annual Report and Accounts for 1966, this list had totalled only £76 million of a total deficit of £134 million. This did not include the cost of its museums, police force, and other minor items for which it was not seeking compensation. Possibly this stress on minutiae was to be expected from an organisation which stuck 'switch out the light' signs on its office walls, but which in the recent past had spent £6 million on building a marshalling yard 105 miles too far north, but 102 miles too far south of where it should have been. In the end, the detailed considerations of the sub-strata of interdepartmental committees (a term as beloved of the civil servant as 'multi-disciplinary team') was not important in determining the amount of recapitalisation, which was based on a global view of the Board's financial prospects. Thus the main result of all this work was to prick the pimples of railway discontent. (One of these, the provision without subsidy of rail replacement bus services, reappeared quickly among the National Bus Company's blemishes.)

These early skirmishes on minutiae like the railway police and the museums were only schoolboy curtainraisers to the big matches on the capital reconstruction and the management reorganisation. The Board had already been excused the interest commitment on £705 million of its capital debt, and was failing consistently to earn interest on the remainder. If it could not pay the interest, the capital debt of £1,612 million was a nonsense. The only question for the JSG was: how much of it should be written off? But another question, of academic interest in the railway context but pertinent to the more general issue of relations between public corporations was: why had the write down not taken place years before? As the JSG was enquiring into BR and not into the Ministry of Transport, that interesting problem had to be left for another time and place.

The quick answer on the amount of capital debt the railways could support was 'none'. To the economists it seemed so simple: if BR could not pay any interest on its capital, the capital debt should be cancelled. Hindsight suggests that we should have recommended more strongly the conversion of the fixed interest capital debt into a Government equity shareholding, on which dividends need be paid only if profits were earned. Because the future looked so bleak, it did not seem important to provide for the eventual payment of 'dividends'. But however appropriate a complete write down of the capital debt (or conversion to equity) seemed to the economists[5], the administrators had misgivings on two grounds. First, on the proposal for a complete write down it was 'judged', on whatever evidence I do not know, that this was 'too much' to ask of Parliament.

As the Government's majority at the time was about 70 seats, Parliament's ability to quibble on this appeared rather limited. But this faint-heartedness was communicated to the JSG, who agreed to their report saying: '. . .we have been informed that the Government would be most unlikely to accept (equity capital), so we have not pursued the matter further'. Any such suggestion was squashed with the throwaway remark that 'the Treasury will not accept it'. At the time the air corporations and the British Steel Corporation were all asking for equity capital in place of their fixed interest obligations, and it was felt that somehow, as the Treasury was resisting these requests,[6] it would be unduly provocative for the Ministry of Transport to recommend this for the railways. As it turned out, the interest on most of the 'new' capital debt to the Government was met by the Government, through the social passenger service grants.

The analysis underlying the finally agreed write off of capital can be found in the JSG's report.[7] The Board were asked to provide a projection of revenues and costs for the year 1974. It was possible to check some of the freight revenue component with the reports of consultants engaged by the JSG. But for most of the revenues and all of the costs there was no alternative to relying on the BR estimates. This led to difficulties because, for many years, the Board had underestimated its deficit of only one year ahead, and now the timespan was six years. A whole meeting was spent in a pedagogical discussion of the difference between a target and a forecast.[8] The railwaymen claimed that their projections were forecasts — statements of the most likely average outcomes. But they also claimed that their annual deficit projections were forecasts, when their poor performance in attaining them had shown them to be rather optimistic targets. This time there could be no Supplementary Estimate pushed through Parliament toward the end of the year; the recapitalisation was supposed to last at least until 1974. The difficulty was that the BR forecasters could obtain a favourable outcome from the recapitalisation exercise by taking a pessimistic view of the future. But in doing so, they would cast doubt on many of the recent claims made by their superiors in requests for Ministry approval of investment projects. Knowing of this inhibition affecting the BR forecasters, and remembering past failures to meet forecasts (or targets), the Ministry tried to be generous. The JSG shied from evaluating the minor items, discussed in loving detail a few months before. These were to be accounted for quickly in a portmanteau amount to be determined by the officials.

After publication of the first two reports,[9] the JSG seemed to disappear. These reports, in the civil service prose which embellishes the end result of all such Government-appointed committees in Britain, foreshadowed 'one or more further reports', but none was forthcoming. All subsequent decisions were to be made by the Ministry of Transport. So much for the capital structure issue. In the next three chapters we will look closely at the other major issues: the track cost (standby) question, and the problem of the loss-making passenger services.

1 This chapter, and chapter ten, are necessarily anecdotal, being intended to give the reader some 'feel' for the inquiry which changed the course of government relations with BR.
2 *Transport Policy, Cmnd. 3057*, London, HMSO, 1966.

3 S.E.Raymond: 'British Railways — Towards a Solution and a Modern Railway', *Institute of Transport Journal*, May 1966, p. 365.

4 Going as far as flying one man from Australia.

5 And to one member of the JSG! See *Cmnd. 3439, op cit.*

6 It later gave way to two of them: BOAC and the British Steel Corporation.

7 See *Comnd. 3437, op cit*, section 2.

8 The Ministry of Transport was so taken with these definitions from the modern manager's vocabulary that they repeated them to the Board in a long letter two years later. By then their worry was that the Board was exceeding their forecasts, a fear which, regrettably, was to be short-lived.

9 Published as an annex to *Cmnd. 3439, op cit.*

9 | The Track Cost Question

'Railways are distinguished by the provision and maintenance
of a specialised route system for their own exclusive use.
This gives rise to high fixed costs'.
Beeching Report (1963)

'. . . the prime cause of the high cost of the signalling
is the amount of permanent way that we have to put signals on.'
A.W.Woodbridge (BR signal engineer) on Euston
Main Line Electrification (Proc. Inst. of Mechanical Engineers,
1966-67, p95)

From the earliest days, railway managements and regulators have been troubled
by questions of the track and its cost. One early proposal was for the owner of
the railway track to permit others to run their trains on the track. This was
quickly rejected because of the need on a railway to control physical and
operating standards within close limits; it could not be run as a toll road, on
which vehicle owners could supply their own propulsion, and, on payment of
the toll, travel at will. In 1850, Dionysius Lardner wrote:[1]

'The operation of the principle of competition was contemplated in the
infancy of railways, as is apparent from the provisions in the legislative
enactments by which the companies have been incorporated. It was expected
that the public should be admitted to exercise the business of carriers upon
them, subject to certain specified regulations and bye-laws. It soon became
apparent, however, that this new means of transport was attended with
qualities which must exclude every indiscriminate exercise of the carrying
business. A railway, like a vast machine, the wheels of which are all connected
with each other, and whose movement requires a certain harmony, cannot be
worked by a number of independent agents . . . Hence it followed, as a
necessary consequence . . . that the companies originally established for the
construction of a road only became, in spite of themselves, the exclusive
carriers upon it; and hence arose inevitably as many local monopolies of
transport as there were separate and independent companies.'

Even if the separation of ownership of the track and ownership and control of
the moving trains had not been rejected on the grounds that it would have been
difficult to manage, the aim of profit maximisation through the optional
allocation of the capacity of a railway would quickly have led to integrated
control of the whole railway operation. For a railway route requires much more
control than a road. Unlike on a road, the driver of a train cannot change his
routeing without outside help. To maximise the net benefit of the use of a
railway route requires close control over the ordering and speed of the train
running. When the control is achieved, very high capacities may be obtained,
especially in relation to the land-use and cost of the track.

But the advantages of the potentially high capacity of railway route are accompanied by the disadvantages that the costs of providing the route are related primarily to its capacity, rather than to its utilisation. This creates two related problems. First, the over-provision of route capacity, relative to traffic requirements, will lead to track costs which are too high to be recovered fully from users. Secondly, once track is installed the invariability of its costs to changes in traffic volumes makes difficult the attribution of track cost to a particular traffic. The allocation of track costs to traffics is perhaps the oldest problem in the field of railway economics.[2]

Competitive railway building in Britain in the 19th and early 20th centuries provided a network having capacity far in excess of the then commercial requirements. Subsequent increases in locomotive power, which permitted the use of heavier trains and reduced section occupancy requirements, and improvements in signalling systems then further increased the effective capacity of the network. The excess of rail network capacity over the commercial requirements is accepted by many writers as inherent in the nature of the railways,[3] and those who questioned the need to construct or maintain excess capacity received litle notice.[4]

Having spare capacity in the network, the ability to run additional trains without significantly increasing the cost of providing and maintaining the track and signalling system was taken to mean that additional traffic could profitably be accepted provided it covered the terminal and movement costs and made a positive 'contribution' to the track costs. We have seen that this principle was broadened to include all existing traffic, on the grounds that its loss to the railways would not permit a reduction in track costs. The alleged fixity of track costs, and therefore their irrelevance for pricing decisions, was the basis of the various railways' policies on pricing and the acceptance of traffic for about a hundred years.

Because the existing capacity of their network was always taken as fixed, it will be recalled from Chapter Two that the main line railways attempted to utilise fully that capacity by seeking the arbitrary diversion of traffic moving by road, and by the use of 'exceptional' rates when setting prices for road competitive traffic. This long-standing pressure for commercial freedom reached fruition in 1957, with the belated approval of the Transport Tribunal for the implementation of some of the provisions of the Transport Act 1953.[5] To match road competition, railway freight rates henceforth were cut selectively over the whole range of traffics, using the recovery of at least terminal and movement costs as a pricing 'floor'.[6] The steady increase in BR's deficit showed that in adopting prices low enough to keep freight traffic on rail, it was failing to recover fully the track costs. Among other solutions to this problem it was argued that BR should not be required to recover its track costs directly from users, but that the railway track should be treated as being analogous with roads and paid for out of taxation. Alternative approaches to parity of treatment of road and rail track costs ranged between levying a toll on users of both modes, to the correction of anomalies on the road side while leaving the railways to recover their track costs through a mixture of charging and deficit finance.[7] However the track costs were to be met, BR argued that to attempt to allocate them to specific traffics was 'an economic nonsense'.[8] If a reduction in capacity was not to be considered, this was clearly the loss-minimising approach.

Dr Beeching reaffirmed this general approach to the treatment of track costs, but with an important variation. In the Beeching report BR stated that:[9]

'Railways are distinguished by the provision and maintenance of a specialised route system for their own exclusive use. This gives rise to high fixed costs'.

and

'the total cost of providing the route system . . . is a fixed cost, in the full sense of the term, all the while the route system remains unchanged'.

Such statements formed the preamble to an argument for the closure of a number of passenger services on the grounds that their revenues failed even to cover their track costs. (Of course, there were other, stronger, grounds for the closure programme. On many services the revenues did not cover even the movement and terminal costs.)

The list of stations and routes to be closed which was provided with the Beeching Report was later supplemented by another published report entitled *The Development of the Major Railway Trunk Routes.*[10] This argued for the concentration of the railways' traffic on to a system of only 8,000 route miles, compared with the then 16,000 route miles. The Trunk Route report was arguing the same points on track costs as its predecessor. The only difference was the apparent priority of objectives. Whereas the Beeching Report had stressed the abolition of unprofitable routes, the Trunk Route Report was more concerned with the benefits to be derived from the concentration of traffic on as few routes as possible.

Whilst it may be possible to quibble with the detail of the Trunk Route Report, its general conclusions were sound. Indeed, it understated substantially the arguments for route consolidation by concentrating on the investment cost implications of having fewer routes to equip with modern signalling, continuous welded rail, etc. Of course, the investment implications of route consolidation are important. It has long been obvious that higher outputs make feasible the use of technologies and large scale plant which otherwise would not be justified. Examples are sophisticated signalling schemes, large gradient reductions and electrification schemes. But the unit costs of the track system are not the only costs to decline in the long run with increases in traffic density; similar advantages are derived in respect of movement and terminal costs. For example, trains must be scheduled to carry traffics which are offered, in a pattern which is subject to unpredictable day-by-day variations. Increasing the aggregate traffic on a route facilitates the matching of services with demands because the greater the aggregate, the greater the likelihood that variations in individual users' demands will cancel each other out. Furthermore, the heavier the traffic density on a route, the more frequent the train service can be. This may have commercial attraction in itself, and provide a gratuitous increase in the 'quality' of the service.

With freight traffic, it is the marshalling function which derives the greatest advantage from route consolidation. This may seem a truism: obviously the fewer the routes the less sorting will be required. But analysis carried out by the Deutsche Bundesbahn has shown that the advantages of reducing the number of routes go far beyond that.[11]

The principles on which the reshaping of the DB operating pattern has been based are simple. They aimed to minimise the time and costs of wagon transits. The time, which the DB called the 'transport speed', is the interval between consignment and receipt, and the other type of speed, the 'technical' speed, is the speed at which trains actually run. It was found, as might have been expected, that the transport speed fell far below the technical speed because of the time spent by wagons in marshalling yards awaiting the formation of a train. The analysis was concerned with the routing of traffic where it touched several junctions and where at least two routes led to the destination of a consignment. It was noted that, on casual empirical evidence, traffic seemed to flow toward the stronger of alternative streams, and a theoretical explanation for this was sought. The main cause of delay in a marshalling yard is the waiting period for an outgoing train, and on the DB this factor is known as a yard's 'power of train formation', ie, the speed at which full train loads can be formed. This power of train formation obviously depends upon the volume of wagons processed through a yard, and here we see the dichotomy between the minimising of transport cost and time, for a train frequency which provides an acceptable transport speed may entail the departure of lightly loaded trains. But if traffic is channelled on to the strongest routes, ie, through the yards with the strongest powers of train formation, these 'powers' will be enhanced. For example, if the traffic on a route is currently moved in ten full train loads per day, a doubling of the traffic will enable the operation of 20 full trains each day, thus doubling the power of train formation. Of course, this is dependent upon the existence of spare capacity over the hump; no change would be necessary in the arrival or departure sidings for they will just double their turnover of wagons.

But the advantages of concentration are associated not only with yards. Raising the power of train formation of a yard raises the likelihood of obtaining full train loads with a commercial desirable frequency of trains, thus reducing the potential haulage cost per wagon. This particular result of traffic concentration on the DB was facilitated by a set of charts issued periodically, which showed the current haulage cost and transit time between all junctions, based on the actual running costs for the standard freight locomotives hauling maximum train loads.[12] The set included 15 schematic maps of the route system, one for each district, on which each route was inscribed with the following data for each direction: distance, maximum load, running time and train cost. Dispatchers choosing the routing of wagons from these charts naturally chose that routing which provided the best time/cost result. In so doing, they tended to concentrate traffic on the route with the lowest haulage costs. In addition, with concentrated routes it is more likely that sufficient wagons will be available to form large 'groups', or even trains for single destinations, permitting them to bypass some yards on route.

Our special interest in the detail of this practice and its theoretical background arises from the effect of traffic concentration on the requirements for fixed plant along the routes concerned. The train costs in the DB charts were determined largely by the gradient profiles of the routes, and the concentration of traffic according to the data meant that traffic was diverted to routes with the most favourable characteristics, even though they may not have been the shortest routes. From this, the choice of routes for electrification was simplified, and of course on the routes chosen for electrification it further lowered the time/cost characteristics of the concentrated traffics. Where the traffic density after concentration was sufficient to support electrification, it may have been able to justify other physical improvements, such as the installation of automatic signalling, realignments, the automation of marshalling yards, and the upgrading of permanent way to take larger and more powerful locomotives. In addition, it permitted the retirement of some or all of the plant from the routes which lost traffic.

Similar results were achieved in France, but by different means. There the haulage and track cost (ie, average cost of output) of each route, which reflects its physical characteristics, is the basis of the rate, and consignors will naturally nominate the route with the lowest haulage and track cost.[13]

Having noted most of the advantages of route and traffic concentration in terms of operations and plant economies, it is interesting to look at the history of route rationalisation on British Railways. Until the last few years, virtually nothing was done to retire the least useful of the great number of competing routes in Britain. Down to the 1923 grouping, of course, these routes were in the ownership of different companies.[14] After the grouping, when the LMS and the LNER had within their control main line routes which formerly were competitive,[15] the routes continued to provide services similar to those prior to grouping. Whilst the retention and operation of full services on duplicate routes by the post-grouping companies may have been thought to have been justified as a *quid pro quo* for their statutory monopolies in much of each's area, this only postponed the inevitable adjustment of railway capacity which had been needed since the middle of the 19th century. After nationalisation of the four companies in 1948, no attempt was made to rationalise the route structure, and when Dr Beeching was appointed to the then British Transport Commission in 1961, the pattern of routes and operation still resembled that of the pre-grouping companies. Under unified control, the possibilities of rationalisation were substantial. BR had often spelled out the difficulties of scheduling trains of disparate speeds on the same track, and shown how the actual capacity of a route increases as the range of train speeds is contracted.[16] But notwithstanding this, all of the competitive routes had continued to provide a complete range of services, from wayside freight trains to passenger expresses.

If certain routes had been selected for specialised freight or passenger operations, the actual capacity of each would have been increased or, alternatively, the operating cost of each could have been reduced. This 'product specialisation' of each 'plant' would have appeared to be the obvious course for a multi-product firm whose main products made competing demands on each set of productive facilities. But the only rationalisations of major competitive routes until 1969 were the closure of the former Great Central route north of Aylesbury, the closure of the Waverley route from Carlisle to Edinburgh, the singling of the old L&SWR route between Salisbury and Exeter, and the downgrading and singling in parts of the former GWR London-Birmingham route between Princes Risborough and Aynho Junction.

To summarise, there are economies of scale associated with the plant and operation of railway routes which arise from both the use of more efficient, but indivisible items of plant at high traffic densities and the advantages of working with large aggregates of traffic in eliminating some of the risk of random fluctuations in demand. The methods of increasing traffic density which are available to a railway administration are to raise the general volume of traffic, or to reduce the number of routes on which the present volume of traffic is conveyed. As the demand for railway services is generally fairly static, the first solution is impracticable; but the second solution is within the control of the railway management. If, after concentration of through traffic, the weaker routes cannot be closed, they can be reduced in both the quantity and quality of physical plant and the services offered, with consequent cost savings. Traffic concentration on through routes, with the improvement of a few routes and the downgrading of others, was a far more profitable course of action open to British Railways than branch closures. The through routes which formed the basis of the network as finally determined and the expenditure in maintaining and operating them far exceeded that of the branch lines, on which so much of BR's managerial effort had been expended in the past.

In considering the powerful arguments for the consolidation of through traffic on to as few routes as possible, it is important to realise that the Trunk Route Report was not necessarily arguing for closure of the remainder. Certainly, without their through traffic the routes 'not selected for development' would have been greatly reduced in function. This has been a bone of contention with supporters of particular routes, and it is worth opening up the topic for their benefit. If only, the argument runs, BR would direct through traffic from other routes to the threatened route, its economics would be greatly improved. For example, G.Clayton and J.H.Rees, in their study *The Economic Problems of Rural Transport in Wales,*[17] suggest that:

> '. . . it might be worthwhile to consider the possibility of making greater use of the Central Wales Line for traffic between West Wales and the North-West of England, given that railways with their high fixed costs should be used to their optimum extent. The Newport-Hereford-Shrewsbury line was not scheduled for development under the (Trunk Route) Report; and the diversion of some of its traffic to the Central Wales Line might make it possible to reduce it to single track over at least some of its length. Such a policy would go far to offset the loss on the Central Wales Line.'

Apart from the claims of those affected by the diversion of traffic from the other route, our earlier discussion of the operating advantages of traffic consolidation has shown that the railway operators would be unlikely to distribute the available traffic over a greater number of routes just to improve the apparent economics of one route. Similar arguments are advanced every time a former main line is scheduled for closure or reduction to feeder status, but the respective cost characteristics of routes of differing capacities dictate that unless massive new investment is required it is always preferable to concentrate traffic as much as possible on one of the routes, and to reduce the facilities (and cost) of the remaining route to accord with the remaining traffic. The future role of such routes would be solely that of providing passenger and/or freight services to the stations along them. The track and signalling costs could be substantially reduced by the reduction in maintenance standards, track signalling and simplification of signalling equipment. Although the Trunk Route report was not followed by any precipitate action on route consolidation, it is important to remember that it did not presage a plethora of railway closures. It just listed the routes for 'development', and left the remainder to survive on their merits as feeder and local routes.

The Beeching Report included a large catalogue of stations and routes which were to be closed to passenger services, but the implementation of the closure programme made relatively little impact on the Board's financial results. The deficit, which had been £133.9 million in the first full year of Dr Beeching's term, was still £134.7 million in 1967.[18] Before any of the route rationalisation foreshadowed in the Trunk Route report had taken place, Mrs Castle and Sir Stanley Raymond made a joint announcement that, in contrast to the 8,000 route mile network postulated by the Trunk Route report for 1984, the system was to be 'established' immediately at 11,000 route miles.

It is not clear that the choice of 11,000 route miles had any more rationale than the fact that it was midway between the then 14,000 route miles and the 8,000 route miles formerly proposed 'for development' in the Trunk Route report. Some time after the announcement of the new 'stable' network, Dr Beeching had this wry comment to make in a newspaper interview:[19]

> 'The plan for the future of British Railways with which I was associated was based upon a forecast of traffic for the next 20 years and upon an assessment of what the capacity of the railways would be when available (or immediately foreseeable) technological advances had been applied to the existing system. Now it's perfectly reasonable for people to say, 'Well, of course, the assessment of traffic over the next 30 years is difficult to make, and we do not agree with yours; our assessment is as follows." But no one said that. The critics just said, in effect, "We ought to have more railways than you said because 8,000 miles does not sound very much; we think it ought to be 11,000".'

The announcement of the 11,000 mile network, which it should be noted was 3,000 miles less than in operation at that time, was followed by the publication of a map entitled *British Railways Network for Development:* This map, and its larger scale supplements for certain areas, delineated the network which the Government and the Board had decided 'should be retained and developed so that the railways can play a full part in the country's transport system'.[20]

It is important to be clear on precisely what this network map and the accompanying notes said, and what they did not say. First, they were not inconsistent with the conclusions reached in the Trunk Route report. It had postulated an 8,000 mile system to be achieved by 1984 of which only a proportion was to be developed by resignalling and relaying to high standards of the permanent way. But if, as had already been announced by the Government, it was intended to subsidise rural branch lines for passenger services, any mileage in addition to 8,000 could have been kept at no net cost to British Railways. But the 'Network Map' and its notes were ambiguous on a far more important point. To say that the basic network would consist of 11,000 route miles was to say virtually nothing at all. They could have been 11,000 route miles of low grade, single track, unsignalled branch lines. They could, but almost certainly would not, have been 11,000 miles of multiple track, automatically signalled main lines. The precise expectations of the Government and the Board as to the mix of high grade and branch line routes were never stated, even if they were known. So all the Network Map did was to say, at a time when 14,000 route miles were in operation, that it was unlikely that more than 3,000 miles of route would be closed in the near future. But any study of the speed at which Governments had been prepared to close routes in the past would have suggested this anyway. So the map and its notes were a presentational exercise aimed at the electors in rural areas, and at the railway trade unions. As an expression of broad railway policy they were meaningless.

Shortly before the 11,000 mile network map was published, Sir Stanley Raymond had claimed that an important reason for the size of the railways' deficit was the cost incurred in maintaining a large amount of 'standby' capacity in the track system. The most appropriate way of paying for this capacity superfluous to the Board's commercial needs was claimed to be a state subsidy.[12] Of all the matters referred to the Joint Steering Group in 1966, the 'standby' issue was potentially the most favourable to the Board. If BR could have convinced the Government that it should shoulder a substantial proportion of the track and signalling costs, it would have removed a similarly large part of its then £135 million annual deficit. In addition to the standby arguments, which were reinforced in more technical terms in the railway trade press,[22] others reopened the arguments for a 'rail track authority'[23] which would take over the ownership and maintenance of British Railways' track and signalling, charging the Board a toll for the passage of trains, as on a toll road.

Unless this was to be a subtle method of relieving BR of part of its track and signalling costs, it is hard to see how a rail track authority could give any advantage to the Board. If it were doing its job properly, a rail track authority would certainly have disadvantaged BR. The idea of the rail track authority was that it would own all of BR's present track facilities, and would maintain and operate them as and when BR required them. It would have charged for *actual* use, and as BR wished to use its track system far less than its present capacity would have permitted, the tolls would presumably have fallen short of the costs of the authority. But presumably the authority would have been given a breakeven financial objective by the Government, so when it found that it was providing more facilities than BR were prepared to pay for, it would have proceeded to reduce its capacity (and costs) to a level more closely aligned to BR's requirements. That is, the authority would have done just what BR should have been doing all along, but would have had the power to incur temporary losses in respect of the capacity which it took over which BR did not wish to use. These losses would have continued until the authority could retire the excess, 'standby', or surplus capacity. But, of course, BR already had, through its deficit grants, the power to incur losses from this cause, and had been doing so for many years.

A rail track authority offered no real solution to BR's problems, because its only effects would have been to spin off part of the BR loss under a different name, and to create enormous problems of co-ordination and integration between the owners of the track and its users. For example, how were the Beeching Report's ideas on: '. . . a specialised route system for (the railway's) own exclusive use . . . the benefits which can be derived from possession of this high cost route system are very great,'[24] compatible with a division of ownership and management of the track system and its users, unless it were to be no more than an accounting device to brush some of the loss under the permanent way?

The Joint Steering Group was therefore asked to:

'Assess whether, and if so, to what extent the cost of the railway infrastructure includes an element of standby capacity.'[25]

It was common ground that BR's track system provided capacity in excess of commercial requirements, but BR was under no formal obligation to continue that state of affairs. On the contrary, the Board's financial duty to 'so conduct their business as to secure that their revenue is not less than sufficient for making provision for the charges properly chargeable to revenue, taking one year with another'[26] imposed an obligation to retire any capacity which incurred costs and which was not profitable to use. The railways' own analysis, in their Trunk Route report, suggested that the system could be divided into three parts: the obviously profitable routes, the clearly unprofitable routes, and 'a part upon which judgement must be suspended because its future use remains questionable.' The obviously profitable routes, which the report suggested totalled some 3,000 of the 15,000 route miles, needed to contain no involuntary surplus capacity, because, as the report added, 'it will be possible to concentrate railway investment upon the selected trunk routes in the confidence that . . . the essential dense flows of traffic will be maintained'.[27] These were the routes on which modern permanent way and signalling were to be installed, and during the course of these works any necessary adjustments could be made to track capacity.

For the other routes, both those which are already unprofitable and those with doubtful prospects, there were two possibilities. First, it was intended to close some routes, reducing the total to 11,000 route miles. Secondly, passenger services on much of the remaining network were to be subsidised on grounds of social need; but outside the commuter areas it was unlikely that social need considerations would require the provision of track capacity on the then existing scale. Assuming that the routes to be closed to reduce the total route mileage to 11,000 were all of single track, this left all but 150 miles of the 'stable' network with double track or more. With a few exceptions, it was unlikely that 'social need' would require the maintenance of the 1966-7 level of rural stopping passenger services, which in 1965 had lost £16 million on direct costs and £42 million on total (including track and administration) costs.[28]

Even if the existing track capacity were tailored to the then level of train services — and the fact that the standby argument was based on surplus track capacity with *existing* train services is evidence to the contrary — a reduction of service to the bare social need level would have permitted a substantial reduction in track capacity. Thus it was obvious that, unless the commercial traffics on these routes, such as freight and Inter-City passengers, could pay for more track capacity than they needed, the future 11,000 miles network should have been planned for a much lower capacity than existed at the time the standby subsidy was requested. This could have been achieved by a combination of track singling and reduction in signalling facilities. If such a reduction were not to be carried out, 'somebody' (ie the Exchequer, through deficit grants) would be paying for the 'standby' capacity. But as it was standby capacity which did not need to exist for commercial operating reasons, and which the community had shown no pressing desire to retain, the obvious solution was for the railways to get rid of it as quickly as possible, not to perpetuate it by obtaining a Government subsidy for it.

This Joint Steering Group set up a special committee to study in detail the concept of 'standby capacity'. As was to be expected, the committee finally agreed that it was highly unlikely that standby capacity could be proved to exist as a permanent element of any foreseeable railway network. In support of their case for a subsidy for standby capacity the Board suggested studies of particular routes. I was asked to carry out these studies working on data provided by British Railways. A summary of my conclusions was published in the Railway Policy White Paper as follows:[29]

'The first route studied was the East Coast main line from King's Cross to Doncaster. The study identified some surplus capacity, which would permit the running of an additional 36 express passenger trains, or 18 slow freight trains per day. Its cause was the need to have a signalling system which would pass express passenger trains at very frequent intervals during peak periods. In consequence, capacity was available for the rest of the day, but it had not so far been possible to sell this capacity to users. It was implicit that the net revenue from peak passenger services adequately covered the cost of providing this surplus capacity.

'The next route studied, Plymouth to Penzance, was a 'secondary' route on which the long term decline in summer holiday traffic had rendered some of the track capacity superfluous to present requirements. It was found, however, that the regional management had plans for completely revised train services on the route, with a consequent reduction of the track mileage, and an increase in track utilisation. The route, which is at present nearly all of double track, is proposed for reduction to mainly single track with appropriate passing loops. The resulting train and track capacity is considered adequate for present and future needs. This was a case where surplus capacity had been identified, but by re-arranging and reducing the train services, it would be possible to eliminate nearly all of the surplus capacity. Some investment would be required for the singling project, but the potential savings were very high in comparison with the investment required.

'Finally, a study was made of the Weaver Junction to Glasgow route, as it would be after electrification. This is a route on which the railways would have almost complete freedom to adjust the capacity to suit future commercial and operating requirements. Even with this freedom, it was proposed to install surplus capacity, so that the day-long rate of utilisation would be only just over 60 per cent. As with the East Coast main line, this high level of capacity was caused by the need to signal the route to carry short-run peaks of traffic at certain times of the day. As these would in themselves be profitable traffics, even including the cost of the extra capacity they required, it was concluded that the existence of the surplus capacity on the route would not impose a financial handicap upon the railways.'

The committee concluded that it was demonstrated by these reports that it is possible to tailor the capacity of a route to the expected volume and mix of traffic at least in the long term. Any surplus was therefore almost entirely a matter of commercial choice or of history. The committee concluded that the surplus capacity which was not required for commercial reasons, ie, to handle peaks of traffic which the Board felt it would be unprofitable to turn away, should be removed from the system and its cost avoided.

Thus four years after the Beeching Report, and with the help of a Government-sponsored inquiry, the ghost of high and necessarily fixed railway track costs was laid. Railway policy could in future be formed on a basis of fact, rather than a myth perpetrated by generations of railwaymen anxious to secure Government help for the transfer of traffic to rail.

At the request of the Joint Steering Group, the Board prepared estimates of the cost of this surplus capacity, which they estimated to be in a bracket from £11m to £17m per annum. The Joint Steering Group recommended that this cost be subsidised on a tapering basis, with the intention that the surplus capacity be removed by the end of 1974. This constituted the greatest single reduction of British Railways track costs ever made. It is only regrettable that the saving was not made 20 years before. Note that the surplus capacity subsidy was really a component of the recapitalisation, and *not* a track cost subsidy. Once the possibility was admitted of removing the capacity and saving the cost, it was clear that the recapitalisation should be based on the level of costs *after* the surplus had been removed. In the meantime, BR would still be incurring the costs, and to keep the recapitalisation calculations simple it was best to compensate BR for the higher costs until it could reduce them. The payment of the annual grant was made conditional upon BR's achievement of the projected rate of progress in removing the capacity, and this was to cause problems when the engineering programme fell behind and when the railway operators decided that some capacity which was claimed to be surplus in 1968 was actually needed. (I hope that this fairly full account of the surplus issue will dispose of Richard Pryke's allegation that the 'surplus' was a crude *quid pro quo* for Government restraint on passenger service withdrawal, and that it was 'very unlikely that the matter was given any careful attention'. As the 1967 decision to keep 11,000 route miles was underwritten by the social passenger service grants, the surplus capacity exercise was a completely separate issue.[30])

The other important change at that time flowed from the Government's decision to subsidise social passenger services on many routes. This gave a completely new dimension to the measurement of railway track costs relevant to commercial decisions. These subsidies were to be paid on a 'full cost' basis, in contrast to the marginal costs of track for passenger service which had previously been the basis of railway passenger service closure decisions. As the services to be subsidised included all of the stopping services over the whole of the network open to passenger traffic, that is, those services which the Board could not withdraw without the permission of the Minister, it was clear that this Government decision imposed on the Board a substantial cost which had to be met through the subsidy. On many of the routes the subsidised passenger services were the primary service, with only a daily or lesser frequency freight service to share the facilities. It was recommended by Cooper Brothers, the consultants, that track and signalling costs should be allocated between subsidised and commercial services according to the weight and number of trains concerned. But on routes which would have been closed if there were to be passenger services, an arbitrary allocation of the type suggested by the consultants would have shifted on to the railways' commercial finance costs which are properly attributable to the subsidised service.

The Joint Steering Group and the Government quite properly resisted this approach, although initially BR were lukewarm to any proposal to vary their pre-existing methods. This problem was solved in the end by the application of what became known as 'Method 2'. This provided that, where the requirements of the social passenger service were the sole determinant of the capacity of the route, the grant would cover all of the track and signalling cost of the route.[31] This acceptance by the Government of financial responsibility for the costs of providing routes for the stopping passenger services meant that there was no longer a problem of deciding whether to allocate or ignore the fixed cost element in track and signalling costs. On those routes the fixed costs were being paid by those for whom they were being incurred — the Government, which required the route to be kept open for social passenger services. In this way, the fixed cost of the passenger proportion of the 11,000 miles basic network was being underwritten by the Government. But decisions on the retention of any route of capacity in excess of that required for the stopping passenger service remained the sole responsibility for British Railways, as did the responsibility for obtaining from the commercial traffics using the route sufficient revenue to pay the costs of the *extra* capacity.

Having in mind the poor profitability of most of British Railways' other traffics, if passenger services were to be subsidised the basis outline above was the only practicable way of doing so. If the Government said to the Board: 'Keep open this route to run stopping passenger trains', it had to pay the costs of doing so. But this underwriting of the 'social need' railway passenger network did alter significantly the incidence of track costs to be met by the users of the parts of the commercial railway. Because most of the social services either (i) had peak requirements, (ii) constituted the bulk of the service on a route, (iii) or both, the track cost which had to be subsidised for the passenger service also paid for some capacity which could not profitably be used by the subsidised trains. This off-peak capacity was then available for the use of the Board's commercial services and as the cost had been met from the subsidy it was a nonsense to allocate any track and signalling cost to the commercial services using it. It has been suggested that this constituted a subsidy to freight.[32] But where the operation of freight trains did not add any cost to that of the route required by the Government to be maintained for social passenger services, the passenger grant clearly did not include a freight subsidy. For a payment to be a subsidy it must involve an expenditure which would not otherwise be incurred. The Auditor-General had clearly been dissatisfied on this point,[32] as was the Parliamentary Public Accounts Committee. Although BR managed to satisfy the Government that the capacity element of the track and signalling cost was not affected by the running of freight trains, in 1970 it was agreed that the Board should pay a 'wear and tear' charge for freight train operation and this was agreed at varying rates per train mile, depending on the type of track.

So far, so good. The 1968 Transport Act provided for the Government to meet most of the cost of track and signalling for social passenger services, and the outcome of the abortive 'standby' subsidy claim was that BR had conceded that it could reduce its total track and signalling cost by £15 million per annum. This left the main lines, and here the picture was not yet very optimistic. In mid-1967 BR had sponsored an Institution of Civil Engineers symposium on 'developments in railway traffic engineering.' Mr C.D.Foster, then director-general of economic planning at the Ministry of Transport, was invited to give a paper. The organising committee hoped that Foster would be able to announce some preliminary results of the 'transport cost model',[33] to the effect that it was in the national interest to make much better use of the railways' track. Foster co-opted me as joint author, and we thought it more realistic to explore the reverse proposition: that it was in the national interest for the railways to *reduce* their track facilities to match the traffic they were currently able to attract.

BR was already charging its users less than the sum of the long run costs other than track costs, and if it could not attract enough traffic to fully utilise its tracks when it was effectively charging nothing for them, the arbitrary diversion of traffic from road to rail was not indicated. Three years earlier, BR's evidence to the Committee on Carriers Licensing (Geddes Committee) had claimed that heavy lorries should pay much higher road charges,[34] but this had been rejected by the Geddes Committee.[35] The approach which Foster and I took[36] was to find the most favourable cost levels for main line track. These were then divided by feasible traffic volumes and compared with a target 'track cost per net ton mile' value 50 percent higher than the maximum 'competitive' track cost per net ton mile in BR's own Trunk Route report.[37] Our target 'unit-track cost' was £0.0021, and aggregate annual costs for difficult capacity routes were developed. These are given in the Table on page 112.

A most important conclusion from this data was the importance of interest in the total cost function. Hitherto, this had been excluded from similar calculations (eg, in the Trunk Route Report), but for the 60% of the trunk system which at that time was yet to be renewed in continuous welded rail, interest on investment was certainly a cost which was relevant to the future operation of the route

The Trunk Route Report had given estimates of the utilisation of what it

| | Number of Tracks (1967 prices) | | |
| | One | Two | Three |
	£	£	£
Interest on average investment	3,020	4,260	7,900
Signalling maintenance and operation	2,600	4,030	8,060
Permanent way and earthworks maintenance*	1,400– 2,840	1,096– 3,442	3,422– 4,472
Totals (rounded)	£7,020– 8,460	£10,190- 11,730	£19,380 20,430

inferred were typical routes,[38] and these were converted into gross ton miles and divided into the total costs to find the following:

	Cost/year £	Average volume (g.t.mls) £	Gross ton mile £	Cost/Net ton mile (freight) £	Cost Passenger mile £
Two track	10,400	6.75m	.0015	.0021	.0166
Four track	19,400	22.9m	.0008	.0012	.0034

Taking out target unit-track cost of £0.0021, and using the 1984 traffic estimates of the Trunk Route Report, we found only *fifteen* inter-regional or inter-zonal flows which could 'afford' two-track route, and only two which could 'afford' four-track route. Thus on a generous interpretation of the railways' own calculations, much of the future main line traffic was going to be unable to cover its track costs if the current route capacities were to be maintained.

Of the BR contributors to the symposium, only the late Arthur Dean, then general manager of the North Eastern Region, reinforced the implications of this analysis. It was attacked by others on the grounds that it looked at the infrastructure costs in isolation. But that was precisely what was needed, because in the past BR had argued its advantages over road in similar isolation. Now someone had taken a generous interpretation of BR's own calculation of the *maximum* which passenger miles or freight ton miles could support in the way of track cost, and had found that very little of the network was able to attract traffic in volumes sufficient to meet this target. The trouble was that the debate had previously been in terms of *potential* average track costs by rail, based on volumes rarely, if ever, achieved.

For example, the *minimum* volume in the BR estimates for the same symposium[39] which we used for permanent way costs was 10 million gross ton miles per year per track. This was 27,400 gross ton miles per day, or about 54 trains per day of 500 gross tons. In 1966, the average year round frequency, *including commuter routes,* was only 26 per day per mile of running track.[40] No

*The ranges of permanent way costs were based on differing postulates of volume: 10 million gross ton miles pa (30m for the 4-track route) at 40mph for the lower values, and 40 million gross ton miles pa at 70mph for the upper values.

one doubted that, if volumes were very high and spread evenly throughout the day, the average track cost per unit of output could be low. But these conditions obtained only on a small proportion of the network; on the remainder the traffics could not support the existing level of track cost. Getting more traffic, which was the aim of the BR initiatives drawing attention to the potentially low unit-track-costs by rail, was not possible, or it would already have occurred with BR's 'below-cost' freight pricing. The Board's alternative approach, the request for the 'standby' subsidy, was in the process of being rejected by the Joint Steering Group. This left only one option: to reduce the total track cost on the routes concerned by withdrawing further capacity. But it was obvious that on many routes any reduction of track capacity would displace some existing traffic, particularly high speed passenger trains. In such cases, if the traffic at risk could not support the track capacity it needed, both the capacity and the traffic should have gone.

That was the last flicker in the track cost argument on the rail side. A few months later the Ministry of Transport was to publish its report on *Road Track Costs*,[41] which argued that even when heavy lorries were made to pay higher taxes to cover the road costs they incurred, which it proposed, the diversion of traffic to rail would be minimal. It was obviously a more fruitful field for BR to manage its own track costs in line with its users' demands, than to try to have its competitors pay more.

1 Dionysius Lardner: *Railway Economy: A treatise on the new art of transport, its management, prospects and relations, commercial, financial and social.* London 1850. p.502.
2 *Ibid*, pp. 38, 52.
3 See, for example, W.M.Acworth and W.T.Stephenson, *The Elements of Railway Economics*, revised edition, London 1924, chapters III, IV and V: and W.Z.Ripley, *Railroads: Rates and Regulations*, New York 1916, pp. 55–61.
4 See A.M.Wellington: *The Economic Theory of the Location of Railways*, New York, 1889, Ch. 1.
5 See *Select Committee on the Nationalised Industries: British Railways*, HMSO, 1960, Appendix 9, para.40.
6 It is alleged that for many traffics this floor has been the effective ceiling; see, eg, National Board for Prices and Incomes *Report No.72, Proposed Increases by British Railways Board in Certain Country-Wide Fares and Charges*, Cmnd. 3635, London, HMSO, 1968, paras. 51, 53, but as shown in Chapter 5 for long periods even this constraint was inoperative.
7 See particularly J.R.Sargent: *British Transport Policy*, London 1958, Ch. IV: D.L.Munby: *Road and Rail Track Costs*, Manchester Statistical Society, Manchester, 1962; H.Osborne Mance: 'Pooling Track Costs', *Journal of the Institute of Transport*, Sept. 1959.
8 See *In the Court of the Transport Tribunal, Transport Acts, 1947 and 1953, In the Matter of the Application of the British Transport Commission (1955 No.2) To Confirm the British Transport Commission (Railway Merchandise Charges) Scheme*, HMSO, 1955–1956, p.368. 9 British Railways Board: *Reshaping British Railways*, London HMSO, 1963 (The Beeching Report), pp. 4 & 9.
10 British Railways Board: *The Development of the Major Railway Trunk Routes*, London 1965. Afterwards known as The Trunk Route Report.
11 See F.Fuelling: 'Zur Wirtschaftlicheit von Leitungswegen in Eisenbahngutenverkehr' in *Internationales Archiv für Verkehrswesen*, Volume 10, December 1958. (I have chosen this German analysis for exposition because it uses manual methods which are readily

understanble. For some years BR has used a suite of computer simulation programmes to obtain basic optimal freight routing strategies. It is now in process of installing a complex real-time freight transit control system based on the Southern Pacific's 'TOPS' programmes.)

12 I am indebted to Dr Bitter of the operating economics department of the DB for providing a smaple copy of these charts, the 'Kostenvergleichskarte fur Durchangsgvterzuge'.

13 See Louis Delecarte: 'Tarifs des Transports ex Prix Revient', *Annales Suisses D'Economie des Transports,* 19e Annee, Zurich, pp. 1—24.

14 The only major attempt at rationalisation prior to the grouping was the uniting of the operations of the railways competing in Kent, in 1899, which resulted finally in corporate merger as the South Eastern and Chatham Railway. See C.Hamilton Ellis: *British Railways History,* Vol.1, London 1954, pp. 307 *et seq.*

15 The LMS had the former L and NWR and Midland routes to Manchester, Liverpool and Scotland, and the LNER had both the Great Northern/North Eastern and Great Central routes to the West Riding of Yorkshire.

16 See, for example, J.W.Dedman, 'Towards fuller employment of the track', *British Transport Review,* Vol. IV, No.1.

17 Cardiff, 1967, p.27.

18 See *BRB: AR&A.* 1963 and 1966.

19 *Observer,* 14.7.69, p.21.

20 Minister of Transport, British Railways Board: *British Railways Network for Development.* London, HMSO, 1967.

21 S.E.Raymond: 'British Railways — Towards a solution and a Modern Railway', *Institute of Transport Journal,* Vol.31, No.10, May 1966, p.365.

22 A.V.Barker: 'Cost of Social Service and Standby Capacity', *Modern Railways,* XXIII, 221, February 1967, pp. 64—5.

23 This idea was revived by Sir Reginald Wilson and taken up for BR by P.H.Shirley. One of the more extreme suggestions at the time was that BR should pay an annual 'licence fee' for each locomotive.

24 See Beeching Report (Ref. 9) p.4.

25 Ministry of Transport: *Transport Policy, Cmnd. 3057,* London, HMSO, 1966.

26 *Transport Act, 1962,* Section 18.

27 Trunk Route Report (Ref. 10), p.47.

28 *BTC: AR&A.*

29 Ministry of Transport: *Railway Policy,* Cmnd. 3439, London HMSO, 1967, paras. B.6.1 — B.6.3.

30 Richard Pryke: *Public Enterprise in Practice,* London 1971, p.254.

31 This was varied slightly in 1969. See Chapter Ten.

32 See, for example, *Committee of Public Accounts: Civil Appropriation Accounts, Classes I—V 1968—9,* London, HMSO, 1970, 1.3361, *et seq.*

33 The 'transport cost model' was a joint MOT/BR project, aimed at developing a valid methodology for making 'total' transport decisions for corridors and, eventually, the whole country. The main conclusion reached was that comprehensive transport planning of this type was not likely to give sufficiently precise guidance to affect the choice of individual investment projects.

34 British Railways Board: *A Study of the Relative True Costs of Rail and Road Freight Transport over Trunk Routes,* London, 1964.

35 See *Carriers' Licensing — Report to the Committee,* London, HMSO, 1965.

36 Stewart Joy and C.D.Foster: 'Railway Track Costs in Britain', in *Developments in Railway Traffic Engineering,* The Institution of Civil Engineers.

37 *Op cit,* p.8. BR's study claimed that 'route costs should be less than about 1/3d per ton mile, if railway transport is to be widely competitive.' (1/3d = £.0014).

38 *Op cit,* Table 3.

39 See A.Paterson: 'Railway track and structures', *loc cit,* p.5.

40 *BRB: AR&A* Tables 5-c & 5-d.

41 London, HMSO, 1968.

10 | The Branch Line Problem

'As to the cross-country and branch lines it is there, I think,
that the main problem arises.''
Sir Brian Robertson (1960)

We must commence our study of this problem by looking back at the recent history of stopping passenger services. Their special characteristics and financial performance do not constitute a new problem; they have been with us for years. In many cases they were not recognised as a problem and in many others nothing was done because the railway management quite rightly (as events have shown) judged that the Government wanted these services retained even though they incurred accounting losses. The traffics on many of these services, particularly outside London and the provincial conurbations, have been falling since the war. There was a significant improvement in their economics in the middle Fifties, through the widespread introduction of diesel multiple-units, replacing the former locomotive-hauled trains. So it is quite likely that the economics of these services were worse between nationalisation and the time the steam loco-hauled trains were replaced, than they were in the ensuing period. An obvious question, then, is why did BR not do something about it at that time, especially when it must have been clear in many cases that the improvement offered by diesel multi-unit working would have been a short-run palliative and would not eliminate the losses. Two factors stand out. First, this type of passenger service had been provided by the railways for over a hundred years on the assumption that it was marginal to the railway's primary task of freight movement and express passenger trains. As long as the revenue for all these stopping services covered their total movement costs, it was thought that they were making a profitable contribution to the railways, because freight and express passenger services were covering all the other costs. Secondly, the railways' freight business was rather taken for granted and questions were not often raised concerning the closure of freight routes or depots. Thus at the same time as there was a general belief that the stopping passenger services were profitable in total, ie, their revenue exceeded the identified specific costs they imposed, there was very little management pressure on the services through the threatened withdrawal of freight traffic. On the routes concerned, freight and stopping passenger services were rather like two men sitting on a seesaw: provided they both sat still the thing would not rock, and each was happy to sit on the seesaw safe in the assumption that the other one would be there to maintain equilibrium.

Inevitably, something upset that equilibrium. Growing motor vehicle population, the movement of factories away from railway routes, reducing coal consumption, decline in the importance of heavy industry, all contributed to a weakening in the demand for railway freight traffic. The historic role of the railway as the universal provider of transport was being usurped by its competitors, and by changing patterns of demand for freight movement. This was recognised very early by railway managers. We saw in Chapter Two how the 'Square Deal' campaign of the Thirties sought freedom from the horse and cart constraints inherited from the 19th century. But it was not until 1953 that there was any real change in the regulatory environment, and the beginnings of railway commercial freedom were enacted in the Transport Act of that year. It will be recalled that this provided for railway pricing freedom, subject to statutory maxima, and this implied the freedom of the railway management to refuse traffic or to accept it only at prices which ensured its profitability. This change was inevitable because there was no longer a large core of profitable freight traffic whose revenues were sufficient to cover all those costs left uncovered by marginal traffics.

The removal of the railways' common carrier obligation, permitting them to quit unprofitable freight traffic or to insist on altered methods of handling, opened a whole new horizon of possibilities with regard to the railway network. No longer was it dogma that freight services would continue to be provided for ever on every branch line of the network, and this raised the need to look separately and sharply at marginal passenger services. But initially not many proposals for closure followed from this new look at the economics of passenger services in the absence of freight requirements, because in the middle Fifties the railways were still only marginally unprofitable and they had just published, with the approval of the Government a modernisation report which claimed that a large amount of investment would restore them to profitability. The old attitude that the railways should be prepared to take the rough with the smooth died hard, especially when railway managers were claiming that the 'smooth' would soon be abundant. In any case, there was a widespread view that many of these branch line passenger services were crucial as feeders to the express passenger trains.

The halting passenger service closure programme was an area specially scrutinised by the Select Committee in 1960. The Committee's primary aim was to find reasons for the mounting deficit, and on the passenger closure cases this involved probing whether the claimed savings were correctly calculated, and whether they were actually achieved. The obvious savings from the few closures made so far showed the Committee the size of losses which must have been occurring on all of the other services. One of its main recommendations was that the Government should pay a specific subsidy for each service. The BTC resisted the Select Committee's offer of an open subsidy, and provided in rebuttal a list of administrative difficulties in calculating the subsidies which proved a remarkably accurate forecast of the experience under the 1968 Transport Act.[2] This was not to be the last time when railway pride and a wish to avoid detailed Government involvement were to cost BR dearly. But, far less easy to explain, the Government rejected the explicit subsidy recommendations, too. Apart from minor changes in the consultation procedures, the 1962 Act did nothing about the loss-making passenger services.

The one major change the Government made was to appoint Dr Beeching, and his 'Reshaping' Report provided long lists of passenger services and goods depots which were to be closed, in the expectation that the loss of revenue would be greatly exceeded by the cost savings. But even the Beeching Report hinted that the measures envisaged at the time would be only a partial solution to the more fundamental problem and that, in the conurbations at least, social benefit criteria justified special financial assistance for railway passenger services.[3] (Looking ahead for a moment, the publication in 1969 of the list of services receiving grant aid, most of which were not even mentioned in the Reshaping Report, showed how far the Report's proposals fell short of the Board's real financial needs).

After initial improvements, the railway deficit started to mount again. The passenger service and goods depot closure programmes, whilst providing substantial savings, did not provide a solution to the Board's financial problems. And equally, the frequency of refusal by the Government of the BR's closure proposals supported an increasingly widely held view that the reduction of the Board's deficit by this means was a subsidiary objective in national transport policy, and was not being allowed to override social considerations. A mixture of knowledgeable pragmatism on the part of railway managers, and the obvious evidence of the Government's closure refusals, led BR to avoid proposing for closure many railway passenger services which were incurring substantial losses but which they could see were fulfilling some social need. If there was no chance of the Government approving a closure proposal, then there was no point in BR incurring the public opprobrium of closure proceedings, and the loss incurred on the service just remained an anonymous part of the deficit grant. With such losses, however calculated, ranging upwards to, say, a quarter of a million pounds per annum, the retention of each such service did not make a big impact on a deficit of around £150 million per annum. As was to be expected, this point was not lost on the Government, either. It was far easier to justify the refusal of a closure proposal when it was clear that the ongoing loss on that service would not be a significant part of the Board's deficit.

The Government's action under the 1962 and earlier Transport Acts, forcing British Railways to provide loss-making passenger services without compensation, was clearly at variance with the financial obligations imposed upon BR by the same Acts: 'To break even, . . . taking one year with another.' A railway subject to massive competition for many of its traditionally profitable traffics cannot be in a fit condition to support loss-making services, however socially necessary they may be. BR was slipping into a situation which was bad for traveller, Government and BR alike. The end result would have been to have BR act as a *de facto* Government Department, providing the services the Government demanded, and meeting their cost out of an annual vote from Parliament similar to the Health Service or Home Office. In a way, this was already happening with deficit grants, but the Board was still expected to observe the fiction that it was obliged to break even. This could only lead to an acrimonious relationship between the Ministry and the Board, for the 1962 Act implied, the National Plan of 1965 assumed and successive statements of Ministers expected, that the Board would soon break even. By 1966 both sides had seen sense, and prominent among the terms of reference of the JSG was:

To establish an acceptable basis for costing and to identify those categories of services (both passenger and freight) which are not covering costs; to isolate those categories which are potentially viable; to examine the remaining loss-makers and to isolate those with no prospects of becoming viable; and to cost in detail the annual loss on each passenger service which is unlikely ever to become viable so that the Government can decide whether it should be grant-aided on broad social and economic grounds. [4]

This general objective of the JSG was quickly transferred into specific remits for the consultants:

Remit 1

1.1 Review and comment on the acceptability of the principles and procedures now adopted by the British Railways Board for the assessment of the costs and profitability of freight and passenger traffic. Recommend any changes in these principles and procedures which may be desirable.
1.2 Recommend the methods by which the profitability of categories of freight traffic and individual passenger lines and services should be assessed.
1.3 Recommend the methods by which any grants for unremunerative passenger services should be calculated, controlled and paid.
1.4 Recommend how, and on what time base, the results of individual loss-making passenger services should be calculated and monitor the preparation of the necessary figures by the Board's staff.

Remit 2

2.1 Consider the results of all loss-making passenger services and recommend any changes, including those in the type and frequency of service, operating practices and fare structure, which would be likely to improve the results of these services in the long run.
2.2 Estimate the effect of the recommended changes on the viability of the services concerned.

Initially, these remits were shared between two firms of consultants, according to their claimed expertise, but after a very short period the JSG dispensed with the services of one of them. The remaining consultants, Cooper Bros & Co, then took up as much of the other firm's remit as was necessary to complement their own. Note that the remits looked at only half of the problem: how to calculate and pay the necessary grants. The other side of the problem — which services to support with Government aid — was reserved for discussion *inside* the Ministry of Transport. As the Government was in the process of publishing its *British Railways Network for Development*[5] map, which specified the passenger network which was to be 'retained and developed', it might seem to have been superfluous to have believed that any further decisions of this sort would be necessary. The BR managers certainly felt that detailed consideration of each of the routes was unnecessary, for all of those with the worst economics (in terms of social needs satisfied per £1 of deficit) had already been proposed for closure by the Board and refused permission to close by the Minister. But clearly there was going to be a big difference between the Minister refusing a closure proposal, (with the inference that BR should just add the loss to its already mammoth deficit) and a Minister saying, every three years, 'this line fulfils such a social need that I am prepared to pay an annual grant in six figures to keep it open.'

Not that most of the Minister's advisers thought that the actual sums involved for each service would be very big, however. This was at the time when all that was known was that BR thought that it was losing £76 million per annum on its total passenger services,[6] but because much of this was on what the Board was claiming were its commercial services, it was expected that BR would take appropriate steps to eliminate those particular losses. For the remainder, the 'stopping' and 'suburban' services, it was hard to understand how a 'loss-minimising' management could 'lose' money on this scale. For example, for every £1 of revenue on the 'stopping' services, ie, mainly the rural branch lines, the Board's annual report indicated that £1.50 was spent on terminal and movement costs alone ie, on stations and trains, and then a further £0.90 per £1 of revenue was spent on track and administration costs.

The trouble was that at the Ministry it was still assumed that it was dealing with an organisation which gave absolute priority to its financial obligation to break even. Thus, even if the Government forced it to operate a particular railway passenger service, we assumed that BR would operate that service in such a way as would minimise the deficit. It was on this assumption that much of the early thinking about evaluation procedures was based, and in 1966/7 this was to set attitudes which in some cases have not yet unbent to accommodate the realities of the situation.

To show how this confusion arose, it is necessary to go into a little detail, but it will be a useful basis for exposing the whole problem. Remember that the starting points were (i) that the Board was required to break even, (ii) the Government had refused a large number of closure proposals, but (iii) even after Beeching, BR had not asked to vary its break-even objective. In these circumstances, it was assumed that when a closure refusal forced BR to run a service it would:

— Provide the minimum level of service.
— Charge the highest possible fares (which at that time was the 'standard' fare of 3¼d per mile).

From this, it looked as if the Minister's obligation to support the basic social railway could be met by paying the cost of a single line of track over the whole of the Government-required network, ie, about 11,000 miles at £2,000/mile, ie, £22 million.

The only remaining net expense would be any cases where the traffic (at standard fares) did not cover the costs of a two-car, collector-guard diesel multiple-unit shuttling back and forth.[7] The first estimates of the shortfall between earnings and the actual cost of running the minimal train service came from the consultants' study of five representative services — it was only £132/mile per annum, or, for all services, about £1.5 million pa. But this left £15.5 million unaccounted for; the 'loss' on stopping services claimed in the 1966 Annual Report was £39 million. Here we must enlarge upon the further assumption implicit in the early estimate of the likely 'cost' to the Government of the social passenger services in rural areas.

Once a closure application had been refused, it was assumed that BR would offer a service in excess of the barest minimum only if the extra traffic thus gained paid in full for the additional cost. The ludicrous nature of this assumption could have been shown in an instant by officials in the same building. These were the people responsible for railway closures, who knew that, apart from minor economies, BR normally continued to offer the same quality of train service after closure refusal as it had done beforehand. And they also knew very well why BR adopted this practice. If it had tried to minimise its losses by reducing service following a closure refusal it would have led to a 'quality of service' complaint to the Transport Users Consultative Committee, and subsequently, an instruction from the Minister to BR to reinstate the former service.

In the experience of the officials administering the railway closure process, there was only one thing a vocal public disliked more than having their train service withdrawn, and that was to have it reduced to save money. The outcry over a decision to close died down very quickly after actual closure, whereas a reduced service was just a running sore to the affected citizen. There was another reason for officials' diffidence about admitting that the difference between the £23.5 million per annum the economists thought should be paid, and the £39 million per annum which BR claimed to be losing, could be explained by past decisions of the Minister on their advice. That was the ease of writing a letter to the Board refusing a closure application, compared with the difficulty, which was now becoming evident, of justifying the massive annual expenditures which these decisions imposed on BR.

It will be obvious from all of this how nonplussed the BR managers must have been by talk of how much of the existing services the Minister 'ought' to have paid for. In their view, subject to (i) any service reductions which might be ordered, and (ii) efficiency improvements which might be found to be possible, the Minister was bound to pay for *all* of the passenger services which were found to be making a loss in the terms of the Remit I to the consultants. To run a little ahead in our narrative, in the end the BR view prevailed.

The fact that nearly all of the losses in excess of the 'basic railway minimum' were subsequently endorsed by the Government in the form of grant approvals only showed that, far from being imcompetent at loss-minimising in this area, the railwaymen had been careful interpreters of Ministers' wishes. When the grant claims started to come in, calculated by the agreed methods, both Ministers and officials began to wish that they had in the part taken more full account of the cost when they were making their decisions about the 'social needs' to be met by continuing lightly-used rail services.

The next problem was to decide the basis on which the grants were to be paid. This was finally enshrined, quite unjustifiably, as the 'Cooper Bros formula'. In fact, it should have been known as the 'Grey & Smith' formula, after the two BR directors of costings who were really responsible for its development. All that Cooper Bros did was to endorse, without significant variation, the existing BR costing practices. The only change suggested by the consultants, concerning the treatment of interest, was rejected by the JSG.[8] Perhaps it is the same with consultants as it is with movie stars, that any publicity is good publicity[9] and Cooper Bros have not minded being labelled with something for which they were not responsible. It was ironic to find in 1968 during the Prices & Incomes Board's inquiry into London fares, that the PIB's consultants, Cooper Bros, required an *ab initio* justification of the formula to which their colleagues had given the firm's name only two years before.

The application of this formula has aroused a lot of subsequent criticism, particularly with the Passenger Transport Executives, and it is worth detailed study. The main points of contention were, and still are:

(i) That it is based on 'full' costs and not marginal costs, thus 'overstating' the grants, or, put another way, that 'joint costs' should not be included.

(ii) That it provides for annual provisions for future maintenance and depreciation on a replacement basis, instead of reinbursing actual expenditures in each year.

(iii) That 'contributory revenue' is not taken into account in determining the grant for each service.

(iv) That the alternative method of handling track and signalling cost (Method 2) resulted in over-compensation.

(v) That determination of the grant in advance may result in overpayment without any compensatory advantage to the Government.

We will deal with these overlapping points in turn.

As with so many railway problems, the 'average or marginal cost' debate has an historical basis. In the present context, it arises where the grant paid for a service under the formula appears to be much greater than the sum the railways would 'save' if the service were to be withdrawn. Following a badly mishandled closure case in 1958[10], the Central Transport Consultative Committee had recommended a new, standard form of costing and earnings information which should be given to Transport Users' Consultative Committee in closure cases. It required provision of data on actual net outgoings (including provision for renewals), and the current revenue, on the line to be closed.[11] This new basis survived only until the Beeching closures began to take effect.

In 1963, the volume of complaints against BR costing led the Minister to ask Sir William Carrington, the eminent accountant, to report on what 'appropriate' figures should be given to TUCC's. Remember that right through this period the railways were in the position of having to justify in public their application to withdraw a service, even though the 1962 Transport Act had removed the right of the TUCC to comment on the validity of the cost and revenue data. Thus allegations of bias against BR were inevitable and, in some cases, merited. In general, Sir William Carrington endorsed the existing practice, with some recommendations for improving the accuracy of the revenue data. But there was one important flaw in the process which was carried over from the CTCC's requirements. In the cost (which by definition were greater than the revenue or else closure would not have been proposed), track and signalling expense savings were included only to the extent that these were incurred through the maintenance of passenger train standards solely for the service under consideration. Thus it was only where the service concerned was the sole user of a route that the cost data included all of the potential savings. Where the only other service on the route was freight, unless the Board signified its intention of withdrawing the freight service at the same time, the track and signalling cost savings attributable to the passenger closure were minimal.

This figure of 'savings from reduction in track maintenance standards' always understated the true potential savings because the cost of maintaining a freight-only branch line was grossly overstated. For example, the Beeching Report claimed that a single track freight-only route (category D) cost £2,000pa to maintain, whereas the same route maintained to passenger standards (category C) cost only £3,500 pa[12] But there was another problem, too. The decision on whether freight services would continue on a route about to lose its passenger service was made on much less certain data. In many cases, the freight service was not worth keeping if it had to bear all of the remaining track and signalling costs, but due to crooked thinking on the question of freight's need to pay for its track[13], this was ignored. There was even one ridiculous case where the Minister refused closure because the Board supposedly intended keeping on the freight, and savings from the passenger closure would therefore not be great, only to find that BR then promptly withdrew the freight service![14]

This inability to look at the total picture often led to the TUCC's and the public being given a completely erroneous view of the potential savings from a closure. Far from deliberately overstating the likely savings, due to the bias in the 'Carrington' data, and its own inability to make valid judgements about the profitability of its freight traffic, BR was understating the potential savings on nearly every mixed traffic route. Information released by the Ministry of Transport for one particular route — the Waverley route from Edinburgh to Carlisle — made this clear. Although the estimated savings advised to the TUCC were only £233,000 pa, the potential savings to BR were at least £536,000.[15] But at the same time, it was estimated that the grant for a full service on the formula basis would have been £700,000! Although the difference between the two lower figures was caused by the lower figure ignoring the savings from closing the freight service and lifting the track, we must now explain why a service whose closure would only have saved BR £536,000 pa would have attracted an estimated grant of £700,000.[16]

Basically, this difference was accounted for by the ubiquity of a loss-making passenger service, and the inability of the few 'profitable' services to pay the whole cost of shared facilities, such as terminals. For example, loss-making passenger services were about one quarter of BR's total activities, and, despite the optimistic Beeching claims of a few years earlier, with few exceptions they were going to stay loss-makers for the foreseeable future. Under the old closure procedures, services had been looked at one at a time, and a single service withdrawal would have permitted no savings in general administration expense. But the time for such a short-sighted approach was past; now it was a fair assumption that if these services were a quarter of BR's activity they were therefore responsible for a quarter of BR's general administration costs. It may be (and often is) argued that BR's general administration costs are far too high,[17] but that is not the point at issue here. Whatever the actual level of these costs, a proportion of them is properly attributable to the loss-making passenger services.

A similar principle applied to other costs, more obviously shared between loss-making services and profitable services. In the Waverley route case, for example, the costs of Edinburgh Waverley and Carlisle Citadel stations were shared between the Waverley route trains and all the other services using them. It was no good to say: 'Ah, but such a small proportion of the trains, and an even smaller proportion of the passengers, at these two stations were from the Waverley route; surely they did not add anything to the cost of the station?' Take Edinburgh Waverley; at that time the only trains using it which were not loss-makers were the East Coast main line expresses. To have forced the traffic in those trains to have supported the whole of the cost of Edinburgh Waverley station, and of Newcastle Central, and Darlington and York and so on, would have turned the East Coast main line service into a loss-maker, too. It was through such glib assumptions that 'some other traffic' would cover all of the shared costs that BR had been allowed to slide into its massive deficits, and there was an iron determination in all quarters to avoid this trap opening again.

If the actual grants payable had been determined on a marginal cost basis, covering only those costs which would have been saved immediately on withdrawal, there would have remained a massive block of shared cost, not attributed to any particular service, and certainly not 'covered' by profits elsewhere, which would have been a millstone around the Board's neck, plunging it straight back into deficit. This was rejected in favour of a rationing of 'full' costs, based on the implicit assumption that in the long run following the loss of traffic, BR could reduce the total cost of any shared facility by the proportion attributed to that traffic. This may appear to be crude, but it does spread the shared costs among services in rough accord with the relative causation of the costs. It is important to remember that the loss-making, social passenger services lean on each other more than they lean on the commercial services or *vice versa*. It was evident from the massive BR deficits that the commercial services were hard put to support themselves, let alone 'carry' other services.

There can be no case in Britain for treating this issue in the way it has been handled in some US cities. A conversation I had in 1969 with an official of the South East Pennsylvania Transit Authority, which was responsible for subsidising the Penn-Central & Reading Railroad suburban services into Philadelphia, showed the other extreme position. Having learned that SEPTA met all the costs of the stations in the suburbs, I asked how the cost of 30th Street Station was shared between the suburban and main line trains. The answer was abrupt: 'It's not; we reckon that any passenger alighting from a suburban train at that station is doing so to catch a main line train — a plausible proposition — and we have done the Penn-Central a favour by subsidising the suburban train which brought him there.' How about the 'Suburban Station' in downtown Philadelphia, then? 'We pay nothing for that either. Penn-Central owns the massive office block on top of that station, and we consider that the railroad should meet the cost of the station out of the rents it obtains.' Subsequent events may have lead to a more relaxed and generous financial relationship between SEPTA and Penn-Central.

Having decided that shared costs should be attributed to the services concerned, there remained the problem of choosing the basis of the attribution. We will deal with track and signalling costs in a moment; for the present we restrict our discussion to terminal costs. The consultants having given a general endorsement to the pre-existing BR method, the officials naturally enquired what the method was, and this was ultimately to disclose one of those many gaps between headquarters instruction and practice out on the railway. The headquarters costing people were adamant that terminal costs were always split on the basis of: booking office costs; ticket issues; other costs; train calls. They were mildly embarrassed to find, during the first Ministry of Transport inspection visit to a division, that a large variety of methods were in use. These ranged from work-study analysis in large stations to an informed guess at unimportant stations, with a wide variety of methods in between. In fact, for the places concerned, all of the local variants seemed to the Ministry people to be more appropriate than the headquarters dicta, and they were approved. The situation reminded me of a staff manual I had used years ago in the airline industry in Australia. Each page, full of instructions for every conceivable eventuality, had printed in striking type at the top and bottom: 'NOTHING IN THIS MANUAL SUPERSEDES COMMON SENSE IN THE FIRING LINE.' For one reason and another the BR headquarters costing men had thought that arbitrary uniformity would appeal to the civil service mind. The rational variety which actually pertained out on the railway was more attractive.

The basic assumption that most of the services would be retained for the foreseeable future bore heavily on the next point of consideration: that grants should be calculated to include provisions for future maintenance cost and depreciation at replacement cost. The alternative — to reimburse only expected actual expenditures — was supported by the Ministry economists as giving a truer picture of the actual resource costs of maintaining each service. But it was rejected, on two main grounds.

First, it was the Government's wish that in future the social passenger services should be managed by BR on the same basis, in terms of accounting practices and reports, as its other services. Secondly, as most of the services were thought to have a long term future, the grant process should reflect this by permitting BR to accumulate funds for eventual repairs and renewals, thus evening out the annual grant payments. There were plenty of safeguards written into the procedures to ensure (i) that wasteful investments are not made, and (ii) that BR cannot in the long run collect more in grant than it actually spends. The first condition is met by the requirement that each grant application must note any investments needed in the grant period, so that when approving the grant, the Minister can weigh the cost of the investment against the social needs being met. The second condition is met by a cumbersome but necessary device for each service: the 'notional capital account.' This ensures that, if a service is withdrawn, any unspent provisions from past grants are refunded to the Government. Equally, any past investments (authorised by the Minister) which have not been fully amortised out of grants at the time of closure are to result in a payment to the Board. This question of 'accounting cost' versus 'cash flow' as the grant basis has really only been at issue in the PTE areas.

The 'track cost' question has beggared railway economics, management and control since the days of George Stephenson, and it was sure to raise its ugly head here. The standard BR practice which the consultants endorsed was to allocate track costs on the basis of gross ton miles, and signalling costs on the basis of train miles. Where traffic has homogeneous physical requirements and is spread evenly throughout the 24 hours this is unexceptionable, but by the very nature of passenger services, if they are mixed with freight on a route, such simple allocations of the track and signalling cost will almost invariably fail to match the actual causation of the costs. But the consultants had endorsed the BR method, the BR costing people had a fear that any more rational method would have resulted in lower grants. There was little time for argument, so the BR method was accepted for general use.[18] This was an area where the consultants were really out of their depth, and they recommend that 'more research' should be done into the variation of track and signalling costs according to variation in traffic.

But there was one area where the blind observance of the BR methods could have led to nonsensical results, and to head this off a variant had to be introduced. Initially, this too was resisted by the BR costing men; later it was to become a sore point with the Government. Its name, given by Mr F.R.Gunton, the first BR manager to recognise its usefulness, was 'Method 2'. The principles underlying Method 2 were outlined in paragraph D.7 of the *Railway Policy White Paper*[20], where the JSG wondered aloud about 'whether it would be more logical, in cases where the capacity' (ie, most of the cost) of a route is determined solely by the peak needs of 'a grant-aided passenger service, for that service to bear most of the costs of the track and signalling, with the other services only bearing a proportion of the wear and tear costs. This would be particularly significant in cases where a line was used jointly by a commuter passenger service and by other passenger and freight services.'

What we were trying to guard against was a situation where, although the grant-aided passenger service caused virtually all of the cost, the standard method of track and signalling cost allocation might, by 'loading' a few freight trains with a large proportion of this cost, cause the Board to withdraw the freight as 'unprofitable'.[21] The net result of such a situation would have been that the freight trains would have been driven off the route by a phoney cost allocation, after which the grant-aided service would have had to pay the whole of the track and signalling cost anyhow. It was felt preferable to short-circuit the possibility of such a resource waste by charging the full track and signalling cost to the grant-aided service from the start, leaving the Board free to fit in freight trains as and when it could so so without incurring a cash penalty for its good management. At the beginning, the 'wear and tear' costs involved were thought to be *de minimus*, and Method 2 charged all of the track and signalling cost to the grant-aided service. But in 1970, after criticism from the Auditor General and the Public Accounts Committee, the practice reverted to the original suggestion of the JSG, and a wear and tear 'charge' was imposed.[22]

1 See *SCNI: BR, op cit*, paras. 232–234.
2 See *Special Report from the Select Committee on Nationalised Industries British Railways Observations of the British Transport Commiswion and the Ministry of Transport*, London, HMSO,1961.
3 *Op cit*, p.22.

4 See the *Railway Policy* White Paper. (Cmnd. 3439), London, 1967, Appendix K, para. 5(a).

5 *Op cit.*

6 BRB: AR&A, 1966, Appendix 1.

7 These estimates were generous compared with claims of low costs emanating from the Eastern Region of BR at the time.

8 See *Railway Policy*, op cit, Appendix E., para.E.2.

9 Excepting McKinsey & Co., it would seem, as anyone who read the issues of the *Irish Times* for October 7, 8 and 15 1971 will know!

10 See *Ministry of Transport and Civil Aviation: Proposed withdrawal of train services from the Lewes — East Grinstead Railway. Report of the Central Transport Consultative Committee, Cmnd. 360*, London HMSO, 1958.

11 The CTCC also recommended that the net sale value of released assets should be shown. This was a particularly sore point as the counting of the revenue from sale of displaced assets as a *benefit* of closure implied that BR was primarily in business to sell its assets, not to run trains.

12 By the late Sixties, however, the civil engineers had been allowed to experiment and find just how far they could reduce the maintenance costs of both kinds of routes, and in some cases this had been reduced to as low as a few hundred pounds per mile.

13 See Chapter Nine.

14 This was the Romford-Upminster branch.

15 See *Modern Railways*, January 1969, p.23.

16 Public discussion of this particular closure case was not helped by a consultant's report (See *Transport in the Borders*, duplicated, obtained from the author, John Hibbs, Saffron Walden, 1968) which failed to take account of detailed costing information which had been supplied by the Ministry of Transport.

17 It is, in fact, the only cost which has grown consistently since Beeching arrived!

18 It was not until I had joined BR that I developed the new cause-related principles of attributing track and signalling costs. See my 'Pricing and Investment in Railway Freight Services,' *Journal of Transport Economics & Policy,* Sept. 1971, particularly pp.7-12. These principles are now being used (in an amended form) for internal BR costing, but they have not yet been adopted for grant calculations. Perhaps it is the Government which is now worried that grant claims might thereby be increased!

19 Some research was done by BR in 1968, but the method used was technically invalid. This was overtaken by a new application of a fundamental principle. See previous footnote.

20 *Op cit*, Appendix D, p.58.

21 I later learnt that our concern was misplaced: BR's freight analysis methods at that time were not sufficiently acute to register this kind of 'cost'.

11 | An Exercise in Mutually Heightened Self-awareness

I hope that this chapter, which, like Chapter Eight is more anecdotal than analytical, will provide the reader with some 'feel' for the problems encountered when the Government became formally BR's biggest customer.

With my penchant for simplifying problems out of existence, I had proposed to the Ministry that the grant application form should be a simple two-page document, with a few boxes to be filled in, multiplied out at annually agreed rates, and the bottom line would show what the Government owed the Board. But this was before I realised that most of the services to be grant-aided were far more than basic railways. Obviously, more detail was required, said the consultants. In addition, my simple scheme assumed that the Ministry officials and the BR managers would sit down once a year and agree national unit-costs for each input — route miles, additional track miles, train miles by different types of DMU, and so on. But the railway costing people rejected this out of hand on the grounds that every mile of route was different from every other, and there were so many different types of DMU, and so on. They were not prepared to use averages, even if the Government was. So it was left to the consultants to devise, test and refine a suitable form of grant application. Their proposal was then augmented by discussions between the Ministry and BR, and the final result, settled around the end of 1967, has been in use, with very little alteration, ever since. With all of its statistical appendices, it has grown a bit from my suggested two pages; the largest I have seen was as thick as a volume of the London telephone book.[1]

In 1968, there was a massive programme of work for both sides. BR had to prepare an application for every service it was putting up for grant, and the Ministry officials had to satisfy themselves on the validity of each application before recommending it to the Ministry for grant aid. On BR, although the rules for preparation of the grant application came from 222 Marylebone Road, each Region decided on its own way of preparing the applications. To the outside observer some of the differences between the Regional practices were informative in themselves. The Southern, it appeared, thought that they had only a few peripheral routes which made a loss, so no special arrangements were considered necessary. The LM and the Eastern each set up special staffs at both the regional headquarters and in divisional offices. The Western, true to their traditions of separateness, decided that no special arrangements were necessary; the grant applications would be prepared by normal staffs as part of their normal duties. The Western promptly fell about four months behind in their timetable, but by the end of the year their administrative machine was in full gear and the WR was as close to the target as anybody else.

There were nearly three hundred separate applications to be vetted. Every Thursday a day-long meeting was held at the BRB to give any explanations the officials might require on a nominated set of applications. In addition to the BR headquarters men, there would be managers there from whichever region's applications were being vetted that day. The LM's teams were led by an assistant general manager of the region. The two gentlemen concerned, who were obviously being groomed for the higher things to which they have now acceded, must have found these weekly explorations of the official mind a useful preparation for later on. The Eastern Region team was led by a wily chap named Ewart Waite, now retired, who had an uncanny ability to sense the topics from the day's applications which would cause the most bureaucratic bafflement, and he always had the appropriate expert with him. The Southern's team was also led by an assistant general manager. But this one was a finance expert who may have felt he should have been at the headquarters settling high principles with the Government. Whatever the motivation, however, he seemed to set out deliberately to prove that the scheme was inappropriate for his region, and oblivious of the embarrassment of his head office colleagues. (More of this anon). He was accompanied, among others, by a volatile gentleman who took an especial delight in telling the officials (and their consultant) that nothing they requested or suggested could be done. He finally met his Waterloo one day when, upon being asked where were the data on alternative bus services, etc, which should have been in the application, snapped back: 'Look in your own files! You refused permission to close this service only eighteen months ago and we gave you all this stuff then! Just how often do you lot need to be told these things?' The answer had to be: 'Once more, if the Southern Region ever wants to receive a grant for the service.' Special arrangements were made for services in Scotland or Wales, because here the Scottish and Welsh Offices had an interest. For these, the whole party journeyed to the respective capitals. The Scottish and Welsh officials were not the most unbiased reviewers of grant applications; after all, it was Whitehall money, from another department's vote, which was being spent.

These weekly meetings were the workshop in which the ongoing relationship between the railways and their newly-found biggest customer was fashioned. There was much gentle probing from both sides. The railwaymen, starting from the premise that the Government must pay the whole loss on every loss-making service they proposed for grant, expected to be treated as the Government's experts on the question of running railways. For this reason, they resisted every attempt by the officials to probe deeply into the 'reasons why' this or that service was operated in a particular way. It was very perplexing; for years BR had been complaining that the civil servants with whom it had to deal had an inadequate knowledge of railway problems,[2] but now, when faced by a group of willing learners, the railway attitude was to say: 'That's *our* business'. This communication problem was not helped by the diffidence of some of the more senior civil servants, who had hoped to avoid going into detail. But, confronted with grant applications which each contained as much information as a small book, if the officials were to give them a proper vetting they were going to be forced to become expert in the detail of railway operation.

Once the need for this learning process had been established, most of the railwaymen displayed great patience. This virtue was sorely tried at times – like the occasion when one very junior civil servant produced his own version of a timetable graph for the commuter services on the Great Northern Line. The task of preparing and justifying the grant applications was an important educational process for the railway managers, too. Never before had such detailed data been available on all the services, and it was clear that in a number of cases action had already been initiated to eradicate nonsenses which were disclosed in this way. A few did slip through the BR regional and headquarters nets. Some of the claimed costs of maintaining track and operating signalboxes were obviously far too high, and a big programme of rechecking was instituted. On one service it was clear that the revenue at the stations along the line did not cover the cost of collecting it. The suggestion that it would be better to let all the passengers travel free, and just put an 'honesty' box at the terminal, was rejected by the BR assistant divisional manager on the grounds that it would 'encourage a tendency toward immorality'. While the Ministry side were conjuring up visions of maidens being seduced in the waiting rooms of unattended stations, it was explained that 'immorality', in the terms of a railwayman born in Aberdeen, was travelling without a ticket.

There was a lot of discussion on which services should be proposed for grant-aid. It was open to BR to propose any service, but it was entirely in the Minister's discretion whether he accepted a proposal. In only one of these discussion did the railwaymen and the Ministry officials reach instant unanimity. That was the day on which a principal from the Treasury had been invited along to see the grant vetting process in action. One of the services being discussed was Newcastle-Carlisle, a mixture of a Newcastle commuter service and a rural stopping service. Following a long tradition of Treasury resistance to spending by the exercise of a brilliant ability to remain unconvinced, our Treasury guest said he could not see why we were wasting time discussing such a service. His reasoning was simple. Both Newcastle and Carlisle were 'cities', so any train service connecting them must be an Inter-City service. He had always understood that the Board accepted full commercial responsibility for the Inter-City network, so why should it not support this service?

One problem was the uneven approach of the different regions.

The Scottish Region had proposed for grant every passenger service in Scotland with the exception of the East and West Coast main lines. In contrast, the Western Region had refused to seek grants for a number of main line services which were obvious loss-makers and which would at that time have qualified for grant-aid if proposed. It was too much to expect the inheritors of the GWR to admit that there were only losses west of Plymouth, or on the Birmingham, Worcester, Hereford and Cheltenham services. The Southern Region started out by being very unhelpful to the Board and the Ministry over its London commuter services. This was due to a mixture of (i) the approach of the finance man from Waterloo, to which I referred above, (ii) a fervent wish to avoid letting the region's commuter network come under Government support and control, and (iii) an inadequate knowledge of the true financial situation of the commuter services which was not far short of shameful for an £80 million business.

The early grant applications for services on the periphery of the Southern

Region's network were all for amounts far in excess of the actual cost of providing a service adequate for the traffic offering. For example, the Ashford-Ramsgate service had eight-car trains when two cars were more than adequate. It was pointed out that this was because the trains ran through to London, and the extra cars presumably were required for the traffic on the main line. What was *not* so readily pointed out was that even though the local and the London services might have been cheaper to operate with the same trains, the net effect was to load much of the cost of the main line service on to the grant application. Operating a separate, two-car service for the grant-aided service would have resulted in a greatly reduced grant claim. Similarly, with the Ascot-Guildford service, it was found that a large part of the track and signalling cost was incurred to maintain reliability on the connecting line to London, and had little to do with the local service. The same thing was happening with every peripheral service. In all of these cases, the Ministry argued that if the local grant-aided service was to be loaded with costs of the through service to London, its 'area' should be extended toward London until it had included enough extra revenue to match the extra cost. This elicited the statement that if such 'profits' were to be diverted from the commuter services to the local services, the commuter network would show a loss. At that stage, the game was up, because it was obvious that Waterloo was hoping to collect enough on its peripheral services to keep the Government's hands off the remainder.

When the unacceptable nature of this approach was pointed out, it was countered with the disingenuous suggestion that the whole Southern Region network should be grant-aided as a single entity. However attractive this might have been to Waterloo, it was totally unacceptable to Whitehall. A fundamental objective of the new legislation was to eliminate the uncontrolled disbursement of deficit grants, and the Government could exercise no control over a 'service' which comprised virtually the total passenger operations of a region. The compromise reached was for the region's London commuter network to be divided into sectors, each a reasonably self-contained operating entity.

Now the surprises began, because when the Southern Region began to do the necessary analysis for such comprehensive grant proposals they found that, far from almost breaking even and needing only the assistance of inflated grant claims on the peripheral services, the region's commuter services were making a substantial loss. The picture looked even more bleak when it was pointed out from headquarters that the region was making a totally inadequate provision for the replacement of bridges. This item had been estimated at Waterloo on the basis of the abnormally low amount the region was then actually spending on bridge replacements. The Waterloo finance man did not realise that the provision for replacement had to be related to the number of bridges requiring replace-ment, and not to the severely restricted number actually being done. When finally added up, the grant claim for Southern Region services exceeded £10m. Had the 'load the periphery' strategem been successful, and the subsequent need to do the sums properly been avoided, this would have been a high price for the Board to pay for Waterloo pride.

Inevitably, many of the services proposed for grant aid raised official eyebrows at the chasm between the cost and the apparent level of social need being met. But the greater the apparent gap, the more likely it was that a service was a 'refused closure' case. Now the Government was being confronted with the true long run costs of its past decisions to retain services, and not the totally inadequate 'marginal cost' data required by the Carrington recommendations. What had been wrong in principle often was wrongly calculated, too. Far from it being a network of 'basic railways' which the Government was about to pay for its own past decisions in closure cases had determined a much higher level of service. And far from the early naive assumption that all these services, fulfilling vital social needs, would be charging the standard BR fare of 3¼d per mile, it was found that except for some of the longer distance services in Scotland, virtually every other service was operating with fares nearer to half the standard fare. In all cases this was because of bus competition.

It was easy for the Minister to accept the arguments of a TUCC that 'extreme hardship' would be caused by a closure. It was far harder for the railways to get the passengers to pay anything more than the competing bus fares for the rail service which was claimed to be so vital to them. In most cases, had the railway charged the standard fares, most of the passengers would have used the cheaper buses, thus proving the negligible 'value' of the hardships supposedly alleviated by keeping the rail service. Of course, all the services had a hard-core of travellers for whom the bus was an impossible alternative,[3] but if the remainder would transfer their custom to bus for the slightest fare differential, it was obvious that the rail service was really being kept for the smaller group. For example, on the Waverley route, which we discussed in the last chapter, although there were about 90 regular passengers, the 'extreme hardship' group which could not transfer to bus was only about 30 passengers. Dividing this figure into the minimum annual cost of maintaining service, the subsidy came to £10,000 *per head* per year.

Although some regions failed to apply for grants for certain services, when they would certainly have succeeded, there were others who applied in cases where the services concerned were more properly adjuncts of the commercial services. Neither BR nor the Ministry had any clear idea of what was 'right' in these circumstances. It was a case of talking it over between the railway managers and the officials, and then for the officials to try to develop a consistent policy to recommend to the Minister. One thing was clear, and that was that the regions which withheld applications did the Board a great disfavour. Where applications, if made, would have attracted grants, it meant that other BR services had to cross-subsidise the services in question. That was a high price for BR to pay for regional pride, because, as it turned out, in the first years of the grant programme the Government was generous in the services it was prepared to grant aid. 'Social need' was defined very freely, and trains whose primary function was to feed into Inter-City trains attracted grant aid. This generosity lasted until about 1971.[4]

Despite all the shock at the seemingly doubtful case for retaining many of the services, after the vetting of grant applications only 133 of them were given one-year grants. Despite some encouragement to BR to renew closure proposals only 29 more services had actually been closed two years later. There was a vast difference between deciding that the claimed grant per passenger mile was excessive, and deciding to overrule the eventual TUCC report on hardship and approve a closure application. At last the responsibility, both financial and administrative, was where it belonged: with the Government. At least the priorities of both parties were now right. The railway managers, freed of the oppressive notion that every £1 which one of these services cost was a £1 added to the deficit, were prepared to go to great lengths to convince the Government that the services should be retained. On the other hand, now that there was a '£' sign in front of their actions with regard to each specific service, the officials took great care to obtain 'value for money' for the public purse.

The only remaining problem was the messy, but necessary, procedure which followed the issue of a qualified grant approval and an invitation to BR to propose a service for closure. Although the Minister's decision to invite a closure proposal is based on a massive quantity of data, when the Board proposes the closure it is again cast in the role of the anti-social villian, trying to close the railway against the interests of its users. The claims of consultative democracy mean that a TUCC hearing is still required, and when the committee has distilled emotion into fact and forwarded its report on 'hardships' to the Minister, he may still refuse closure, thus acting as the protector of the public interest from the rapacious railways. Hardly any member of the general public knows that BR only makes it closure proposals at the invitation of the Minister, and after he has decided that a prima facie case for closure exists.

1 Only because someone at Waterloo thought it better to Xerox about 100 pages of the Southern Region timetable, instead of handing over a copy of the complete, and much thinner, timetable.

2 See, eg, *First Report from the Select Committee on Nationalised Industries, Session 1967-68*, London, HMSO, 1968, Volume II, Q.572 (Evidence of Sir Stanley Raymond.)

3 The smallest 'extreme hardship' group I have seen reported from a TUCC hearing was nine persons; closure of that service was approved by the Minister.

4 The Grant approval list at the end of that year excluded two services — Chesterfield-Sheffield and Bradford-Huddersfield — which although incurring deficits and meeting social needs, were claimed by the Minister to merit cross-subsidy from commercial services.

12 | The Transport Act of 1968

'They have nothing to strive for now because they are in such
a state of total irremediable deficit.'
*Sir Thomas Padmore, Permanent Secretary, Ministry of
Transport, in evidence to the Select Committee on
Nationalised Industries, 1967*

In the last few chapters we have concentrated on the recommendations of the
Joint Steering Group for reshaping BR's future. Looking back at the terms of
reference of the JSG it is clear that the Government foresaw the necessary
financial and subsidy changes and really only wanted the JSG to endorse them
and fill in the financial and procedural detail. It is equally clear that BR did not
have in mind quite the changes which the JSG recommended, and this can be
attributed to a lack of understanding of the direction and scale of its own
problems. It was a serious misjudgement to expect the Government just to
package a set of financial crutches for BR without exacting a *quid pro quo* in
terms of tighter control and some guarantee that the railways would not drift
into a similar predicament again. The Board's approach was simply to state that
BR obviously needed help, and to offer a few suggestions on how this might be
wrapped up in a form which would not attribute any fault to the railway
management. We have already looked at the ill-fated 'standby' issue in Chapter
Nine. Elsewhere, BR's 'social obligations', which may have included 'standby',
were claimed to cost the Board £100 million a year.[1] There was nothing wrong
with BR, the argument ran, that could not be fixed with continued Government
subventions, ie, deficit grants under a nicer name, and 'co-ordination'.

'Co-ordination' had been the aim of the Transport Act of twenty years before
and for a variety of reasons, which we discussed in Chapters Two and Three, it
had failed. Now, in the mind of the chairman of the BRB, future transport
policy was to have BR as its centrepiece, propped up to a large extent by
'co-ordination'. The first strategem was to have the Government approve and
jointly produce the Network Map, and then to argue that once the Government
had determined the network it should make sure that BR had enough traffic to
fill it. Thus the Government was asked to take into account the railways' need
for traffic when setting its policies for the future of the National Coal Board
and on the question of home produced ore for steelworks.[2] Other 'co-ordination' proposals concerned the freight and passenger activities of the Transport
Holding Company. Here, too, the Government and the Railways Board had
divergent views of suitable means and ends. What was at stake was the future
scope of BR non-rail activities, which could have been changed in either
direction — widened or narrowed. The arguments for widening came from the
Board, and reflected a hankering to return to the British Transport Commission
situation (without London Transport). The 1962 Act had transferred the
separable non-rail activities — British Road Services, Pickfords, the Tilling bus

companies and Thos Cook's travel agency were the main ones — to the Transport Holding Company (THC). This was a new idea in public ownership, which effectively sterilised the various businesses from Government interferrence. The components of the THC had performed passably well under the BTC, but to focus the attention of the new top management on the main problem, the railways, it had been thought best to remove these potential distractions.

Since its formation in 1962, the Transport Holding Company had lived up to its name, with only a small headquarters,[3] and had maintained the delegation of responsibility to the operating companies which had been practised by the BTC. This strategem effectively isolated the operating companies from Parliamentary interference, because if the Minister dealt with the chairman of the THC, he could not reasonably expect to delve into greater detail than the THC used for its own transactions with its subsidiaries. Of course, there was not nearly so much call for Parliamentary surveillance with the THC companies as with the railways. Only the bus companies had any monopoly power, and this was regulated by the Traffic Commissioners. The other subsidiaries were all regulated quite effectively by the market. Over the years, the THC (and its chairman, Sir Reginald Wilson) had blown its own trumpet on the virtues of its chosen form of organisation and wide delegation of authority,[4] and this was echoed by outside commentators.[5] This chest-beating by the junior offspring of the BTC was aimed primarily at the giant sibling: BR.

It was connected with the fact that, by following the non-rail activities into the THC (whether voluntarily or having been pushed), the senior management of the THC had been cut off from the power and the glory (and the deficits) of the much bigger BR organisation. Evidence of this nostalgia for the larger scale of activity can be found in a remarkable address by Sir Reginald Wilson (chairman of the THC) to The Institute of Transport.[6] Sir Reginald drew many damaging comparisons between his own THC and BR, seemingly forgetting that virtually every criticism he made of the BRB could have equally well been made of the BTC between 1948 and 1961 while he was comptroller, and later a member of the Commission.

Judged on some limited criteria, the THC *had* done well. It had caused no trouble for the Government and, operating in competitive fields, it had satisfied its customers. But the same businesses had met the same criteria under BTC rule. When we come to look at the operating performance of the THC, and its stewardship of the assets and businesses placed in its care, the best that can be said is that it failed to do any worse with them than the much-maligned British Transport Commission. In his *Public Enterprise in Practice*[7], Richard Pryke argues that technical efficiency is much more important than allocative efficiency. That is, that it is more important in national product terms for whatever is produced to be produced as cheaply as possible than for the price/quality relationship to be optimal. This was where the THC fell down, for large parts of its activity were less efficient than comparable firms in the private sector, and the lack of 'interference' from head office meant that they could go their own quiet way. Thos Cooks is the prime example of this. Starting under THC control with the best world-wide chain of retail outlets in the travel trade, Cooks managed to miss the boom in inclusive tour business and stagnated in most other fields of its activity. The main determinant of Cooks' profits was the volume of travellers cheque business, which supported the other activities.[8] From 1967, Thos Cooks was under the personal management of Sir Reginald Wilson, who himself became chairman of Cooks on the retirement of Sir John Eliot.[9]

The subsequent history of Cooks, and the disastrous purchase of Lunn-Poly by the THC,[10] suggest that the THC style of organisation and management was not an attractive blueprint for other public sector activities. Elsewhere in its oprations, we can find other evidence that the THC 'hands-off' management was not necessarily conducive to efficiency. The 'THC' bus companies, for example, appear to have been less efficient than their private sector 'British Electric Traction' contemporaries. The purchase, in 1968, of the BET operations improved every THC bus efficiency statistic.[11] Further evidence of this, admittedly tenuous, is to be found in a study of bus company profits by M.E.Beesley and Janet Politi.[12] They found that for one 'holding company group', ie, either BET or THC, the fact that an individual bus company was a member had a significant effect on profits for all years of the study, while for the other, membership of the group was significant only in one year 1964-65, and almost so in 1965-6. The fact that these were the two years of THC ownership in which aggregate bus profits were significantly higher than the other two, suggests that of the two 'holding companies' it was the Transport Holding Company whose ownership and control made only a patchy contribution to the performance of its subsidiaries.

This overdue look past the trumpeting of the Transport Holding Company, to see that just the earning of profits (however small) is too low a hurdle against which to judge a management, should not divert our attention from the one important conclusion which was drawn from the THC experience. There was obviously great virtue in the subdivision of activities into 'profit-centres', whether separably incorporated or not. This practice had been adopted by the BTC for the activities which had been transferred to the THC, and the THC had continued the arrangements with obvious, although not spectacular, results. It was clearly an advantage over the unmanageable mass of BR, and the Government was very impressed with the possibilities in this direction.[13] Apart from British Transport Hotels Ltd,[14] and British Rail Hovercraft Ltd, there were no important operating subsidiaries. Although the shipping services had recently been organised into one division, it was not yet operating in an 'arms-length' relationship with the BR rail activities. Substantial businesses such as property letting and development, the Sundries division, the railway workshops and Freightliners were divisions in name only, separable profit and loss accounts were not produced. The latter pair, which operated in the fields most directly competitive with the private sector road haulage industry and the THC subsidiary, British Road Services, Ltd, were the greatest bones of contention with BR's competitors and enemies (which are rarely coterminious).

Freightliners' glowing future had been heralded in the Beeching Report,[15] but that initial prospectus had attracted widespread criticism.[16] In their early years there had been widespread surprise in the road haulage business at the low prices charged for Freightliner movements,[17] and it was therefore alleged that BR was squandering public money on a new loss-making activity. As long as Freightliner costs were mixed up with all other BR costs there was no way of satisfying its critics on this point. But there was more at stake than just obtaining a set of accurate accounts. The way in which the Freightliner concept was being 'sold' to the Ministry of Transport gave rise to serious qualms about its commercial future under direct BR management.

In many of the Joint Steering Group discussions the apparently bleak future of BR's wagon-load freight services was brushed aside by the senior BR representative as being of no consequence. He foresaw the day, in the not too distant future, when BR would operate only 'company' (ie, full train-load for one customer) and Freightliner trains.[18] Now it was clear that, in some narrow technical senses, Freightliners were more 'efficient' than conventional wagon load services.[19] But whether they were sufficiently 'efficient' to attract a large volume of traffic from road haulage was far from clear. At the Freightliner prices quoted in 1967, and with only scanty knowledge of BR's costs, it was clear to any outsider that Freightliners were not operating profitably, and this suspicion was reinforced by BR's reluctance to provide detailed information on the question. It was argued that, so far, only 'stage 1' of the Freightliner Network was in operation, and that the extension of routes and services to 'stage 2' was necessary before conclusions could be reached on the profitability of the concept. But some of the evidence offered in support of the investment necessary for 'stage 2' only raised further doubts[20] that Freightliners could ever attract BR postulated volumes of traffic at profitable prices.

The Government had just seen BR sink many millions into the wagon-load freight business since 1955, only to be told now that the Board intended getting out of the business because it could not be made profitable. It was naturally chary about bank-rolling a new technique which, to attract the share of the market being proposed, would have to offer such a high and costly standard of service that it would inevitably lose money. For the Freightliner concept is not a cheap solution to the problem of moving freight. On the shorter routes, and through low volume terminals, it is an inflexible high cost operation which can survive in competition with road haulage only by offering a commensurately high quality of service. With all the then current allegations of under-pricing, and with the careless statements about the future volumes of traffic which Freight-liners would attract,[21] the only way to isolate the operation from cross-subsidy by BR was to shift the major part of it into a separate company, Freightliners Ltd, to be majority-controlled by the NFC. BR was to provide the line-haul, but would be only a minority shareholder in the more risky terminal and collection and delivery activity. This division of activity was in line with the general BR aim to withdraw from 'retailing' activities, and to concentrate in fields where the size of the offered units of traffic more closely matched the optimum capabilities of the rail technology, ie, the train-load, not the wagon-load.

This decision met great opposition from BR, largely on the grounds that the marketing of its most promising development was being placed in the hands of its major road competitor. The NFC, of course, did not see the transfer in quite the same light. It saw itself taking responsibility for 51% of the losses of a so-far-unproven operation, which would be totally dependent upon the good graces of the minority shareholder. In theory, BR could have raised its charges for the line-haul enough to suck any potential profit out of Freightliners Ltd. To guard against this sort of thing, a Government-sponsored committee[22] spent a great deal of time working out transfer-pricing rules which, in the event, have not been needed. (Looking ahead of the narrative for a moment, the Freightliner company has served both owners well.[23] Some railway managers claim that it would have done much more business under full BR ownership, but these claims are usually based on the original, unrealistic traffic estimates, and take no account of the profitability question. It is just not credible that the Freightliners Ltd management would pass up *profitable* traffic growth, nor would the NFC.)[24]

The Sundries Division was a problem of a different order, having a volume about seven times greater than Freightliners. Only recently organised as a 'division', under one of the most vigorous BR managers, the Sundries Division was the inheritor of all that was worst in a transport operation. Overmanned (vans still carried drivers' mates, originally boys, but since World War II, women, presumably to hold the reins of the long deposed horses), and underpriced (because of the traditional belief that any price was better than no price), it was the poor relation in the BR organisation. Thought to have been losing £21 million on revenue of £38 million in 1961,[25] by 1967 it was claimed to be losing £26 million on a greatly reduced revenue of £22 million. The establishment of the quasi-separate Sundries Division had come too late to save it under direct BR ownership and management. BR had done far too little about the losses. The Beeching Report had claimed a potential improvement of £20 million per annum, but instead, traffic had been lost far faster than costs had been reduced. The formation of the Sundries Division had been a necessary preliminary to any attempt to rationalise its activities with those of BRS (Parcels) Ltd, its main competitor. In the long run,[26] a merging of the two organisations was an obvious solution, but equally obvious was the fact that this was more likely to be carried out satisfactory in the hands of the NFC than with BR, which had performed so poorly in this field. For BR ever to have imagined that the Government would, in these circumstances, have given it control of any of the BRS companies was ludicrous. Incidentally, the claimed Sundries 'loss' of £25 million in 1966 was to cost BR something in the recapitalisation.

In its first two years under NFC control, National Carriers Ltd (as it was renamed) was able to negotiate many lower rail rates for its line-haul activities. This suggested that the old Sundries Division of BR was being 'overcharged' for the same services, thus overstating its loss, but understating the true loss on the wagon load business. As the recapitalisation was based on the latter, this error will have a lasting effect on BR.[27]

So much for the creation of subsidiaries, in which the Government placed so much hope.[28] (I have ignored the creation of British Rail Engineering Ltd out of the BR workshops organisation. With the bulk of its activity priced on a cost-plus basis to its owner, BR, it must be clear that separate incorporation has little meaning in this case.) Before turning back to consider the other direct effects of the new Act on BR, we should consider briefly some indirect effects of changes in the road haulage industry. In 1965, the Geddes committee had recommended abolition of the 'economic' regulation of road haulage,[29] but the Conservative Government of the day had failed to enact this return to *laissez faire*. Now a Labour Government intended replacing the old *quantity* licencing[30] with *quality* licencing, aimed to reform the haulage industry's practices on vehicle maintenance, observance of drivers' hours, etc. After 35 years of economic regulation of road haulage, it was difficult to identify any beneficiaries of the system, with the key exception of some established hauliers.[31] It had certainly not protected the railways.

Even if that had at some time been a valid objective of the policy, the widespread growth of 'own-account' operations meant that BR derived little benefit from the 'protection'. Of course, BR always acted as if the protection of The Road Traffic Act of 1930 and its successors was important. Hardly an issue of *Motor Transport* passed without reporting a BR objection before a Licensing Authority, to the effect that a licence application should be denied because the railways could handle the traffic.[32] But with the own-account loophole, restriction of the number of lorries licensed for commercial hauliers could not prevent the railways losing traffic. More important for BR, but not really tackled until the 1968 Act, was the competitive advantage the hauliers derived from the much looser control over the conditions of work in their industry. Tightening up on these standards, and their observance, would have an immediate effect on hauliers' costs, and therefore on the prices they charged. These, in turn, would affect the prices which the railways could charge, and were therefore of far more importance to BR than the ineffective restrictions on entry to the haulage industry.

It was, of course, the Labour Government's intention to retain quantity licensing for 'rail-competitive' hauls of greater than one hundred miles in heavy lorries. But the protection offered was illusory; instead of driving the proverbial coach and four through the regulations, it was going to be possible to drive a 16-ton lorry through them instead.[33] (In the event, the following Government did not gazette the necessary regulations for the quantity licensing, and from the end of 1970 Britain became the first European country to allow a completely free market in inland freight transport.)

Taking account of all the other changes affecting BR, it was necessary to determine the Board's likely future earnings to find how much capital debit on which it could be expected to pay interest. That is what any recapitalisation (or capital reconstruction, as the Americans call the procedure which has befallen most railroad companies over there) is still about. A railway (or any other company, for that matter) finds itself unable to meet its interest commitments, and selling up assets would not raise enough to wipe off the capital and other debts. So the only feasible solution is to adjust its interest commitments to a level which the railway can afford to pay, and this is done either by cancelling some of the capital debt, or by altering the owners' entitlement to regular interest payments. (An example of the latter step in similar circumstances is the conversion of fixed-interest debt into equity capital, on which interest, in the form of dividends, need be paid only when the Company can afford it. The suspension of £705 million of BR's capital debt, under the provisions of the

Transport Act of 1962, was an example of this.) On the British Railways Board's own estimate of its likely financial performance from 1968 to 1974, the Government decided that, in addition to its liabilities to others, the Board could in future afford to pay interest on only £365 million of its debts to the Minister of £1,627 million. That is, £1,252 million which had been invested in BR by the Minister (either as the initial price paid to the shareholders, or as subsequent loans), had been lost. Certainly, many of the assets which had been bought with this sum were still around and in use. But as they could not earn the interest on the debts they represented, to the lender of the money they were worthless.

Once the Government had decided the amount of capital debt to be written down, it was up to the BR accountants to decide the pattern of adjustment to the asset values in the Board's books. For that is what a capital write-down means: that the assets are no longer worth (in earning power, or scrap value) the amounts at which they stand in the books. Thus, for future years, in addition to the reduction in the annual interest bill (£27 million lower after the Act), the provisios for depreciation and amortisation which had to be set aside in each future year were reduced by £24 million per annum. We can now summarise the financial effects on BR of the Transport Act of 1968:

	£ million
Interest bill reduced by	27
Provisions for depreciation and amortisation on reduced book values, reduced by	24
Pension obligations assumed by Government	6
Sundries Division and Freightliner loss transferred to NFC	25
Social passenger service loss, now met by grants	58
Surplus capacity grant	15
	£155

It was no coincidence that this was near to the railway deficit in 1968 of £147 million; the aim of the Act was to eliminate the deficit. But eliminating the deficit did not ease BR's long-term difficulties with what remained of its commercial services; all it had done was to change the scale on the financial 'thermometer' by which the Board's performance was judged. On January 1st, 1969, BR's commercial customers were not paying a penny more for the services they used than they had paid the previous day, before the recapitalisation. And in terms of resources consumed, there had been no change either. The change was confined to the financial accounts; to the future profit and loss accounts and balance sheets. Few senior BR managers realised that in January 1969 they were still running the same commercial railway they had been running the previous month,[34] and that if they tried to continue doing so for too long, they would end up with the same deficit on commercial operations that had just been eliminated by the 1968 Act. For the way the Board had applied the capital write-down to its book values of assets implied that, apart from operational land, less then £600 million worth of the 'renewable' assets could actually justify renewal when the time came. Compare this with about £1,000 million actually invested in commercial services between 1955 and 1968, not including those on London and other grant-aided services, and the chasm between what existed, and what could be justified for replacement, is disturbingly obvious. The only way in which the Board could justify the replacement of a greater proportion of its renewable assets, ie, to maintain a greater proportion of the services it then offered, was so to improve the efficiency of their use that future profits would both justify and pay for the extra replacements. In the absence of higher profits justifying the extra replacements, to borrow the money to do so would, in any normal circumstances, be financial suicide.

1 See *First Report from the Select Committee on Nationalised Industries: Ministerial Control of the Nationalised Industries.* London, HMSO, 1968, Vol.II, Minutes of Evidence, Q.562, (Evidence of Sir Stanley Raymond.)
2 Speech by Sir Stanley Raymond at the Annual Conference, Transport Salaried Staffs' Association, Hastings, May 17, 1967.
3 Albeit with gold-braided footmen in the railway tradition.
4 See, for example, *Transport Holding Company Annual Report & Accounts* each year.
5 See, eg, George Polanyi: *Contrasts in Nationalised Transport since 1947,* London, (Institute of Economic Affairs, 1968).
6 See 'Transport and Common Sense', *Institute of Transport Journal,* Vol.31, 1969. The address printed differs considerably from the address actually given.
7 *Op cit*
8 Through inter-company loans, the cash float generated by Cooks' travellers cheque business supported other THC subsidiaries, too.
9 It is of interest that for nearly two years Sir Reginald filled both positions.
10 Bought by the Transport Holding Company in 1968 for between £450,000 and £1m only days before the collapse of the parent company (British Eagle) would have forced its sale at a much lower figure, Lunn Poly managed to lose £500,000pa in successive years under THC management, and was finally sold for £300,000. The business was described by the new chairman of the THC, Mr Lewis Whyte, as a 'disastrous investment' (see *The Times,* 4 June 1971).
11 See *Transport Holding Company: Annual Report and Accounts,* 1967 and 1968. A noteworthy change in these ratios was in 'capital expenditure per man'; for years the BET companies had been operating with a bus-life policy five years longer than that of the THC subsidiaries. On amalgamation, this was found to be the better policy and has since been adopted by the THC's successor, the National Bus Company.
12 'A Study of the Profits of Bus Companies, 1960-1966' *Economica,* May 1969.
13 For the clearest statement of this, see the speech of Neil Carmichael, MP, Joint Parliamentary Private Secretary to the Minister of Transport, to the 'Management of Transport Workers Conference', June 25, 1968.
14 Which had been incorporated at the time of the 1962 Act, but had been found impractical to transfer to the THC due to complications relating to the hotel buildings in many cases sharing the structures of stations.
15 *Op cit,* see Appendix
16 See, eg, A.J.Harrison: 'Investment in Liner Trains', *Bulletin of the Oxford University Institute of Economics and Statistics,* Vol.26, No.3, August 1964, pp.205 - 2-2.
17 The initial rates were set to be competitive with road hauliers' back-haul rates. This could have been taken (and mostly was) by road hauliers as an attempt to drive them out of business. In fact, it was no more than an attempt to relieve the road operators of only the line haul, concentrating them on the collection and delivery part of the haul on which rail could not compete. But BT had not counted on the union opposition to 'open terminals', to which hauliers could bring containers. The cartage division of the National Union of Railwaymen claimed that work for themselves. On top of that, BR's collection and delivery charges implied an unattainable efficiency of operation.

18 These statements were to fix Government attitude to the 'wagon-load' freight business for years to come.

19 This applied particularly to the utilisation of rolling stock and locomotives, the maximisation of which had been an exclusive goal of railway managers for many years.

20 For example, one diagram purporting to show the 'trend of Freightliner carryings' showed the *cumulative* total of containers moved over time, thus shooting off the diagram in the top right hand corner.

21 In 1965, BR had claimed *potential* Freightliner carrying of 26 million tons, even with no industrial growth, but by the end of 1969, the actual volume was only 4 million tons.

22 See C.D.Foster: *Politics, finance and the role of economics*, London, 1971, p.22.

23 For a general discussion of its economics, see B.T.Warner & Stewart Joy: 'The economics of rail container operation in Britain', *Rail International*, April, 1971.

24 One hope of the framers of the 1968 Act was that, under NFC ownership, Freightliners Ltd would make those optimal modal choice decisions, so beloved of proponents of transport co-ordination. The idea was that Freightliners would give unsuitable traffic to BRS and *vice versa*. In discussions for the paper on Freightliners which I wrote with B.T.Warner (*ibid*), I gathered the distinct impression that BRS had a closer operating relationship with BR's wagon-load service than with Freightliners. This was not necessarily a bad thing. The stronger is the competition *between* NFC subsidiaries, provided that they remain profitable, the stronger will be competition between the NFC (as a whole) and its private sector competitors.

25 Beeching Report, *op cit*, Table 1. (The comparison with Freightliner (above) is on the basis of Sundries: costs, Freightliner: revenue.)

26 In the event, it was to be a 'long-run' of considerable length. The first real progress in integrating the two operations did not occur until the third year of NFC ownership.

27 The apparent financial improvement achieved under NFC ownership was also greatly assisted by the profits it was to make on wagonload and parcels collection and delivery activities for BR, which had been separately counted up to 1968.

28 See, particularly, the speech by Neil Carmichael, MP, *op cit*.

29 *Carriers Licensing*, op cit.

30 Except for vehicles carrying more than 11 tons on hauls of over 100 miles. These provisions were not brought into effect.

31 A key argument for economic regulation was always to protect the revenues of established hauliers, to avoid a temptation to skimp on maintenance and other safe operating practices. But profit maximisation appears more important than satisfying the regulators. For evidence of this trait in an even more closely regulated system — the USA — see Robert Fellmuth: *The Interstate Commerce Omission*, New York, 1970, Chap.6.

32 BR's objections under the old legislation to licence applications for large lorry loads were so widespread that a leading maker of diesel engines for heavy lorries believed that the railways had the most comprehensive statics on the potential demand for new lorries.

33 Provided a shipper was prepared to accept the cost penalty of the less efficient lorry, it was possible to avoid the remaining quantity licensing provisions. But the fact that road was in other respects so favourable that the coal penalty could be suffered, would have been strong *prime face* evidence in support of an application for a heavy vehicle licence to handle the traffic at lower cost.

34 Excepting, of course, the activities transferred to the NFC.

13 | What Went Wrong?

'Inland transport is much discussed, but the progress made is not in proportion.'

Sir Reginald Wilson (in a 40 page paper presented to an Institute of Transport Congress) 'The Framework of Public Transport', Journal of the Institute of Transport, July 1953

The main blame for the mismanagement of British Rail in its first 20 years must be shared between the British Transport Commission and successive governments, with by far the greater share resting on the former. The massive staff economies made during the Beeching era proved that the BTC had been running a very inefficient railway. Even without the excessive and obsolescent investments of the modernisation plan, the inefficiency of British Rail under the BTC would have brought about the same financial collapse. Just 50,000 too many workers (and there were many more than this) employed in each year from 1948 to 1957 would have cost about £200 million. That this inefficiency was allowed to persist for so long was an obvious cost of nationalisation, which relieved management of the pressures which would have existed if they had not had the Exchequer there to meet their debts.

But where individuals might be singled out for particular criticism, it is important to remember that they were only exploiting opportunities created by the inertia of those above them. Possibly, they might have been expected to know better. Perhaps some of them *did* know better, but were prepared, cynically, to accept the rewards of high office in the BTC and the railways in return for the unpalatable task of tricking the government on a mammoth scale. Those men were either fools or knaves: at this stage it does not matter much which tag we apply.

The rail users, of course, were happy to sit idly by while all this was going on. Their objective, to have lots of train service, coincided with that of the trade unions, the management, and the political sense of the government. It was the financial sense of government which was, seemingly unbeknown to anybody, being violated. More and better railways were what everybody in the country was expecting. The British people had never admitted that the invention of the motor car and truck changed the railways from exploiters to exploited. By the time the nation achieved the ability to bleed the railways white, the red corpuscles had already been killed by the speed and convenience of the internal combustion engine. Then nationalisation reversed the tubes, as it were, and the BTC was able to give itself a transfusion at the nation's expense, while declining to do anything about its basic disease — inefficiency. But the nation could only exploit the railways because of the failure of the railway managements of the Thirties, Forties and Fifties to understand their predicament. They too, failed to realise that the car and the truck meant the end of the first railway age. They constantly hankered for a return to those glorious (?) years when railways had only to compete with each other. There were great attractions in a return to the quiet life of total regulation; as we have seen, Sir Reginald Wilson was still wanting to put this particular clock back as late as 1959. The railway managers, offering an eldorado of cross-subsidisation in return for stiff regulation of the road hauliers, failed to see that the nation wanted all of the benefits and none of the costs. It took what the railways offered, and gave none of what they claimed in return. It did this in the Thirties, when the Road Traffic Act limited, but failed to extinguish, the threat of the professional road haulier. It did it again in the late Forties, when the Transport Act of 1948 imposed on the British Transport Commission all of the obligations its railway predecessors in the Thirties had offered to assume in return for the end of competition from the hauliers, whilst leaving intact the 'own account' hauliers.

Of course, Governments could accept such one-sided 'deals' as long as the railways retained some residual monopoly powers to exploit, or some share-holders' equity to consume. With nationalisation, the question of financial responsibilities was changed. Governments could now do what they wished with the railways, because they stood ready to pay the bills if the customers refused to. But the railway managements, both BTC and Railway Executive, believing their own myths of the Thirties that the power to co-ordinate the competing modes at last secured their future, took on an impossible task. Admittedly, they made it even harder by their leisurely pace, in both the speed with which they did things, and the yesteryear look of many of their acts. Possibly what appeared to outsiders as a leisurely pace was in fact the best the BTC could ever have achieved.

It is likely that co-ordination, as required by the 1948 Act, was impossible, and the BTC's lack of progress was just a blind for a refusal to admit defeat at a self-sought task. Possibly the unimaginative technical and operating developments were the best which could be achieved by managers whose development had been in a precarious day-to-day existence in depression and war. Possibly the monolithic railway organisation *was* unmanageable by the BTC. If so, by concealing these inadequacies from the public and Parliament, the BTC did themselves and their successors a disservice. The Nation had been led to believe that nationalisation would solve more problems than it created. Hiding the new problems only delayed their solution.

We can now see that nationalisation created more problems than it solved. More than ten years were to pass before significant economies were achieved from the unified system, and most of the other claimed benefits of the BTC were never achieved. But nobody could have been convinced of this at the time. Who could have predicted that the first five years would be consumed by an unproductive squabble between the BTC and the Railway Executive? Even those who opposed nationalisation did so for reasons which, in the event, proved unimportant. Hardly anybody saw that the primary reason for nationalisation, the 'co-ordination' preached by the railway managers (and just about everybody else in the transport industry), would not work. For had not the railway managers and the *established* road interests always wanted it? Had they not offered to run true 'public services' if only they could be freed of competitive pressures? Everyone was supposed to benefit by taking the railways and commercial road haulage into public ownership. The unions and the Labour Party were sure that getting rid of the shareholders would create a new era.

So when nationalisation had sent those greedy shareholders packing, with their money or their two percent British Transport Stock, the public sat back and waited for this supposed transport utopia to restore the quality and scope of service it had last enjoyed in 1939. The managers, or at least some of them, had got what they wanted. The unions had got what they wanted.

Now it was the public's turn. They never saw the basic inconsistency between 'co-ordination' and 'public service' for those whose range of choice is to be 'co-ordinated'. Few who rode the 'pirate' buses in the Twenties thought that they were better off when London Transport 'co-ordinated' them out of existence in 1933. Of course, those using the new routes, which LT was able to cross-subsidise out of its profits from the elimination of competition, did not mourn the passing of the 'pirates'. But for there to be gainers from transport co-ordination there must also be losers. Co-ordination can only mean the restriction of choice to reduce costs; 'public service' implies the widest possible choice.

For the BTC, and ultimately for the Nation, the difficulty arose because the increasing availability of competitive substitutes meant there could be no 'losers', from whom to mulct the monopoly profits to subsidise the 'gainers'. Yet the BTC set out to create and retain 'gainers' as if it had the necessary revenues. In a sense it did have the revenues, in the guise of an indulgent government.

The Beeching 'efficiency' type economies which, despite the uproar over the passenger service withdrawals, constituted the bulk of the savings of the Sixties, could have been achieved at any time since 1948. But the BTC was allowed to take its time; as long as it could meet some undefined 'public service' objective without making an overall loss, the Government was happy. And even when it increasingly could not satisfy this condition, the Government first lent the money, and later gave it as deficit grants. As fast as the would-be 'losers' from the now-forgotten co-ordination deserted to the roads in their cars and trucks, the Government made up the BTC's losses and lent it money for capital works so that it could provide for the traffics it still had *and for all of those it had lost*. But most of the disaffected losers refused to become gainers from the railway modernisation plan bonanza.

No one can deny that the BTC tried to give the public what it wanted. It was still trying to do so when the Select Committee read it some home truths in 1959. But 'co-ordination', which was to provide the profits which would in turn provide the public service, had failed very early. With the change of government in 1951, Ministers were quick to see this. Some senior managers in the BTC never saw that the impossibility of co-ordination meant the impossibility of the 'public service' dream.

Until the railway modernisation plan, the railways and the government were just feeling their respective ways. Not as efficiently as possible, to be sure, but that was not the aspect which interested public or Parliament anyway. The elimination of complaints about the railways was *their* mutual objective. For the public, that would have meant the railways were spending their revenues in ways which kept the complainers quiet; for the Government it would have meant the suppression of a potential embarrassment.

Had it been possible to ask the public or MP's, collectively or individually, whether they thought the modernisation plan was 'a good thing', there would have been unanimous approval. Even if the BTC's hopeless arithmetic had not blinded supposed experts to the plan's flaws the public and its elected representatives would have remained convinced that the BTC's prospectus of improvements would be giving the country the railway system it 'needed'. Quite naturally, in the public mind, 'more' is better, whether it applies to hospitals, schools, policemen or railway services. But what distinguished the railways in this group was that it was possible to state, unambiguously, how much was 'best'. For the railways had substitutes, and users and governments could make choices. Users exercised this choice, and during the Fifties they left the railway in droves. The Government's 'choice' was not really exercised until Dr Beeching confronted it in 1963; it simply provided the money for the BTC to make decisions on its behalf, mostly bad ones as it turned out.

The results of the exercise of such an implicit delegation of power could only have begun to match the intentions of the Government if the railways' objectives had matched those of the Government. Here we see how easy it was for the Government to hide behind the vague statements of the BTC's duties in the 1948 and 1953 Acts. And how irresponsible it was for not acting, when it became clear during the Fifties that the BTC was one Act behind in the objectives it was following. The position was confused by the 'implicit under-standings' which passed for objectives in the minds of the BTC Members. They knew that the Government had been wrong in lumbering the BTC with the massive capital debt at nationalisation, and they knew that it had repeatedly been wrong since then, when price increases had been rejected and delayed. Furthermore, there were crucial elements in the BTC who still thought that 'co-ordination' remained the answer, and that in permitting competition with the railways the Government was unjustifiably harming them. Of these issues, only the capital structure issue had substance. The 'pricing interference' question was, with the exception of London commuters, of little importance. When all other prices are rising, delaying a railway price increase effectively reduces the real price of rail services. But such effective price reductions did not increase traffic to any measurable extent, so we may infer that it was largely the exploitation of the railways' few remaining monopolies which was being restricted. On the remaining yearning for 'co-ordination', the BTC had no case at all. If nothing useful could be done between 1948 and 1951, when the BTC had nearly all the powers its railway predecessors had longed for, it was vacuous to expect the country to put up with a further period of experimentation at its expense. In any case, the Government had set its mind firmly against such a course, and accordingly had made appropriate alterations to the BTC's formal duties under the 1953 Act.

But the BTC was in a mood for thinking that (i) the Government owed it something, and (ii) it knew, better than any government, what its objectives should be. The attractions of its services to users were clearly not all that they could have been, and the BTC mistakenly attributed this more to the low standard of its own services than to the increasingly higher standards of its competitors. To be sure, its service in crucial areas was worse than it need have been; the steam locomotive enthusiasts had seen to that. But the BTC saw the building of its pigeon-holed projects as a panacea for all of its ills. It was encouraged in this by the Government's newfound willingness to lend for investment, after years of capital rationing. But much of what it built was either for traffics it no longer had, or for traffics it should not have been trying to retain. Add to this the wasted construction to obsolescent designs, and Britain had the makings of the most wasteful civil public investment programme until the Concorde, ten years later.

Regardless of the financial consequences, the BTC had an inherent bias toward more and newer assets. The reasons for this range from the wildly romantic to the severely practical. Just like officers in the armed forces, railway managers are intensely interested in the 'hardware' which they operate, and they derive great satisfaction from having the latest models. The old railway companies used to place great emphasis on their latest locomotives, and this tradition is not yet dead. At the practical level, the men operating the railway naturally preferred new equipment, with its implicit reliability and low maintenance costs. As there was no absolute profitability analysis of investment decisions, the bag of gold of the modernisation plan was open for grabs on all sorts of non-financial criteria. The BTC assumed that virtually all the existing railway services would be provided for an indefinite period, and that if users would not pay their full cost, taxpayers would be forced to. Any obligation to cover costs with revenues was ignored.

Where were all the checks and balances to prevent this? The whole idea of the public corporation as a form of government-owned activity was that the need to maintain the commercial accounts in balance would provide a spur to management efficiency. But the BTC, led first by an ex-permanent secretary of the Ministry of Transport and then by a General, never embraced this fundamental requirement of a commercial organisation.

The BTC's first defence for this apparent defiance of the Government's intentions was that its interpretation of 'taking one year with another' was fairly elastic — the modernisation plan of 1955 offered a return to a break-even (but not a repayment of the losses in the interim) by 1961 or 1962. And six or seven years in the life of a railway is not a long period, provided that the trends are favourable. For the BTC they were totally unfavourable, but nobody seemed to know or care. Certainly the Government was happy to carry on underwriting the BTC's mismanagement and misplaced optimism. For the rebuilding and the persistence with unprofitable services which the BTC had set its heart upon were precisely the things which ministers, civil servants and laymen would have expected from a capable and optimistic management. Unfortunately, there was too little capability and too much optimism, and the latter is a disastrous substitute for the former.

But what if the BTC had been the very model of a modern public corporation? What if, in 1955, it had announced to the Nation that, in the light of the Government's aim to have a competitive solution to the transport problem, it could only afford to invest in main line passenger services and bulk freight traffics? It is hardly credible that Englishmen, whose first big toy had always been a Hornby train on the parlour floor, would have believed such a dark prognosis, however true. The BTC and its railway managers were not the only once to believe in the inevitability of railways, but they happened to be the supposed experts in such matters. Would the Nation have listened? Would the Government have immediately legislated for subsidies for socially necessary services? Or would it have looked for a new BTC, in the same way that it looked for Dr Beeching to resolve an impossibility a few years later? The members of the BTC were not faced with this risk to their careers, because they, too, had failed to see that the breach in the 'inevitability' dogma, started by the car, the bus and the motor truck in the 1920s, had now become a deluge. They could not see that spiralling deficits meant fewer people wished to use the railways, but the BTC had declined to reduce its capacity (and costs) in consequence.

If the BTC were blind to this, can we blame ministers and their advisers for accepting the excuses and optimism, and continuing to find the money? For had not the members of the BTC been chosen by those same ministers and their advisers, as being the men best fitted for the job? Until 1958 or 1959, the Government acted, in defiance of the bleak evidence of the BTC's Annual Accounts, in the hope that somehow the BTC would pull it off. Until that hope evaporated, there was no call to look closely at just what the BTC was doing, providing loss-making passenger and freight services all over the country in defiance of its duty, under the Act, to break even. Or to look at the efficiency with which the Commission carried on its other railway activities. For until that time, both Government and BTC had the same ultimate objective: to provide as much railway service as possible, even though each had different reasons for ignoring the bit about breaking even.

For the BTC to have taken its break-even objective seriously, ie, in any way other than the vain hopes of jam tomorrow, would have required managerial skills which were just not there. The evidence of some of its members to the Select Committee in 1959 shows that, even after the gross error of their ways had been pointed out to them, they still did not understand. (The fact that some of them survived in nationalised transport industries for up to another ten years shows that those responsible for such appointments did not understand, either.) And if the top management had no understanding of the basic problems, the middle management had no capacity for carrying out the necessary cures. It took a Beeching to force those through.

If the BTC was incapable and unwilling to spill the necessary blood within the railway, the Government was no more willing to face realities in the country at large. This unwillingness to do what is right, when it might show that many previous acts must have been wrong, was a fairly natural reaction. Railway services which should have been reformed, repriced or closed from 1948 onwards, were still operating in pre-nationalisation form in 1960, and all the intervening governments had been spared the nuisance and embarrassment which would have ensued if the BTC had vigorously followed its formal instructions. Nobody had wanted the BTC to succeed more on its chosen course than the governments which had pumped in the money. But when it failed, it was a case of 'sack the Chairman, reorganise the industry, and all will be well.' The government ignored the warning signs as the BTC collapsed, and it ignored the need for *total* reform, of its own approach to the problem as well as that of the railways, if the BTC's successor was to succeed. To extend the simile of Chapter Four, in 1962 the Government invited the new British Railways Board to find its own way to the door, necessarily stepping on the wet paint left on the floor by the BTC. Had the Government attempted to clear up the mess before putting in the new management, it would have been necessary to admit responsibility for supplying the excessive quantity of paint.

So Dr Beeching accepted an impossible remit, and the Government was able suddenly to assume the role of protector of the public interest against the rapacious railway managers who were trying to close all the railway lines people loved but did not use. Now the Government's and the Board's objectives were both formally and practically in conflict. For the break-even objective is quite inconsistent with the attempted cross-subsidisation of social passenger services, as there are no monopolies left from which to gain support for the other services. Except for the fundamental error of the Board's in accepting the impossible remit, the 'blame' for the period 1962-1968 rests squarely on the Government, and all the praise is due to the Board for achieving in six years what the BTC had failed to do in 14.

But was the Government under any real pressure to act differently? The way in which the BTC incurred self-inflicted wounds right through the Fifties, and the way in which Beeching accepted the impossible task for the Sixties, put no pressure on successive Governments to act more responsibly toward BR. Instead, they had an incentive to leave the railways in an impossible situation which was largely of their own making. It can be argued that individuals (and whole organisations) will try harder if faced with extremely difficult goals. Governments were prepared to see the railway chug uphill with difficulty, hoping that at least they were performing more useful work than if they had been permitted to chug easily downhill. Of course, it can also be argued (but not proved) that the amount of rail service provided under this arrangement was, possibly by accident, the optimal amount, and that with the best possible relationship between governments and BR the net result would have been the same. Such an argument ignores the BTC's poor efficiency record. And it is a little hard to imagine that had governments been more decisive and realistic in their management of the railways, the results would not have been much better.

In the event, the Government, the Nation, and ultimately the railways, got the worst of all worlds. The ways in which the Government did influence BR between 1948 and 1968 only left the railway management with a sense of outrage and a determination that they knew what was best for the country. Then, when the railways' view of what was 'best' for the country directly contravened the Government's formal wishes (but not those of the remaining rail users), the Government strung along with the railway managers' optimism.

We do not need to reach new conclusions here, only to summarise the arguments which have been documented in the previous chapters. We can answer much of our chapter-title question: 'What went wrong?' by simply stating: 'All the things which the Joint Steering Group recommendations put right.' But things happened in the years 1948-1968 which have cost the nation, and the railways, and future rail users, very dear. In our final chapter we will look at some of these, and at the possibility of their recurrence.

14 | Has the Runaway Train Been Halted?

'All the legislation we are carrying through at the moment is concerned to enable each particular form of transport to play its part in the total mix as effectively as possible.'

Richard Marsh, Minister of Transport, London 23 April 1968

The writing of business history is not an end in itself. Looking backward is useful only for the clarification it can offer to the much more important process of looking forward. So the questions to be asked are: can the first 20 years' sorry story be repeated, and if so, will they? Will the government allow BR to paint itself into more corners? Or should it enlarge the room, by finding a social case for some hitherto commercial services?

The 1968 Act was adamant on this point: with the exception of the long overdue grants for social passenger services, BR was to provide only those services for which the customers were prepared to pay the full cost. The need for the massive write-off of capital showed that, up to 1968, many railway customers were paying far less than the full cost of their service. Because the prices those customers were paying BR were set competitively (ie, had they been higher, the traffics would have gone by some other mode) BR was faced with two alternatives. Either it had to increase efficiency, so that the hitherto uncovered 'full cost' would come down, or it had to abandon the traffics gradually. This was not as bad as it may sound; provided steady progress was made, there need have been no violent hurry to turn traffics away.

The reason for this temporary, but reducing, breathing space was that although the capital write-down indicated an inability to repay the principal and interest on any assets, particularly freight rolling stock, it left those assets for free use by BR until they wore out. Provided the revenues from traffics covered *all other costs,* it was profitable to retain them until the assets they were using required replacement. But the problem was not limited to the question of whether BR could afford to replace the assets which had been written down. It was more concerned with whether losses on out-of-pocket operating costs would use up vital cash generated elsewhere, and thus prevent the replacement of fully profitable assets.

The recapitalisation and the belated subsidy arrangements could only provide a temporary respite for BR. Unless the underlying malaise of unprofitable 'commercial' services was to be tackled, the deficits would recur, even if, initially, on a much smaller scale than those of the Sixties. It was clearly the intention of the Government that the withdrawal of its power to pay deficit grants would provide a tight financial restraint on the Board's future activities. The Joint Steering Group report had stated the intention and given an appropriate warning:

'Nevertheless it is also recognised that recapitalisation is merely an accounting device to align the book value of British Railways' existing assets with their earnings and of itself does nothing to render British Railway more commercially viable in the future when assets will be replaced at the full cost of such assets at that time. The recapitalisation is, however, recommended in the expectation that it will help British Railways' management to solve the basic problem of *aligning the actual value of their future assets* with *future earnings,* that is, to ensure that the quantity and types of assets that are actually replaced in the future are only such as can be *supported by future earnings.* '[1]

This was the inescapable lesson of the recapitalisation at the end of 1968, that BR's traffic did not at that time justify commercially the volume and scope of service then being offered. It was considered by the Board and Government of the day that future prospects justified a total investment in renewable assets of only about £600 million. Assuming an average commercial life of 15 years, this meant an annual rate of re-investment of about £40 million. Because about £10-15 million per annum of that was bespoken for London and grant-aided services, the rate of annual investment in the rest of the railway which the Government considered could be justified in normal commercial terms was only about £25-30 million per annum. If more money was to be profitably invested in the 'commercial' services, their profits would have had to be improved substantially by increased efficiency and, more plausibly, the elimination of loss-making activities. As the Board wished to carry on immediately investing at a rate of more than double this, and to increase the amount in the early Seventies, there was a big gap which somehow had to be covered.

There were two other immediate possibilities: the sale of assets no longer required for use in the rail business, and profits from subsidiaries. In the *Railway Policy* White Paper in 1967 the Joint Steering Group and the Government had tacitly ignored the stock of non-operational assets, particularly property, which could be sold off to provide funds for additional railway investment. But it was its clear intention that any railway investment additional to the annual rate implied by the recapitalisation should be limited to what could be financed from asset sales and that which was justified and financed by profits.

In practice, net proceeds from the sale of assets and the profits from subsidiaries are to a large extent mutually exclusive. The subsidiaries themselves are heavy consumers of investment funds, and a decision to apply subsidiary profits and the proceeds of the sale of assets to the railway business would not go down well with their managements, who tend to see themselves as running independent businesses which should be left to develop by themselves and not be milked to support the further rebuilding of the railway. On the other hand, it is unlikely that any government would accept the development of the subsidiaries at the expense of railway operations. And for the property business in particular, the spectre of the Penn-Central collapse lends weight to the argument that funds should not be diverted to long-gestation property projects when the basic aim of the organisation is to run trains profitably. None of the Board's non-rail subsidiaries have ever produced outstanding profits relative to the amounts invested in them, although some improvement might be possible.

So the railway business must generate most of the resources necessary to replace its assets. Its ultimate size as a commercial undertaking will depend on its own efforts, just as it does with every other company supplying competitive products or services. A lot of confusion still exists over the conflict between what BR is trying to do, and what its financial results say it can *profitably* do. The Joint Steering Group said, in effect, 'improve profits, by increased efficiency or eliminating loss-making activities, or else the Board cannot sustain present levels of investment.' Increased efficiency is not very promising here, because all improvements from that source have in the past been immediately absorbed (and more) by 'real' wage increases. These are increases in railway workers' wages over and above the rate of general price increases (and railway price increases) — the way in which railwaymen's standard of living is increased.

To maintain British Rail's railway operations at about their present size would require annual investments of well over £100 million per year. This is even without replacing the obsolescent freight rolling stock and renewing freight locomotives, which will be necessary if the wagonload freight system is to survive into the Eighties. On present indications, around one-fifth of the railway investments planned will attract government grants of various kinds, particularly Infrastructure Grants for conurbation public transport improvements and replacements. So the remaining four-fifths (around £90 million per annum) must be financed by (i) depreciation provisions, (ii) sales of assets, (iii) profits from subsidiaries, (iv) railway profits, and (v) new borrowing.

Depreciation provisions[2], on the reduced asset values following recapitalisation, amount to only about £40 million per annum. They represent cash available for reinvestment in the business *only if profits are earned.* If a loss is incurred, it means that revenues have failed to cover costs, including depreciation. The gap to be covered is about £50 million per year.

Sales of assets produced about £18 million in each of 1969 and 1970, well down from the peak £33.6 million of 1966. This is not an unhealthy sign, in that an over-eager seller is not likely to get the best prices, and a very high volume of sales does not necessarily represent the best disposal of the assets, particularly land and scrap. These do not deteriorate, and the Board can afford to take its time in selling them.[3] But there is not an unlimited supply of assets to sell, and it is unlikely that future sales will, on average, exceed the 1969-70 levels, in real terms. Profits from subsidiaries are not likely to help very much, for they have investment plans of their own and will aim to reinvest all of their profits in their own businesses.

To cover the gap by new borrowing[4] will only propel BR back into deficit again unless profits can be improved faster than the interest bill rises. The investments themselves will not have a striking effect on profits, as they are mainly required just to keep the present, barely profitable, operations at their present level. We have already seen that all the normal efficiency[5] improvements which can be obtained will be needed to meet railway workers' legitimate wage claims (this was the point which both the BTC and Beeching ignored). The recapitalisation deliberately and inevitably created a profits 'knife-edge' for the Board; its basic effect was simply to reduce the capital debit to a level on which the Board could just pay the interest bill. So with depreciation and asset sales providing something short of £60 million per annum, and profits from the subsidiaries or the railway (at its present scope of operation) being at best neutral, and more likely consuming cash to meet rail deficits, how can the gap be covered?

There are three ways of looking at this gap. The typical railway manager's view is that unfortunately cash generated within the business is insufficient to finance *necessary* investments. The typical finance man's view would be that the level of necessary and *profitable* investment for an industry which is at best static and probably still declining, will be no more (and probably less) than what can be financed internally. The man who has an emotional commitment to a large railway operation, without regard to profits[6], sees not enough funds. The man who accepts the avoidance of deficits as the basic aim sees too much investment. The third viewpoint is to say that neither the present level of cash generation nor the present planned investment level are sacrosanct, and to ask whether a smaller railway operation would both reduce investment requirements *and* have an improved ability to pay for them. This is implicitly the view taken by successive governments in recent years, or else they could not in conscience have approved any BR investment in excess of what could be financed internally. The Treasury's rules for the appraisal of investments in public corporations require that only *profitable* projects should be undertaken. As BR's planned investments are aimed only at keeping the present services running, how can all the individual projects be profitable, when to carry them out will require borrowing on such a scale as to make the whole business unprofitable?

The two possible answers to this question disclose the key to the whole railway problem in Britain. One possible answer, which I would support, is that there is, within the mass of BR, a moderately profitable railway waiting to be stripped of its constricting surround of loss-making activities. Those activities, which are unable to cover their cost let alone provide for the replacement of their assets, should be stripped off as quickly as possible. The long run health of BR demands that surplus cash be invested in the areas, like Inter-City passenger, train-load freight, and London commuters, which it is good at, and not dissipated in activities which have higher costs than rail's competitors. The social passenger services have a key role to play here. BR is automatically 'good' at them, because the government grants the difference between costs, calculated on a generous basis, and revenues. These services are then able to share staff and other assets with commercial services in a way which helps the profitable retention of the commercial services.

The other possible answer means that the Nation must take BR at roughly its present size or not at all. It is to the effect that any attempt to slim the railway further will cause revenue to fall faster than costs and thus increase deficits. This view, which is held by some senior BR accountants, is a damning indictment, either of their management colleagues' abilities or of their own management information systems. To assert that any attempt to get rid of activities which now cost far more than they earn will cause the loss of all their revenue but only a small part of the costs, is to say that the managers are incapable of reducing their costs proportionately with reductions in output. If that is true, British Rail must be unique among railways. The evidence from statistical cost studies of railways in other countries suggests that the long-run elasticity of rail costs to output is at least 0.85; that is, that a 10 percent reduction in output will be accompanied by a reduction in total cost of at least 8½ percent.[7] The reason for the difference between the proportionate reduction in output and the related cost reduction is to be found in the track cost 'indivisibility' — a certain low level of track cost is needed regardless of the level of output. But on most routes in Britain this particular cost is covered in full or in part by the social passenger service grants, so reductions in the outputs of other services should be accompanied by proportionate reductions in costs.[8]

In the USA, where the large number of railway systems makes such studies possible, there is evidence of diseconomies of scale with very large systems; ie, the bigger they are, the higher will be their unit-costs. This is for two reasons: bigger railways seem to be harder to manage than small ones, and, associated with this, bigger railways seem to find it much more difficult to use their clerical and managerial labour to the best effect. The result is that, unlike every other industry, big railway organisations need a disproportionately large administrative staff than small ones. This would be an argument for reducing the output of BR only if it is believed that the Board can drop pieces of its administrative tail in step with any rundown in railway activity. But since Beeching, general administration expenses have risen from 10.3 percent of railway working expenses (1963) to 15 percent.[9] This is disturbing; as the railway has been slimmed down, the administrative effort should have become proportionately less, not more.

Assertions to the effect that if BR were to lose traffic its deficit would inevitably rise are a disturbing indictment of its managers' ability to manage. They rest on a notion of the total rail system, Thurso to Penzance and Inter-City passengers to railway letter-carrying, being an inviolate whole. If they are true, the Nation must choose between all the railway and no railway. It would be faced with a threat of total collapse and unheard-of deficits if it tries to trim anywhere. Such a threat could not be taken seriously.

Nearer to the true position, maybe, is the possibility that the accountants are unable to identify the costs of particular activities, so that even if they knew the revenues they could not say whether they were profitable or not. That is, the managers can manage all right but the problem is in the data they are forced to use. Assertions that any attempted reduction would raise the deficit may be no more than a blind to hide the fact that the management information system, faced with an operation which is unprofitable overall and certainly not able to replace itself, cannot tell managers where to act. If true, this would be a sorry admission to have to make, 20 years after the establishment of a traffic costing service. There has been a lot of talk over the years about the difficulties in railway costing — the shared costs, joint products, etc. But it is really no harder than in a complex manufacturing industry, if Ford or the BSC can find the cost of each of their products, so can railways, and many other railway systems have developed reliable systems.

What is required is simply for BR, unlike the BTC, to have and to exercise the will to find an independent solution to its problems. This was the opportunity provided by the 1968 Act, but the Board has not so far availed itself of the offer, and is still acting as if the size of railway operation it thinks the country wants is the size which users failed to pay for up to 1968 and since. Certainly, stripping out the loss-making activities could mean a smaller railway, with less jobs, and nobody likes to be associated with a declining industry, least of all its managers. So it is both natural and correct for them to try to keep the railway as big as possible; that way they will keep more users happy and they will retain more jobs. But keeping the railway at anything like its present size will require government assistance in ways which will require a wholesale revision of British transport policy. BR cannot go on as a free-standing public corporation if it is allowed to cover the gap between the investments its users are prepared to pay for and the investments which will maintain its size, by incurring capital debts it has no hope of servicing or repaying. That would be no more than a cynical return to deficit grants, under another name, and in a way which avoids too much Parliamentary criticism until the next, inevitable, recapitalisation.

Right now, the BR services which have the brightest long term futures are in better condition, and offering higher quality of service than ever before in British railway history, or anywhere else in the world for that matter. But the funds they generate must be reinvested in them, and not frittered away meeting current operating losses elsewhere. Neither can the benefits the Nation derives from keeping the prosperous services be adduced as reasons for propping up the rest, unless the 'inviolate whole' theory is accepted. And if the government were to accept this, it would quickly find itself pouring money into a 'hole' of a different kind, called a bottomless pit.

Clearly, a large part of BR's operations additional to the social passenger services can survive only with overt government assistance. The 1968 Transport Act, the work of a Labour government of which the present Chairman of BR was a senior minister, clearly intended that such services should not survive. With the exception of the social passenger services outside the London commuter area,[11] BR was to be a wholly commercial operation. But in the three-and-a-half years since the passage of the Act, BR has not made any steps in that direction, indeed it has slipped back into deficit. So the present Government must either reaffirm or reject the policy of its predecessor before the Board will act. In the meantime, it is hedging its bets by approving railway investments at a high level, and lending the money to pay for them. Such general assistance to BR will have to cease with British entry into the European Economic Community. Then assistance will be possible only on a service by service basis, whereby BR identifies loss-makers *and measures the losses,* and threatens to close them. In effect, this already happens with the social passenger services; the new development will be the application of the same methods to freight services.

So far, British governments of both persuasions have been adamant that they will not subsidise unprofitable rail freight traffics, for which a suitable road alternative exists. (Traffics which have no feasible road alternative need never be unprofitable, because BR can charge rates high enough to cover its costs.) The Department of the Environment is clearly not very impressed with the environmental costs of diverting rail freight traffic to the roads. If half of BR's present freight traffic were to be diverted, it would only add between one and two percent to road traffic.[12] Provided that BR can work out its costs, the total social costs and benefits of retaining particular freight services can easily be quantified. If the government agrees that such traffics should stay on rail, it will have in the EEC regulations a suitable framework within which subsidies can be paid.

As with all such potential benefits, there is a catch in this for BR management. To gain subsidy for any loss-making services BR will have to be prepared to submit to all kinds of enquiries by civil servants, to satisfy them so that they can satisfy the minister that he is getting value for money. In principle, this will be no different from the existing procedure for reviewing social passenger service grants. But in practice, matters will not be so simple. It will be recalled that, at the time of the Joint Steering Group enquiry, very senior railway managers were saying that the wagonload freight business was finished, and that the railways' freight future lay in Freightliner and train-load operations. The reason for this poor prognosis was that, for much of the wagonload traffic, the full costs of rail operation exceeded the prices which road hauliers would charge. The government recognised this, by cancelling the capital debt re-presented by the freight wagons. The expectation of the government at that time was that BR would withdraw from the unprofitable wagonload freight activities as quickly as possible, so husbanding funds for investment in the remainder of the railway. The whole affair would have been under BR's control. But the Board's decision to maintain these services, leaving it no alternative but to seek subsidy for them, puts the boot on the other foot. Even if the government approves rail freight subsidies in general, the process of obtaining freight service grants for specific routes or areas will be a torrid event in BR/DOE relations.

Before the Department will be able to advise the Minister to pay a grant on environmental grounds,[13] it will have to be satisfied that the loss is being minimised. This is where the Board's troubles will begin. Even if the Department accepts that the whole of the existing rail traffic should be kept off the roads, it will require a lot of convincing that (i) the traffic is being worked at minimum cost and (ii) the rates being obtained for it are the best possible.[14] The 'minimum-cost' point should not be too hard to satisfy; for all the grant-aided passenger services there have been very few situations where the Department has successfully suggested economies. It bears remembering that the people most likely to know the best way to run a railway are the railwaymen.

It is on the revenue side that the difficulties will arise. Unlike the passenger business, with its simple fares structure, freight moves under a myriad of rates, privately bargained and not previously disclosed to outsiders. How civil servants will be able to satisfy themselves that these negotiated rates are being maximised is not clear. But unless they do so, there will be no defence against allegations that BR is deliberately under-pricing its freight business so as to keep an uneconomically high volume on the railways, knowing that the government would eventually foot the bill. There has been a suspicion of this among road hauliers and certain civil servants, from as far back as the mid-Fifties. If BR chooses to apply for explicitly freight subsidies, instead of quitting unprofitable traffics, the allegation will colour the enquiries the Minister's officials have to make.

The only way in which the Board will be able to avoid such annoying detailed surveillance of its activities is to get rid of the loss-makers, but it has so far not done this. Of course, there is no certainty that all freight subsidies applied for will be approved. Unless the government agrees to underwrite the whole of the present rail freight operation, which would be as unfair to the taxpayer as it would be to the competing road hauliers, there will inevitably be a reduction in the number of railway jobs.

This will come as a shock to many, particularly those railwaymen and union leaders who heard the then chief executive, Mr Geoffrey Wilson, paint an optimistic picture of the Board's future in early 1971. This was based on the first 'Corporate Plan',[14] which assumed a virtually static system size, and increasing borrowing to finance it in the face of a failure to come to grips with the underlying problems. The 'stability' which the first Corporate Plan seemed to promise can be of help to neither management nor labour, because it depends much more upon the Board's ability to convince the government to keep the cash flowing than upon actually managing the railway. The Board are thus taking on a task, the success of which is right outside their hands. If they fail, the time they have spent trying is time which could have been better spent attacking the problems within the railway. There may be some who would consider this a worthwhile gamble, arguing that if the government has to pick up the pieces after the Board's failure to come to grips with its own problems causes another financial crisis, at least they will be bigger pieces than if the Board had set about the government's intention of slimming itself down. Such arguments display a begging-bowl mentality which ill befits supporters of what could again be among the proudest railway systems in the world. Dieting is better than surgery as a way of losing weight, but it does require a will to pursue an active independent life. One thing is certain: the need for continual doses of drugs to keep an overweight person functioning will shorten the life expectancy. A railway system is very like a living organisation in this and many other ways. Unless those working in it can be assured that their masters know where they are leading it, and be proud to seek the goal, their personal contribution to the enterprise will be diminished.

The train which ran away in the Fifties was brought under some control in the Sixties. It may not survive another, but slower, runaway in anything like the form which we know today.

There is, of course, another argument for increased subsidies as an alternative to really attacking the fundamental problems highlighted by the JSG studies and the recapitalisation of the 1968 Act. That is the suggestion that any attempt to actually carry out the intention of the 1968 Act would cause such a collapse in the morale of railway management and staff that the resultant chaos and inefficiencies would be worse than those existing now. If that is the view of the present senior management, who all received their early training in the lotus-land days of the British Transport Commission, then its sins will truly have been visited on its successors, 'even to the third and fourth generation'. If this horrendous prospect did turn out to have substance, the railway system of the nation which invented railways could have no honourable future. Not only railwaymen's pride is at stake here; it is a great national asset which is at risk.

1 *Railway Policy* White Paper, Cmnd. 3439, 1967, para. 2.35. (emphasis added.)
2 For a full explanation of these, see Chapter Eight, above.
3 Provided that the potential sale price increases over the years at a faster rate per annum than the Board has to pay for borrowed funds.
4 Even the very sophisticated 'tax allowance-farming' methods of leasing assets can only soften the blow. They do not eliminate it entirely.
5 Of course, simply quitting loss-making activities will improve the efficiency indicators. They are only loss-makers because their efficiency is so poor.
6 Or even to the need just to break-even.
7 Evidence on this point is cited in my *Railway Economics* (forthcoming) Chapter Three.
8 The same applies to passenger terminal costs on BR.
9 *BRB: AR&A* 1963 & 1970, Table 2A.
10 For ways in which BR's costing systems could be improved, see my *Railway Economics* (forthcoming), Chapter Four.
11 London Commuter services were to be put on a break-even basis — see *Transport in London*, London, HMSO 1967.
12 See 'Freighting Week in Parliament', in *International Freighting Weekly*, March 8, 1972, p.12.
13 The other possible ground, regional development, will hardly be appropriate when rail carries such a small proportion of any region's traffic.
14 Even convincing the Department that it knows the cost of the operation will be difficult enough, given the inadequacies of the present costing system.
15 The Plan itself was never made public, but it was summarised in most newspapers. See particularly, the account given by Wilson after he announced his shock resignation: 'Will Government buy British Rail's new Timetable?' *Sunday Times, May 23, 1971.*